FINAL APPROACH:
THE CRASH OF EASTERN 212

Final Approach:

The Crash of
Eastern 212

William Stockton

Doubleday & Company, Inc., Garden City, New York, 1977

Library of Congress Cataloging in Publication Data

Stockton, William.
    Final approach.

      1. Aeronautics—Accidents—1974. 2. Eastern Air
Lines, Inc. I. Title.
TL553.5.S74   975.6′76′04

                           ISBN: 0-385-11628-4
Library of Congress Catalog Card Number: 76-50794

To Those Who Would Make Flying Safer

FINAL APPROACH:
THE CRASH OF EASTERN 212

Tuesday 3 P.M.

ITS TWO JET engines whining shrilly, the Eastern Airlines DC-9 waddled carefully toward the man in blue coveralls and protective earmuffs standing by Gate 37 of Concourse A at Atlanta's Hartsfield International Airport. He stretched his arms above his head, marking the spot where the airliner must park to disgorge its passengers. The whine grew intense as the purple and white behemoth with its black bullet nose lumbered slowly closer. The heads of the two pilots grew larger until their colored glasses were clearly visible and then the shock of graying hair and the dapper moustache of the man in the left seat could be seen.

Just as it seemed the airliner might bowl him over, the man in coveralls suddenly crossed his two outstretched arms, the airplane abruptly halted with a bob of its nose and the whine subsided slowly as the pilots began systematically flicking their hands over the banks of switches above their heads. Shortly, the thick door on the left side of the fuselage behind the cockpit moved and then swung open and a tall stewardess leaned out and reached around to shove the door fully open.

"Hi there, y'all," she called to the other men in blue overalls. They stood waiting to service the craft and unload baggage, the fronts of their overalls unzipped in deference to the September heat.

The stewardess pressed a switch on a control panel just inside the door and the airplane's metal steps suddenly began extending from a compartment beneath the door, jerking outward like the single tentacle of a dim-witted creature, groping for the asphalt. Soon, the passengers began filing down the shaky steps, blessed with a cheery farewell from the stewardess, whose name tag announced "Mrs. Watson."

"Good-by now. You come back now. See ya later. Have a nice day. Good-by now. Good-by. Have a nice day. So long," she said, again and again.

In the cockpit, the pilots completed their aircraft shutdown checklist and turned to their flight time pay forms and other paperwork. Captain James E. Reeves, a short, portly man, sat slumped. He felt drained. Weary. Not fatigued, just tired. He raised up slightly and glanced out the windshield toward the interstate highway that circled the airport perimeter in the distance. He could make out a steady stream of cars flashing past. He glanced at the cockpit clock, a circle of glass staring back from among dozens of circles of glass: 3 P.M. It would be four before he finished everything and could leave the airport. Just in time for the beginning of the evening rush hour.

Reeves sighed, mentally ticking off his evening ahead. Home by four-thirty, supper at six, watch some television, go next door and say good night to his grandchildren, into bed early, at least by nine. Then up at . . . what? He worked backwards. He had a 5:30 A.M. takeoff. That meant a four-thirty check-in. So he should get up at three-thirty. If he could get to sleep by eight-thirty, that would be seven hours sleep. At the airport the next morning he would begin the same two-day trip just completed. Atlanta to Charleston to Charlotte to Chicago O'Hare to Orlando. Overnight in Orlando and on to Dallas-Fort Worth and back to Atlanta. Then, a glorious long stretch of time off—time to enjoy his parents' visit and anticipate his annual fall hunting trip.

As Captain Reeves stepped down the airplane stairs, not far behind the last passenger, resplendent in his uniform jacket and gold-braided cap, conscious of the coveted four stripes of the captain on his coat sleeve, he smiled with pleasure at the thought of his two grandchildren. Aaron James, four, and Toni Jo, eighteen months. The little girl was just beginning to talk. He was proud of his close-knit family, proud of raising respectable children. His oldest daughter had chosen to live with her husband and children next door, giving Grampa the pleasure of constant access to his grandchildren.

There had been so much flying lately—days on end of flying, restaurant meals, motel rooms, early check-ins, late check-ins, a *most* erratic schedule. But as soon as he got this next flight out of the way, as soon as he finished these next two days, there would be a long stretch of time off. He could spend as much time as he wanted with his grandchildren.

CHAPTER ONE

Wednesday 12:51 A.M.

THE FOG ROSE UP into the midnight darkness, settling into ravines and hollows, hiding trees beyond the meadows and cornfields, obscuring winding roads that dipped to quiet streams cloaked in mist.

A blimp-shaped area of barometric high pressure had settled over the Atlantic Seaboard the afternoon and evening before, bringing a calm to the atmosphere, a paucity of wind and turbulence in a moist but cloudless air mass. Through the night the sun-warmed Carolina Piedmont radiated its daytime heat skyward, cooling, as a result, the first few hundred feet of becalmed air above the ground. An inversion slowly formed, a layer of cold air trapped against the earth beneath a layer of warm. As the temperature dipped degree by degree through the night, the water vapor, the stickiness of the trapped air rose steadily. After midnight, the air became oppressively moist, nearly saturated with water vapor.

Then, with another degree temperature drop, the delicate balance between temperature and water vapor tipped and the water vapor began to condense. Slowly, almost imperceptibly at first, the fog rose up from the red clay earth. It ascended in wisps and bellows, thickest in the low spots where pockets of the coolest air had settled, thin and translucent on the warmer ridges. Within minutes it hid fields and roads, houses and stores, rising a few tens of feet at its shallowest, a few hundred at its deepest.

At 12:51 A.M., September 11, 1974, Robert P. Green, a veteran of twenty-three years observing the weather, climbed the concrete stairs outside the National Weather Service office on the second floor of the Charlotte, North Carolina, municipal airport. He stepped through the door onto the wooden catwalk atop the terminal building roof. The control tower cab—a glass-walled room—loomed above him in the darkness. He could barely make out the solitary graveyard shift air traffic controller on a high stool, illuminated dimly by the control panel lights.

Green, a balding man with a rapid-fire voice who began his career as a weatherman in the Navy during the Korean War, methodically scanned the horizon, searching for the familiar markers —a lighted water tower, the office buildings of downtown Charlotte, the blinking red lights of radio antennae—used to pinpoint airport visibility. He took his time, giving his eyes a chance to adjust to the darkness.

"Yep. I thought so. I said so," Green said, half aloud and half under his breath, and to no one in particular except his early morning loneliness. When he drove to work he had seen the first wisps of fog.

"Visibility . . . oh . . . five miles," he said, squinting into the dark, the visibility marker chart burned into his memory after years of use. To the east he could just see the lights atop the oval water tank, 4.7 miles away. The buildings of Charlotte five miles away were only dimly visible. He couldn't make out the lights of the three WBT radio station towers, 5.7 miles to the southeast.

"Yep. Five miles," he mumbled to himself, turning and retracing his path over the catwalk, down the stairs and into the office. He studied the bank of instruments that rise above the observer's desk and then jotted down his findings on the surface weather observations chart: estimated ceiling 12,000 feet, broken clouds, visibility five miles, ground fog, temperature 67 degrees, dew point 65, wind calm, altimeter setting 30.14 inches of mercury.

"It'll get worse 'fore the sun comes up," he said to the room, turning into an alcove and sitting at the teleprinter keyboard to punch out the weather observation in paper tape. His fingers flew over the keys and the yellow tape belched from the machine. Green stuck the tape into the transmitter and waited. A central

computer somewhere sent an electrical pulse which set the transmitter to chattering as it read the tape. Within seconds, then, the
strange symbols that are the grossest gibberish to the layman but
quickly tell the aviator the latest weather at Charlotte were tapping
out on teleprinters throughout the country.

The new shift of air traffic controllers began arriving in the
parking lot of the Charlotte, North Carolina, municipal airport
about 6:30 A.M. They climbed the back stairs beside the airport
barbershop to the unmarked door on the second floor down the
hall from the Weather Service office. They gathered in the preparation room to get a cup of coffee from the pot, store their sack
lunches in the refrigerator and take their tiny headsets, the badges
of their profession, from personal lockers.

The new shift goes on duty at 7 A.M. in time for the morning
nose-to-tail rush of airplanes at Charlotte, which begins about
seven twenty-five, when two propeller-driven airplanes flown by
small air taxi feeder airlines arrive from nearby communities.

Then the surge of big jets commences. Delta 608 from Atlanta
en route to New York and Hartford; Piedmont 917, Fayetteville to
Cincinnati; Eastern 370 from Atlanta and Greenville and on to
Washington and Boston; Piedmont 952 from Greenville, en route
to Greensboro; Eastern 590 from Augusta, then on to Philadelphia; Eastern 212 from Charleston to Chicago; Eastern 352
from Chattanooga to New York; and Eastern 350 from Columbia
to New York. All but one arrive within a ten-minute period, most
take off a few minutes later.

The Charlotte controllers orchestrate this ballet of multimillion-
dollar machines. They direct by remote control with little tolerance
for a reckless glissade or hasty pirouette. From four states and an
infinity of airspace the airliners are drawn to Charlotte, like moths
to a flame, to squat in rapid succession in the same spot on the
100-foot-wide ribbon of concrete, tires belching tiny puffs of
smoke in protest as they grab the concrete, engines rising to an unexpected crescendo as thrust reverse levers are slammed forward.

The airliners sometimes arrive in ground fog, for which Charlotte is famous. Any airline pilot who flies the Carolinas can tell a

story about sitting on the Charlotte runways waiting or circling interminably at some holding point, or finally diverting to another city, all because a layer of fog twenty or thirty feet deep sat upon the runway.

Like all workers who must report to an early job, the controllers were quiet as they sipped their coffee, stowed their lunches and mentally prepared themselves for another day. The boisterous, often ribald jokes that frequently mark controller banter were absent or subdued. The talk was desultory and sparse, interrupted by yawns and stretching.

"Man, that fog's thick. I could just barely creep along in some spots," said Dennis Hunter, entering the room.

"So what else is new?" somebody commented sardonically.

"How's school, Pete?" somebody called across the room at William Hogan, who drove forty miles each day from the small farm at Locust, where he lived with his wife. Each semester he juggled college classes with his erratic work schedule.

"Aaahhh," Hogan replied, waving a hand in dismissal of the question.

One by one the controllers filled their coffee cups a second time, gathered up their headsets and headed down the hall to the tower cab steps or moved through a door into the darkened radar room, where the fluorescent glow of the radar screens and the orange flush from the control panels cast an alien hue upon their faces. They sat down, positioned the headsets, inserted the custom-fitted earplugs, inserted the long black coiled cords into the jacks at each position and waited for the morning rush.

Today, they would have fog.

CHAPTER TWO

5:55 A.M.

JIM WILKES PAUSED halfway across the lobby and sighed. It was five minutes before six and the first flight of the morning wouldn't depart for another sixty-five minutes. But already passengers were lined up at the Eastern counter. "It's that dadgummed National strike," he said to himself. "Two twelve'll have a full load today."

He stepped past the as yet unstaffed security counter and opened an unmarked door into the Eastern Airlines operations office behind the ticket counter. Danny Poe and Bill Aldridge already had arrived.

"How're you fellas this morning?" he asked. Then, "Good morning, Happy," as Happy Lempesis, the new man among the Eastern passenger service representatives at Charleston, came through the door.

"We're gonna have a big day today. All those National tickets."

The four men were each dressed in the blue pants and blue blazer, cream shirt and red and blue checkered tie of the Eastern Airlines passenger service representative uniform. Tiny pins on the left blazer pockets bore the Eastern symbol and their names.

Poe adjusted his tie, rubbed a hand over his moustache and said, "Well, let's go." Trailed by Aldridge and Lempesis he walked down a short hall flanked by glass-walled alcoves and emerged

behind the ticket counter. Flipping on the lights, he smiled at the
man at the head of the line, waiting with an elbow propped on the
counter top.

"Be right with you, sir," Poe said, fishing for a key.

In the pecking order of airports served by Eastern Airlines,
Charleston is at the bottom, a class C small potatoes station that
never sees a jumbo jet and has no VIP lounge. The Eastern ticket
counter closes at 10:30 P.M. and reopens at 6 A.M., and the
twenty-one employees can handle any job from busting bags to
figuring aircraft weights.

Charleston Municipal Airport shares its two-mile-plus-long runways with Charleston Air Force Base. The passenger terminal and
the military hangars stare at one another across a half mile of asphalt and grass. The runways sprawl beside Interstate Highway 26
ten miles up the peninsula from Charleston, where the famous an-
tebellum mansions and church spires look across the confluence of
the Ashley and Cooper rivers to the ruins of Fort Sumter, where
the Civil War began.

Like many towns that feed upon the memory of events gone by,
that which is viewed in some cities as down-at-the-heels dilapida-
tion is regarded as rustic charm in Charleston. So it is with the
small airport terminal building. It is of weathered brick, oblong,
with two stories, vines climbing up part of the outside, a half
dozen palm trees set about to break the monotony of the parking
lot on one side and the aircraft ramp and taxiways on the other. It
is dingy, outside as well as in, but nevertheless charming if viewed
as an extension of old Charleston.

The first floor is laid out in the shape of a letter T with airline
ticket counters along the crossbar. The passenger security checkpoint waits at the bottom of the T and beyond that is Charleston's
most visible concession to modern airport accouterments—a new
"holding" lounge, in which only passengers passed through security screening await boarding.

The new holding lounge is a garish contrast to the rest of the
drab building—brown carpet, contoured blue and yellow vinyl up-
holstered seats and tall narrow windows that look out on the flight
line.

While Poe, Aldridge and Lempesis moved out to the counter to cope with the steadily growing lines, Wilkes, who this morning doubled as operations manager and ticket agent, sat down at the scuffed desk in the operations office. He set about preparing the dispatch documents for the two pilots who would arrive shortly with the empty DC-9 brought each morning from Atlanta to begin Flight 212.

Eastern's operations office is no larger than a suburban bedroom. It looks out upon the flight line through dirty, high wooden framed windows that once, before air conditioning, opened on sultry days to admit a breath of air. Dusty venetian blinds that seldom are cracked and even more rarely raised cover the windows. The room is painted in that pea soup color known as institutional green.

The operations desk sits at a right angle to the windows and a bank of pigeonholes rests along one edge. An altimeter is mounted in one pigeonhole, papers protrude from the others, and a telephone with a speaker where the dial should be sits at one end of the desk.

Behind the operations agent's desk is a cathode ray tube computer display hooked to Eastern's central computer—the electronic messenger that links the Eastern system. A printer beside it can, at the push of a button, print out on paper what is displayed on the screen. A teleprinter shoved up against the venetian blinds, when not turned off to conserve paper, prints out an incessant stream of reports from the National Weather Service. From his desk, the operations agent can look through a door with a window, into the baggage handling area, another bedroom-sized space directly behind the ticket counter.

Wilkes pulled a dispatch release form from a pigeonhole and began filling it out. He jotted the flight number and the day of the month in the first block in the upper left corner, writing first a ten and then, with a glance at the calendar, writing a one over the zero. The month and year followed in the next block, then the airport symbol—CHS for Charleston. He noted the time in the lower right corner—10:30 Zulu or 6:30 Eastern Daylight—then turned to the weather teleprinter, tore off the block of weather reports for Charlotte and adjacent airports and tucked everything under a clip.

The attitudes of airline passenger service agents toward the traveling public can be divided into two categories—those who detest it and those who embrace it. Danny Poe happily fit into the latter category. He was particularly enjoying the early morning bustle, the extra activity caused by the National strike as he and Happy and Bill scurried about the two ticketing positions and an express baggage check-in.

A big man with tight, curly hair stepped up, a woman in a nylon sweater and slacks at his side. He clutched a bank charge card in a meaty fist.

"Toohey. John Toohey. I'm getting the seven o'clock flight. To Philadelphia and then Bridgeport."

Poe stepped to the computer console, tapped the flight number and passenger name into the keys. He waited, tapping his foot. The screen flashed.

"Let's see. John Toohey. Two twelve to Charlotte and then 590 to Philadelphia and then—" He paused, studying the unfamiliar notation.

"Then I see you're taking a commuter line to Bridgeport?" he asked. Poe turned to the thick book of fares and routings, jotting down figures there on a scratch pad and then running a total.

"That's going to be $167.73," he said finally.

Toohey frowned and glanced at a piece of paper in his hand.

"The girl on the phone last night said it would be $138.61," he said. "That's almost thirty dollars cheaper."

"Just a minute, sir," Poe said, glancing at the growing line. At times the impatience of a waiting queue seemed palpable.

He ran through the figures once more and then raised his head.

"What I don't know is whether Eastern has a reciprocal arrangement with this commuter line," he told Toohey. "If we do, then it's the cheaper fare. If we don't, you'll have to pay the higher fare."

"Don't you know? Can't you find out?" Toohey asked. His voice was growing edgy.

"It would take a few minutes to find out and . . ." Poe glanced at the line again and then the clock.

"Why don't you go ahead and pay the full fare and then later,

when you get back, we can make an adjustment, if that's necessary," Poe suggested.

Toohey hesitated.

"All right," he said, handing over the card.

If Danny Poe thrived on the challenge of the ticket counter, Jim
Wilkes, who by now had moved from the operations office to the
flight check-in counter in the holding lounge, detested it.

"Thank goodness things are smooth today," he mused, opening
a ticket envelope, ripping the flight coupon out and then plunking
a large stamp down that imprinted "SEPT 11 212" on the envelope back. He scrawled a *"Y"* for coach class in pen beside the
stamp.

"Sit anywhere you want, sir," he said, returning the envelope.
"We'll be boarding in a few minutes."

A tall, heavy-set man stepped up next. "I'm on standby," he
volunteered.

Wilkes studied his ticket. It was Steve Boireau, a Lexington,
Massachusetts, real estate broker.

Boireau was in a good mood. His hip didn't hurt. He had felt
genuine pride in his son the day before as he watched the Marine
Corps boot camp graduation ceremony. He had telephoned Eileen,
his new wife, the night before. The outlook for adopting the two
children was improving. Life was looking up. He would be in Lexington by early afternoon.

"We'll call you after the other passengers have boarded,"
Wilkes said after checking Boireau's status. "Your chances look
good."

One after another the passengers presented themselves to
Wilkes.

"This whole damn thing of lifting tickets, selling tickets is a
pain," Wilkes mused. "I can't stand it at times. I just don't like the
hassle. If everything is smooth like today, it's O.K., but it's like an
assembly line. You don't notice anyone unless a short skirt . . ."

He stared at the girl standing before him, smiling, proffering her
ticket envelope. He hastily took it and looked down so as not to
stare. She was pretty. Long hair down to her shoulders. He
glanced at the name. "D. Tracy." Going to Columbus. Lucky
Columbus.

"Have a nice flight," Wilkes said, smiling.

"The worst part is the bad weather," he once told a friend after an annoying day. "One of Charleston's fogs can move in and you can't see six inches in front of your face. A 7 A.M. departure and all of a sudden some guy runs up at five of seven and starts cussing because it usually takes him ten minutes to get to the airport and today it took forty-five. And he'll say, 'Hey, is that flight on time?' And you'll say, 'No, sir. That flight was canceled.' Then he says, 'Jesus Christ. God damned Eastern Airlines.' Then he'll say, 'So what are you going to do for me?' Some people love the counter, but I don't know why. Anybody working for an airline that can put up with the counter for more than a year is doing dadgummed good."

John Merriman tucked the book he had been reading under his arm, ducked through the security checkpoint's metal detector and stepped up to Wilkes's check-in counter. He stared absently into the brightly colored holding lounge as Wilkes ripped out the ticket coupon and stamped the envelope. "Smoking in the rear of the aircraft. Have a nice flight."

Merriman was the news editor for the CBS Evening News with Walter Cronkite. With the rigors of months of grueling Watergate coverage finally ended by Richard Nixon's resignation, Merriman had taken some vacation. A visit to his mother in Walterboro, South Carolina. Now back to New York to pick up Eileen and a long weekend in Maine. He and Eileen had to sort out what their future together was to be.

What Danny Poe liked and Happy Lempesis, too, although he'd been on the job for Eastern less than a year, was the familiarity that a small station permitted. Poe prided himself on recognizing a passenger and greeting him by name as he walked up to the counter. He especially liked to stand at the bottom of the airplane stairs and personally welcome the Charleston businessmen he knew who traveled Eastern Airlines regularly.

"How are you, Dr. Colbert?"

It was Dr. James Colbert, an official of the Medical University of South Carolina, a regular customer. Always off on university business.

"Good morning, gentlemen," Colbert said. His two sons, Paul, who had turned eighteen two days before, and fifteen-year-old Peter, stood nearby.

"Where to today, Dr. Colbert?" Happy said, taking the ticket envelope and attaching labels to the bags they had hefted up for transfer to the luggage belt.

"Boston. Paul and Peter are going back to school," he answered, smiling at the boys.

"Gettin' to be that time of year again," Happy said.

"Good morning, Mr. Seal." It was Danny's turn again. Walter Seal, the anchor man for WCIV-TV's evening news. Heads were turning. Seal seemed to enjoy the attention.

"Good morning, Admiral," Happy said, taking the ticket envelopes of the gold-braided naval officer and his two aides at the express check-in line. It was Rear Admiral Charles W. Cummings and Captain Felix Vecchione and civilian Paul Mergenthal, the admiral's aides. They were going to Washington, as most Charleston admirals and their retinues seemed to do. Happy snapped on baggage checks with "DCA"—the identifier for Washington National Airport.

Ward Cummings had been promoted to rear admiral the year before while attached to the Office of the Chief of Naval Operations in the Pentagon. Soon after, he had been assigned as commander of the Navy's Mine Warfare Force in Charleston, hardly a glamorous billet for a new, aggressive rear admiral.

Richard Arnold stood in the line behind the admiral's party, staring disdainfully at Cummings as if to challenge the naval officer to remark about Arnold's beard. Arnold was an IBM engineer and not in the Navy, but the admiral didn't know that. And it was no secret that many of the traditionalists among naval officers opposed beards. Arnold had caught the admiral giving him what had seemed a fixed stare. Arnold had returned the gaze and then suddenly smiled in challenge. The admiral had glanced quickly away.

"They look like flies buzzing around something," Arnold thought, watching an aide bend to whisper something in the admiral's ear. Then they laughed. Arnold turned away and found himself staring into the face of a smiling baby hefted up on a woman's shoulder. The baby was gurgling with happiness and looking directly at him. Arnold raised a hand and waggled his fingers at the child in greeting.

The lobby filled quickly. Passengers stood in line at the ticket counter and then at the security checkpoint, waiting to have hand luggage searched by two harried women behind the table. Then they stepped through the doorlike frame that scanned their bodies for metal. A sleepy-eyed policeman with a paunch and a service revolver on his hip watched from nearby as they moved to the line at Jim Wilkes's check-in counter.

Mike Gagnon and John Pinheiro eased closer to the metal detector. John could feel the nervousness mounting in his stomach. He glanced at his buddy. Mike looked uneasy, too. They weren't carrying anything that might trip the alarm and create a ruckus. But if something went wrong and the policeman had cause to question them and then someone asked for their orders and then if the Shore Patrol was called . . .

The night before they had persuaded the yeoman—against Navy regulations—to give them their orders early. So instead of standing in line at the airport, they should have been back at the Charleston Naval Base dressing for the decommissioning ceremony of their ship, the destroyer tender U.S.S. *Yellowstone*. But by ducking out of the ceremony, which would get them into trouble if caught, they could board the early flight to Charlotte instead of the 11 A.M. flight. They both would get into Boston by 11 A.M. rather than just before supper.

John took a breath and stepped through. His heart seemed to thump an extra beat in the second after emerging from the detector and realizing it hadn't rung. Then Mike stood beside him, free too. They glanced at each other and smiled.

One of the ramp service workers eased through the door at Gate 4, carefully locking it behind himself, and crossed the brown carpet to where Wilkes continued his methodical lifting of ticket coupons and stamping envelopes.

"The girls are ready," he said.

Wilkes picked up the microphone for the holding lounge's public address system.

"Ladies and gentlemen, Eastern Airlines Flight 212 is now ready for boarding at Gate Four. Please extinguish all smoking

materials and refrain from smoking until your flight is airborne.
Thank you for flying Eastern Airlines and have a good day."

The ramp service man unlocked the metal door beneath the
large numeral *4* and the waiting passengers quickly bunched up to
pass out onto the asphalt, where the first light of the coming sunrise glowed in the east. They mounted the shaky metal stairs that
protruded from the purple and white DC-9's open door. The passengers emerging from the air conditioning into the early morning
stickiness could just make out the two pilots' heads above the
lighted cockpit windows.

Charles Weaver heard the boarding call just as Danny Poe
finished straightening out a problem with his return ticket from
Philadelphia. Weaver peered about.

"Now where did Harry go off to?" he thought irritably.

"Damn. It was bad enough, Grady, just being late."

Weaver and Harry Grady, boss and trusted aide, were en route
to business meetings in Philadelphia and New Jersey. They lived
just a few doors apart on the same street, but happy-go-lucky
Harry had been late, as usual. Weaver had squeezed his big frame
into Harry's tiny sports car and then held on as they careened
down the dark roads, the headlights sweeping giant oaks bowing
under burdens of Spanish moss.

Weaver turned and took the stairs two at a time. Damn Harry.
Probably dawdling over a cup of coffee.

Bruce Thingstad held Karen Ostreim's hand. He could sense her
nervousness.

"Well, I'll leave it up to you to take care of everything you can
at your end," he said. "And then I'll be there in six weeks and that
will be it."

Karen snuggled closer.

"It's going to be fun to plan for a wedding," she said. He
smiled. Her mood had changed from the night before. She hadn't
wanted to leave at all then. They'd had another argument.

"I'll just stay here in Charleston and we'll get married right
now. I'll just call the hospital and tell them I'm not coming back,"
she had said, pacing the floor of Bruce's trailer.

And Bruce, mature because of his seven years in the Navy, had patiently argued with her. She could be such a little girl at times, even though she was twenty-three.

"That would break your mother's heart. You should have a church wedding. And you need to give proper notice at the hospital. We need to have an apartment."

He had won out in the end. But it made him uneasy.

Bruce glanced at his watch. It was six-fifty. "I guess it's time to go," he said, bending to kiss her.

Jim Schulze and Roy Hendrix waited their turn with the metal detector. Hendrix went first. Then Schulze, who winced when the detector's high-pitched whistle sounded.

"I'm sorry, sir," one of the uniformed women said. "Will you empty the contents of your pockets into one of the cups and go through again?"

"Hey, Roy," Schulze called. "Save me a seat." Hendrix already was halfway to the door. Schulze stepped through again grinning ruefully at Lynn, the college sweetheart he'd married in an ROTC ceremony three years earlier. She stood to one side in the lobby watching. The whistle was silent and Schulze scooped up the contents of the cup, waved to Lynn and hurried after Hendrix. The two submarine officers, their captain and the skipper of another Polaris missile submarine were going to Norfolk for the periodic secret meetings in which the Atlantic fleet's operations were reviewed.

Jo Jo and Cleve Willis handed over cash for their two round-trip, first-class tickets Charleston to New York and return—$380 total. Cleve, wearing an exaggerated denim touring cap with a tiny bill placed ever so carefully at a cocky angle on his Afro haircut, peeled the bills off a wad he carried in his pocket. Danny Poe started to comment on the hat and then thought better of it.

Following their usual custom the Willises had made the reservations under aliases. Williams. C. Williams and J. Williams. It was to protect them from potential ripoffs by other heroin dealers as much as to cover their tracks should any narcs be on the prowl. They, and the big wads of cash they carried with which to consummate the heroin coup in New York, would be easy marks to streetwise dudes in the first uneasy minutes after they left the pro-

tective cocoon of airport security at LaGuardia Airport and before
they could arm themselves.

Poe checked the tickets over again.

"Here you are, Mr. Williams. Have a nice trip to New York,"
he said, handing Cleve Willis the two ticket envelopes.

"Hey, Mama. We're goin' to New York," Cleve said, turning
and waving the envelope at the young woman standing with Jo Jo.
"We're gonna take a little trip to Noo York."

"Eastern Airlines Flight 212 for Charlotte and Chicago O'Hare
is now in the final boarding process. All passengers with confirmed
seats should be boarding," Wilkes said into the microphone.

Out on the asphalt ramp beside the jet airplane's metal stairs
two Eastern Airlines workers dressed in blue coveralls with yellow
armbands gently eased their hands under Steve Lane's bony frame.
They slowly helped him come erect and move shakily from the
wheelchair to the narrow, high-backed chair waiting beside it. The
chair had no arms and they buckled a seat belt about Lane while a
middle-aged woman, apparently his daughter, hovered anxiously
nearby. The old man seemed particularly small and frail, particularly exposed and vulnerable strapped in the incongruous chair
with no arms, the chair back towering over him.

One man grabbed the top of the chair, the other lifted the bottom and they slowly carried Lane backward up the stairs, jostling
him as each man took each step. There is no graceful means for an
eighty-five-year-old man to get from his wheelchair to a seat in the
first-class section of an airliner.

Three floors above the asphalt in the control tower cab the
headset of air traffic controller James C. Baines came alive.

"Charleston clearance delivery, Eastern 212. How about a
clearance for Charlotte?"

Baines sat up and reached out for the plastic holder in which he
had stuck a strip of heavy paper when it came out of the computer
printer a few minutes earlier.

"Just happen to have one here for Eastern 212," he said into
his microphone.

CHAPTER THREE

6:55 A.M.

No ONE KNOWS with certainty how many Americans are afraid to fly. There is wide agreement that the number must be large—tens of millions, perhaps 25 million or more. Some—probably a distinct minority—are so fearful of flying that they won't set foot in an airliner no matter how urgent the need. Others are fearful, but fly nevertheless.

America's airlines have committed much time and money to market research determining what movies, food and stereo music will lure business away from competitors in a market where prices are set by government. But they remain ignorant about the public's fear of flying and the depth of that fear or what to do about it.

Periodically, airline spokesmen attempt to deal with this fear by wheeling up statistical artillery and blasting away, often forgetting that statistics mean little in the face of irrational emotion. Even so, the statistics are impressive. In 1974, 207 million Americans boarded airline flights. Often it was the same people, because an elite 15 per cent of airline passengers each year generally account for half of all flying. They are the lifeblood of the airline passenger business, apparent victors over their fear although little is known about them.

These 207 million individual passengers flew a grand total of

163 billion miles during 1974, but only 420 of them lost their lives in the six fatal crashes involving U.S. air carriers. And that was a bad year—a year with about twice as many fatalities as U.S. carriers normally experience. That means there was one fatality for every 388 million passenger miles flown. Or to put it another way, the average passenger in 1974 could have expected to fly 388 million miles before being killed in an airline crash—whatever his personal fears.

Such statistical reassurances, however, don't revive bodies in makeshift morgues erected at the scenes of air disasters. There were, with certainty, an uncounted number of first time fliers among those 420 victims who overcame their fears and strode through the open airliner hatch, only to die.

U.S. air carrier spokesmen also load their artillery with bus, train and automobile statistics. Air travel statistics, when viewed beside these other forms of transport—particularly the automobile —become even more reassuring. In 1973, for example, when 197 passengers died in U.S. airline accidents, the average passenger could have expected to fly 833 million miles before dying in a crash.

In the same year, however, the average American bus rider could have expected to die in a highway crash after logging only 588 million miles. The average motorist—there were 33,700 motor vehicle fatalities that year—could expect to drive 58 million miles before experiencing his fatal pileup. Thus it has been argued that airline travel was fourteen times safer than auto travel.

The practitioners of such statistical gymnastics have their detractors, of course. These critics raise a valid point. Namely, all the comparisons are in terms of *passenger miles* traveled—that is, the number of passengers multiplied by the total number of miles traveled. But, the argument goes, why shouldn't the comparisons be in amounts of *time* spent exposed to the mode of transportation? For example, an airliner streaking cross-country in an hour will move a passenger 600 miles while a car at best will eclipse sixty miles. Thus the airline passenger spends much less time at risk while traveling far more miles. The auto traveler, on the other hand, spends ten times or more time at risk for the same distance.

This argument is cogent, but one that can't be resolved to satisfaction because no accurate data exists. No one knows how much time Americans spend traveling about in their tin palaces—only approximately how many miles are covered.

When Jim Wilkes heaved the DC-9 door shut, there were certainly people strapped into the contoured seats of Eastern 212 who felt a dampness on their palms or chewed a fingernail or wished for a cigarette or tapped a foot or simply felt apprehensive.

John Merriman was one. Probably no other person among the seventy-eight passengers, with the possible exception of the admiral or his aides, had traveled more widely by air. As news editor of CBS Evening News Merriman constantly flew, not only to the far-flung places world events sent him but for pleasure as well. Travel was a hobby for John Merriman—an avocation, really, along with his love of fine food. Single, with a large salary and ample vacation time, he traveled to Asia, the Middle East, innumerable times to Europe, Africa, the Caribbean and on and on. Name a major world city and John Merriman could tell you the best restaurant to seek out and the best hotel bed to sleep in. But each time a trip loomed, his fear of flying surfaced.

Merriman, like everyone else who crossed the threshold of Eastern 212 and showed his ticket envelope to Collette Watson, the senior stewardess, had reached a reconciliation with the fear. Each had performed, probably unconsciously, a crude risk-benefit analysis. The benefit of flying to Charlotte, a thirty-minute ride costing twenty-five dollars, had outweighed the five-hour drive or the seven-hour train ride. So the passengers pushed down the aisle to seats, their fear subdued to manageable levels but playing a subtle role in seat selection, nevertheless.

Charles Weaver didn't smoke and preferred to be near an emergency exit. But he sat with Harry Grady so Harry could smoke. Jack Toohey didn't smoke, but because he only recently had quit, cigarette smoke didn't bother him. Hendrix and Schulze took the very back row and then moved up two rows when they discovered the rear seats in a DC-9 don't recline. Francis Mihalek always grabbed the left window seat in the first row in first class.

The two people aboard Eastern 212 that morning least afraid of flying were Captain James E. Reeves and First Officer James Daniels, Jr., who sat in the crowded cockpit. Flying was, for each, his life, a love that sometimes only other pilots understood. Their fears had been confronted and conquered long ago—Reeves as a dashing young fighter pilot during World War II and Daniels as a flight instructor who taught eager young kids to fly, a job nearly as risky as crop dusting.

Fear was the farthest thing from James Daniels' mind as he dialed the Charleston clearance delivery frequency into the number one radio and pressed his microphone switch.

"Charleston clearance delivery, Eastern 212. How about a clearance for Charlotte?"

Each morning a pilot in the cockpit of 212 radioed clearance delivery, and each morning the controller read down the same clearance. Eastern had a preferred flight plan route for Flight 212 stored in the FAA's computer in Jacksonville. Each morning the computer clicked it out on the printer in the Charleston tower at six-forty.

Sometimes it seemed to Daniels as if he should just call up and say, "Hey, normal route today?" And the tower would call back, "Yeah. Have a nice flight."

But if any one thing governs exchanges between pilots and air traffic controllers, it is adherence to the formalities of language and procedure.

"Just happen to have one for Eastern 212," clearance delivery replied. "Cleared as filed. Maintain . . ."

Daniels cocked his head. The voice seemed to fade.

". . . one six . . . DME north, after departure turn right on course. One nineteen three. Squawk code one thousand just before departure."

"I might have missed that first one," Daniels replied. "That's as filed to maintain sixteen. Turn right on course. Nineteen point three. And a thousand."

Clearance delivery gently corrected.

"Yes, sir. That's cleared as filed. Maintain three thousand. Expect one six thousand three zero DME north," he repeated.

"O.K. . . . Maintain three. Expect sixteen thirty DME north."

"Roger."

Daniels copied down the clearance in the cryptic shorthand

pilots develop and stuck it among the flight papers in the metal clipboard. To the layman, of course, the clearance might as well have been delivered in Sanskrit by an Irishman with a head cold. But it made perfect sense to him: fly from Charleston along airway Victor 53 to Columbia, South Carolina, along Victor 37 to a radio navigation station twenty miles south of Charlotte and then straight in to Charlotte; after taking off turn right and intercept Victor 53; do not climb higher than 3,000 feet until thirty miles north of Charleston; expect permission then to climb to the assigned cruising altitude of 16,000 feet; radio the departure radar controllers on frequency 119.3; dial 1,000, 212's unique code for this segment of the flight, into the transponder.

With the two engines whining on either side of the tail and the ramp service man giving his "All clear" signal, Captain James Reeves eased the throttles forward gently until the 95,000-pound airplane began to inch forward. He turned a small steering wheel in the left corner of the cockpit to the right to bring the nosewheel around, then, advancing the throttles a bit more, brought the entire airplane into a lumbering right turn onto the taxiway.

The engines thundered and as the tail swung around the hot jet blast, pungent with the smell of kerosene, washed over Jim Wilkes, who stood watching at the holding lounge door, hands over ears.

"Eastern 212 for taxi," Daniels said into his microphone.

"Eastern 212, Charleston ground," a controller in the tower cab said. "Taxi, uh, runway two one or three three if you like. The wind is three six zero degrees at three. Altimeter three zero one two."

"Runway two one," Daniels shot back, although it would mean taking off with a slight tailwind. The threshold of Runway 21 was a quarter mile closer than Runway 33, so the extra fuel and the shorter taxi time outweighed a three-knot tailwind.

As the jet lumbered along the taxiway past rows of small single-engine airplanes, Daniels and Reeves ticked off the taxiing and before takeoff checklist.

"Fifteen degrees flaps," Daniels said.

"Got it," replied Reeves, clicking the flap handle down.

"One thirty-five. Five and a half," Daniels called.

"Got it," Reeves said, twisting the small knob to set the reminder bug on the airspeed indicator at 135 knots, the takeoff airspeed. He spun the stabilizer trim knob until the pointer stood midway between the five and six.

"Fifteen by the gauge," Daniels said, verifying that the flaps had, indeed, deployed fifteen degrees.

"Airfoil and engine heat, off," he said, touching the switch above his head.

"Flight instruments . . ." He paused, scanning the artificial horizon, the turn and slip indicator and the RMDIs to see that they functioned.

". . . checked," he said, satisfied.

"Yaw damper set."

He pushed the yoke full forward then hauled it back between his legs, twisting the wheel first left and then right, wagging the ailerons on both wings and the stabilizer on the three-story-high T-tail to check operation.

"EPR set. Flight controls set," he said.

The list was complete just in time. The end of the taxiway loomed ahead. Reeves pushed down on the top of each rudder pedal with the balls of his feet, gently braking the airplane to a halt. Daniels clicked his radio transmitter selector switch to radio number two, set on the tower takeoff clearance frequency.

"Uh, Eastern 212, be ready," he said.

"Eastern 212, Charleston tower," a controller replied. "Taxi into position and hold."

"Roger," Daniels responded.

Reeves relaxed his toes on the brakes, eased the throttle levers forward a bit and then used the small steering wheel to begin swinging the nose around. The DC-9 slowly rolled out onto the runway, lining up with its nosewheel on the white stripe. Reeves let the airplane ease forward a few feet to make certain the nosewheel pointed straight down the runway and then hit the toe brakes again. He reached up to the overhead switch panel and hit the stewardess call button twice—the signal that takeoff was imminent.

Collette Watson sat in the stewardess jump seat just outside the open cockpit door.

"See ya later," she called, sticking her head around the corner.

"O.K.," Daniels said without turning around.

"Awright," Reeves said, smiling. He waited until she pushed the door shut, clicking the outside key lock, then he shoved the inside bar latch into place. The latch had been installed at the height of the skyjack fever to augment the key lock.

Daniels turned to the final pre-takeoff checklist.

"Yaw dampers on."

"Closed and closed," he said, reaching down to the very rear of the control pedestal between the seats and making certain the two pneumatic cross-feed valves were shut. They needed no protection from wing ice in Charleston in September.

"Radar and transponder . . . ignition is continuous. Takeoff . . . anti-skid . . . oscillators . . . black." He touched the switch panel making certain each switch was in its right position.

"Got the brake?" Reeves asked, relaxing his feet on the rudder pedals.

"Yes, sir," Daniels said, pushing down with his feet. He was to fly the DC-9 on the Charlotte leg and this was the moment at which the captain relinquished control of the aircraft.

The radio crackled to life.

"Navajo six nine Lima, contact departure control," a controller said, instructing a twin-engine Piper Navajo that had taken off a few minutes before.

"Oh, there's a Navajo," Reeves said, raising an eyebrow. "With a Nigaho on board."

They both laughed. It was an old racial joke among pilots.

The tower had left them sitting on the runway while a giant C-141 Air Force StarLifter cargo jet made a low approach to Runway 33—coming down to just above the concrete and then suddenly taking off again without landing. Peering out the left windshield they could see the landing lights of the big-bellied airplane as it neared the runway.

"I think that big one out there's making a low approach. I'm not sure," Reeves said.

"Probably. They've got a lot of airplanes."

"They sure do, don't they?" Reeves answered.

Both men looked across the airport at the Air Force ramp, where a half dozen StarLifters were visible under the high intensity lights.

"Boy, I tell you. Over in McCoy they don't anymore though," Reeves said, recalling the empty ramps at McCoy Air Force Base in Orlando, where a Defense Department cutback had closed the air base—all but the control tower. McCoy, which shared its runways with Orlando civil traffic, was the two pilots' last stop of the day. After a night in a motel they would fly on to Dallas-Fort Worth, and back home to Atlanta.

"Yeah, McCoy's really dead, isn't it?" Daniels said. "I guess they've taken every damn airplane out."

"No, I guess there aren't any. No military left."

"Well, I wonder if they're still running the tower."

"Yeah. They're still running the tower."

"That's pretty plush duty." Daniels chuckled, remembering his own Air Force days. All those Air Force controllers and no traffic.

"At least they don't ask you this shit about your wheels down and three green," Reeves said.

It seems an unwritten obligation that civilian pilots carp about military air traffic control procedures. Every military controller when giving the final landing clearance also asks, "Wheels down and three green?" It's a pointed reminder not to forget to lower the landing gear.

"Sure a nice facility, that McCoy," Daniels said.

"Sure is. Look at all that money going to waste."

The StarLifter had crossed the threshold and was settling closer to the runway.

Smoke suddenly poured from the StarLifter engines as the pilot thrust the throttles forward. Reeves and Daniels could hear the roar in their closed cockpit as the StarLifter began to climb.

"U. S. Air Force. Go, man, go," Reeves cheered.

"Comes right off, doesn't it?" Daniels said, watching the fast climb.

The radio crackled again.

"Eastern 212, cleared for takeoff."

Reeves hit his microphone switch.

"Two twelve rolling."

Daniels grasped the two throttle levers and steadily thrust them forward, watching the EPR gauges. The engines thundered to life. He held the toe brakes for a second and then released them. The DC-9 began to roll, slowly, almost creeping at first. Then it gathered speed and the white stripes on the runway began disappearing beneath the nose faster and faster.

Daniels' eyes flicked to the engine gauges.

The N-one dials. One for each engine. Both O.K. Exhaust gas temperature. Again, both O.K. N-two gauges. Both O.K. Fuel flow, left, O.K. Fuel flow, right, O.K.

The engines screamed more loudly now, the roar penetrating to the farthest corners of the airport. The palpable sound waves washed over the line service men at the gate who paused to watch. The thunder bounced off the hangars and echoed and re-echoed. The sheer power, the ecstasy of a fifty-ton machine about to take flight, as unlikely as it always seemed, turned heads everywhere. It was the most exciting moment of flight.

Incredibly oblivious to the tension of takeoff, Reeves and Daniels casually contemplated their fatigue.

"O.K. Let's go to Charlotte," the captain said.

"Yeah."

"Go to Chicago and then McCoy and some rest."

"Yeah."

"That's what I need. Rest. I don't need all this damn flying."

"Yeah. I get enough of that."

"Boy, you know if you fly real hard for about . . . twenty . . . twenty-five hours, you can see why they've got that thirty hours in seven days rule."

"Damn right. All this damned noise in a jet."

"Sticking around at thirty-five thousand feet with your cabin altitude at almost nine thousand gets to you."

Reeves's eyes had been flicking over the airspeed indicator in front of him, watching the needle creep toward V-1, the go, no-go decision speed. Before V-1 they could shut the engines down and stop before plummeting off the end of the runway. After V-1, they were committed to flight, regardless of what happened.

"V-one," he called.

"Roger."

The runway stripes were a blur now. Reeves could make out the approach lights racing at them from the end of the runway. The needle crept slowly to V-R, 128 knots, the "nose up" speed at which flight began.

"Rotate," he called.

Daniels eased back on the control wheel and the nose slowly rose. The airplane seemed to hang for a moment, then came the shudder as the main landing gear let go of the runway. Daniels' eyes flicked to the vertical speed indicator, searching for an indication of climb. The needle started moving upwards.

"Gear up, please," he barked.

Reeves reached across the center instrument pedestal and yanked the black lever.

"Rollers up," he announced. The nosewheel could be heard spinning in the wheel well. Some pilots call, "Skates up," others, "Anti-grinding devices retracted."

The vertical speed indicator needle now had leaped sharply. The airplane seemed to sit on its tail and rocket upward. Daniels glanced out the window, flicked his eyes back to the altimeter and then turned the control wheel slightly to the right. Eastern 212 dipped its right wing gently and came around in a graceful right turn.

Richard Arnold peered out his window on the right side in the forwardmost row in the coach cabin.

"Nice of them to lower the right wing," he thought, drinking in the steadily growing view of Charleston. He could see Interstate 26 winding down the peninsula until the road petered out at the edge of the city. He picked out the Naval Station beside the Cooper River with the destroyers and submarines lined up in neat rows. His eye moved down to the Battery and across the harbor to Fort Sumter. The streetlights of Charleston seemed to be winking off in anticipation of the sunrise.

Arnold shifted a bit in his seat and peered back behind the tip of the wing, trying to spot his house. His eye picked up the Ashley River and followed the coast down to old Fort Johnson. He followed Fort Johnson Road inland to Fort Johnson Estates. There . . . but the airplane rolled out of the turn and the view was gone.

CHAPTER FOUR

6:57 A.M.

MARY COFFMAN GREW up in Frostburg, Maryland, an Allegheny mountain village sandwiched in Maryland's western neck between Pennsylvania and West Virginia. She lived there until middle age approached and then in 1968 moved to Charleston to escape the snow and cold. She found her place in the sun as night auditor at the Airport Holiday Inn, which sprawls beside Interstate 26, separated from the airport boundary by a quarter-mile-thick stand of oak and pine trees.

Built in 1967, the Airport Holiday Inn is typical of the motel chain's smalltown facilities thrown up across the country in that period. A trio of two-story wings surrounds the swimming pool and a one-story dining room-bar-registration desk-meeting room building. A fourth two-story wing, built a few years later, is set on a slight hill behind the main complex.

The Holiday Inn marquee announces the familiar structure to travelers on the interstate. The buildings are the usual blend of brown bricks, azure doors, yellow and green panels and cinder block walls. Each room has a wallpaper mural looking down on two double beds, gold and brown shag carpet, a Motorola color television, a dial telephone, a Gideon Bible and a complimentary copy of the Holiday Inn magazine. In the lobby, inexpensive paneling and a wooden artificial fireplace in which a revolving wheel trails streamers of cellophane to simulate a fire have been arranged according to a decorator's perception of hospitable congeniality. In September 1974 a solitary traveler could spend the night for $14.04, including a fifty-four-cent tax.

The night auditor arrives at midnight. It is a lonely job through the first hours of the morning, registering the occasional late arrival, posting the bills for each guest and monitoring the sleeping motel.

The pace picks up about 5 A.M., when the wake-up calls begin and the early risers straggle through the lobby to plunk room keys on the counter and settle bills. On most mornings the tempo peaks about six-thirty, when the guests booked on the Eastern Airlines flight to Charlotte stream through the lobby's double glass doors.

Each evening when a retiring guest requests a wake-up call, the desk clerk notes the room number on a form in which each quarter hour has a column. Then a small brass key for that time is thrown on the large alarm clock sitting beside the switchboard. Each key corresponds to a given quarter hour. Then each morning when the alarm sounds for, say, six-fifteen, Mary Coffman steps to the switchboard beside the registration counter and calls each room listed in the six-fifteen column.

"Good morning. It's six-fifteen." "Good morning. It's six forty-five." "Good morning. It's seven o'clock."

Sometimes the alarm is silent on one of the quarter-hour intervals because no one requested a call then. But such lapses are rare after 5 A.M.

Placing the wake-up calls is a tedious task which Mary Coffman nevertheless performs conscientiously. Partly it is a pride in her work and partly the knowledge of a guest's wrath if he or she oversleeps.

"It's a thankless job, but there's nothing they'll fuss at you more about than missing a call," she would admonish the youngsters who relieved her each morning at 8 A.M.

"The plain fact of the matter is a lot of rooms that leave a call don't answer when you ring them. They leave a wake-up call and then leave early and don't tell anyone. It's not unusual. We're frequently ringing an empty room. You can't send somebody by to check every room that doesn't answer. 'Course we should if they ask us to.

"Then you never know what you're going to get when they do answer. You're always getting the phone slammed down in your ear. A grunt and a slam. Some people are in a daze. They don't know what's goin' on. But we offer the service. So we should do a good job."

A good job to Mary Coffman meant going back fifteen or thirty minutes later and calling again a room that hadn't answered. When a slack moment presented itself she would scan the list, running her fingers down the "N.A.s" scribbled beside room numbers earlier. Then she would dial the room again, unconsciously counting the rings, one . . . two . . . three . . . ten in all. Sometimes the line of guests checking out would mount and the "N.A.s" might receive no more attention. She did the best she could.

Sixteen of the Airport Holiday Inn residents on September 10 had reservations on Eastern Airlines Flight 212 the next morning. Between six and six-forty a steady stream piled their bags in the lobby by the glass doors and stepped to the counter with key in hand, glancing at a wristwatch. She took their credit cards, traveler's checks and cash, stapling credit card invoices to the motel invoice, counting out change, carefully thanking each guest.

One by one they paid their bills and carried their bags out to the yellow and green Ford Club Wagon. The driver piled their bags in the back, closed the sliding side door and gunned the truck down the drive and onto the service road for the five-minute ride to the Charleston air terminal. In front of the old brick building the driver hefted the bags onto the sidewalk, accepting the tips— usually a quarter, sometimes two—and then hurrying back to the motel driveway for another load.

The last couple of guests booked on the 7 A.M. flight checked out about six forty-five, clearly worried they might miss their airplane. Three or four other guests not going to the airport paid their bills, and then the alarm clock gave its 7 A.M. buzz. Mary Coffman rang the four rooms with wake-up call requests. "Good morning. It's seven o'clock."

She ran a finger down the list looking for the rooms that hadn't answered earlier. Room 138. They had left one wake-up call for five forty-five and then another at six—slow risers. Some people had been known to leave four consecutive wake-up calls.

"One more time. I'll ring 138 once more."

Outside, the dim shapes of the chairs and lounges beside the swimming pool loomed more clearly in the dawn light, silhouetted by the greenish hue from the underwater pool lights. The busy hum of dozens of air conditioners mounted in the wall below the window of each room filled the air, punctuated by the roar of big trucks on the interstate heading out for Columbia.

Behind the motel, up the hill and beyond the pine and oak trees, the rumble of a jet airplane could be faintly heard over the air conditioners and the traffic.

Behind the tightly drawn curtains, Room 138 was dark. The steady whir of the air conditioner on high speed bathed the room in a shapeless sound that drowned outside noise.

Guy Henderson and Steve Moore lay in each of the double beds, asleep.

As a regular guest at the Charleston, South Carolina, Airport Holiday Inn eventually learns, the telephone system is sometimes plagued by mysterious gremlins. The telephone on the night table between the two beds sat silent.

CHAPTER FIVE

6:59 A.M.

THE EARTH'S ATMOSPHERE is a hostile frontier through which the airplane pilot must fly. It is an environment of swirling air masses and cycling temperatures continuously generating more thermodynamic energy than a thousand hydrogen bombs. Never constant and only crudely predictable, it usually appears seductively benign but always waits to entrap the unwary aviator.

The weather observer mans a lonely outpost along this frontier. His information about current conditions becomes a haven to the pilot not unlike the nineteenth-century western Army post to the pioneer in a covered wagon. The pilot embarking on a journey has a threefold perception of the weather at hand and the weather awaiting him: a forecast that may be several hours old and is sometimes seriously wrong; what the weather observers at the nearest stations to his route saw at their latest hourly observation; and what he can see from the cockpit window at the moment.

In the end the pilot must rely upon an almost intuitive sense of the weather. Without all the information the National Weather Service can feed him, he would be severely handicapped. But weather information is not carved in stone; nothing is more outdated than an hour-old observation or a three-hour-old forecast.

The synergism of experience and intuition is the pilot's best defense against the atmosphere.

As the destination approaches, the last weather observation becomes a forecast of how the flight will end. Clear or partly cloudy skies or an overcast several thousand feet above the ground promise an uneventful, "piece of cake" approach and landing. Low ceilings, poor visibility and an airport lashed by a storm offer at best an adrenaline-producing approach and landing on instruments, at worst a diversion to a nearby airport where conditions are better.

Throughout the United States twenty-four hours a day, seven days a week, thousands of National Weather Service observers—officially called weather service specialists—step outside their offices at fifty-five minutes past the hour to record local conditions. Theirs is a workday of rigid structure, careful adherence to routine. It can become tedious.

They must make the hourly observation and keep records; monitor hundreds of hourly weather reports and update them for pilot weather briefings; study weather system movements, area forecasts, airport forecasts, pilot reports of weather, winds aloft forecasts, radar weather summaries; answer the steady stream of telephone calls from the public, reduced to a manageable level by telephone answering machines. There are bursts of excitement when raging thunderstorms approach, tornado conditions develop or airport weather conditions become so bad that pilots must push their machines and their skills to the limit to slip in for a landing. But mostly it is a job filled with tedium, especially in a small quiet station like Charlotte and particularly on the lonely midnight shift.

Through more than two decades as a weather observer Robert Green had learned to balance the tedium of his job against his fascination with the weather. He had a ready answer when anyone asked him about his job, the words tumbling out on top of one another.

"I just love to follow the weather. What's happening in California, their temperatures, or whatever they're having in the Rockies. Do they have blizzards? And how strong a pressure system is and how intense the low is and is it going to affect us here in the Carolinas or move up into the Great Lakes? They get freezing rain in Tennessee and you worry about it. Is it going to come into Charlotte tomorrow night? I've always been impressed by the weather. I love to follow it."

Green's lifelong fascination began on a small farm in Timmonsville, South Carolina, a village 100 miles south of Charlotte. The gangly young boy dogged the footsteps of the grandfather he loved and respected. The boy and the old man worried together about the weather. Too much rain. Too little rain. Hail. Wind. Tornadoes. An early freeze. A late freeze. Slowly, patiently, the old farmer passed on to his grandson a lifetime of weather folklore. A wind shift to the southwest meant rain. If the wind shifted to the northwest, the chance for rain was lost.

The old man died before the boy matured enough to appreciate fully the knowledge passed to him. It was later in high school science books that he discovered meteorology and realized that his grandfather had learned to monitor the passage of a frontal system although he was ignorant of low-pressure systems and their movements.

Green joined the Navy in 1951 and asked in boot camp to become a weather observer. He spent part of the Korean War on an aircraft carrier off the coast of Korea observing weather. He joined the National Weather Service—known then as the U. S. Weather Bureau—at Greensboro, North Carolina, in 1955, went to the Huntington, West Virginia, station six years later and then transferred to Charlotte in 1962. He and his wife and two girls bought a house and put down roots. Secure in a well-paying government job that he liked, Green settled back to enjoy his gardening and bass fishing in the Catawba River and Lake Norman and Lake Wiley.

The Charlotte weather observers must rotate shifts—day shift, evening shift, midnight shift. Green seldom knew the luxury of regular hours.

"The midnight shift is the hard one. Some stations have it every third week. One week of day shifts and one week of evening shifts and then one week of midnights. We rotate here more frequently, though. Only work the same shift about three days in a row. As a rule here you have about two midnights every week. Something like two day shifts, two evenings, then two midnights and a couple of days off. Split shifts every week. It's hard on you sometimes."

Green drew the midnight shift for September 10. That meant reporting for duty at 11:30 P.M. and manning the station alone until 7 A.M., when a relief man would come on. Green's shift would end at seven-thirty.

September ground fog in the Carolina Piedmont is one of the more easily predicted weather phenomena. When Green kissed his wife, picked up his sack lunch and drove away from their brick ranch-style house in a southeast Charlotte development at 11 P.M., his twelve years in the area told him at once there would be ground fog by morning.

Several hours earlier—while Green ate dinner and then settled down to a bit of television—meteorologists at the National Weather Service's Suitland, Maryland, forecast headquarters had reached the same conclusion.

The signs were classic: a large, flat high-pressure system over most of the East Coast moving slowly out to sea; a cloudless sky that would radiate ground heat directly into the upper atmosphere, creating an inversion; and a high relative humidity that would provide the moisture to condense into fog.

So at eight-forty that night weather teleprinters throughout the East had tapped out a forecast for the Carolinas effective until 3 P.M. the following afternoon: no significant clouds; visibility unrestricted except by 1 A.M. it might drop to five miles in haze with occasional periods of three miles' visibility or less in ground fog after 3 A.M.

By the time Green walked into the Charlotte Weather Service office the Suitland forecasters had enough early evening weather observations in hand to see with certainty that ground fog would be a problem in the Carolina Piedmont. They issued Airmet Alpha One. It warned of visibility below three miles and ceilings of 1,000 feet or lower caused by ground fog, haze and smoke beginning in southern Ohio and West Virginia and spreading to the Carolinas by 7 A.M. The fog would persist into midmorning.

The most imposing object in the Charlotte weather station is the instrument rack, a wall of instruments six feet high and ten feet wide shoved up against the windows that look out on the terminal building concourses and the runways beyond. The weather observer can sit at a desk before it to monitor the gauges and fill out the observation logs.

A pilot briefing counter is to the left just inside the office door and rows of clips hold various categories of weather reports and forecasts that stream in over the teleprinter. Maps depicting current and forecast weather systems tower over the counter. Pilots can sit at a small table to study weather reports or prepare flight plans.

The station chief's desk is set in a small alcove at one end of the office and a room filled with teleprinters is at the other end.

Gauges on the instrument rack give an immediate reading of current weather conditions, and slowly moving paper strip charts over which mechanical pens dance provide a permanent record. The instruments monitor temperature, dew point, wind direction and speed, precipitation, amount of sunlight, height of clouds and atmospheric pressure.

The cloud height instrument, called a ceilometer, begins functioning when cloud bottoms move within 4,000 feet of the ground. The instrument—located one-half mile from the touchdown zone of Runway 5—projects a beam of light on the cloud bottoms. The flash of the light beam on the clouds is measured by another detector, which then uses high school trigonometry and the angle at which the light was beamed to calculate cloud height. The answer is displayed on a strip chart in the Weather Service office.

Airport visibility is measured by the observer on duty from the terminal building roof using known landmarks. But when visibility drops below one mile, the human eye is augmented by an electronic system sitting beside the touchdown zone of Runway 5. Called the RVR—runway visual range—the instrument measures a light beam projected 500 feet from one tower to another, each sixteen feet high. On a clear day the light travels uninhibited. But when obscuring weather intervenes, the light is impeded. Another strip chart in the Weather Service office records how much light gets through, and the observer uses a table of figures to convert this to a visibility distance.

When the RVR visibility falls below one mile, the observer reports the high and low values recorded in the ten minutes before the official weather observation. This gives the approaching pilot an idea of how widely the runway visibility might be fluctuating.

The RVR also is monitored by a computer that averages the RVR readings once a minute and displays the visibility in a small window. The control tower and the radar room use this RVR reading to advise pilots who are about to land. The computer has an alarm that Charlotte weather observers often set to go off if the RVR visibility falls below 6,000 feet.

When ground fog engulfs Douglas Airport, it usually forms to the southwest first, rising off the Catawba River four miles from the approach end of Runway 5. The first heavy fog bank rolled in from the river and settled over Runway 5 at about 3:30 A.M., triggering the RVR alarm. The sudden visibility drop from five miles to less than one mile required a special weather observation, so Green scurried up the stairs to the roof.

The night was perfectly still. He stood patiently, waiting for his eyes to grow accustomed to the darkness. The fog had closed in. Shifting white billows—heaviest in the southwest—had obscured all but a patch of sky directly overhead. He could see broken high clouds through the hole.

The details of the airport became more definitive as his eyes adjusted. The spinning radar antenna 1,000 feet to the southwest was visible. He could see Avis and the Air National Guard a half mile to the east. But that was all.

Back in the office, Green dialed the tower operator, who also must monitor airport visibility when it drops below four miles. They agreed. Three-fourths mile. In ten minutes the RVR had dropped from more than a mile to 1,600 feet.

Through the next hours the fog surged and retreated. The RVR pen swung to and fro on the paper chart—a mile-plus, then down to 1,600 feet, then up again. At 5 A.M. the lighted buildings of downtown Charlotte five miles away were dimly visible through a small hole in the fog. By 6 A.M. the buildings were gone but more sky could be seen. On Runway 5 the fog had grown shallow and covered the concrete like a white blanket. The tips of the two RVR towers protruded from it. "Ground fog depth 10 feet," Green noted in the remarks section of his log.

Green climbed the stairs for the last time at 6:45 A.M. He stood on the warped catwalk boards and studied the east, where the first light of dawn glowed through the fog. The sun would rise in twenty minutes. Clouds had returned above. He could make out two layers. The fog had risen up higher. The RVR towers had disappeared.

Downstairs, seated at the instrument rack, he dialed the tower again.

"I'd say it's still a mile and a half. I can see downtown a bit again, but it's just a hole."

He listened to the reply.

"O.K. A mile and a half."

He hung up the telephone and began to fill out the log with the weather observer's shorthand symbols which every pilot must learn to read. Translated, it read: "Partial obscuration, layer of broken clouds estimated 4,000 feet, a second layer of broken clouds at 12,000 feet; visibility one and one-half miles; ground fog; sea level atmospheric pressure 1,020.5 millibars; temperature 67 degrees Fahrenheit; dew point 65; wind calm, altimeter setting 30.16 inches of mercury; fog obscuring two tenths of the sky." For the first time in four hours the RVR had remained above 6,000 feet in the ten minutes preceding the observation, so there was no mention of its reading.

Green picked up a large circular slide rule lying on the desk and quickly used the temperature and dew point to calculate the relative humidity. Then he picked up the telephone and tripped the switch that set a recorder running. Each hour the weather conditions were recorded on a special telephone number so radio station disc jockeys could quickly obtain a weather report.

He spoke into the receiver.

"At 7 A.M. the sky is partially obscured by ground fog with scattered clouds above. Temperature 66 degrees. Relative humidity 97 per cent. Wind calm. Barometer 30.16 and steady."

Green scooted his chair to the right end of the desk, picked up an electric stylus and began to jot down the same shorthand weather report he had noted a few seconds before in the observer's log. In the tower, the radar room, and the Air National Guard and Eastern Airlines operations offices electric pens hooked to Green's started scratching out what he wrote. Charlotte airport personnel wouldn't have to wait for the weather report on the teleprinter.

Green glanced at the clock: 6:57. He grabbed the log and hurried into the teleprinter room and sat down at a keyboard. He paused for a second, like a concert pianist about to begin a concerto, then sent his fingers flying over the keys. He tore off the tape and carefully positioned it in the transmitter for the computer's call.

It was 6:59. He had made it.

The sun rose four minutes later. As it steadily climbed into the sky it began to warm a Piedmont bathed in patches of fog clinging to the ground. Hills and hummocks, water tanks and radio antennae, high-rise office buildings and amusement park observation towers all protruded from the silky floss—silent, sunbathed sentries guarding a whitewashed plain.

CHAPTER SIX

7:06 A.M.

BRUCE THINGSTAD GLANCED in the side view mirror for traffic coming up on the inside lane and then eased down on the accelerator and pulled into the left lane of Interstate 26 abreast of the truck. He urged the old green Camaro forward a bit more and then, with the exit sign rushing closer and closer, cut back in front of the truck, hit the right turn signal to blinking and braked for the Cosgrove Avenue exit ramp.

He had wanted to stay and watch Karen's airplane take off, but Navy discipline left little room for reporting late for duty. Thingstad was an electrician. Today they would continue work on some satellite communications gear on a destroyer escort tied up at the Navy's Cooper River piers.

He thought of the diamond ring as the Camaro threaded its way through the rush hour traffic. How careful over the summer he had been to learn Karen's ring size without letting her know. When he was home for the Fourth of July, she had admired some rings in a gift shop.

He asked to see them, and while the smiling girl behind the counter watched he tried to slip several on Karen's finger.

"Oh, that won't even fit my little finger," she laughed at one. He tried again until they found one that fit. They didn't buy it but he carefully noted the size: 6½.

One day at work shortly after Karen arrived he picked out a ring at the PX. But they didn't have it in the right size. He ordered it, counting the days remaining until she would return to North Dakota. He wanted to surprise her.

"It should get here in time," the clerk reassured him, promising to rush the order.

He called Monday and then again Tuesday, but, no, the clerk said after leaving the telephone to check, the ring hadn't come. Karen had gotten on the airplane without it.

Marian Sineath carefully switched on the right turn signal and took her foot from the accelerator, slowing the old Ford even more in anticipation of the Summerville exit ramp. She and her sister Julia Bell Merriman had left the airport shortly after six-thirty, when Julia Bell's son John seemed settled.

They headed west on Interstate 26 toward Summerville, with Marian, who was seventy-four, at the wheel. A steady stream of cars kept pulling past them.

"You think Claudia will be surprised to see us so early in the morning?" she asked, turning her gaze briefly from the highway. Marian raised her voice out of habit when she addressed her eighty-four-year-old sister, who seemed to have more and more difficulty hearing.

"She certainly will," Julia Bell said, brushing back a wisp of hair that the breeze from the open window had laid on her forehead.

Marian turned left across the overpass above the interstate and started west on Route 17A.

The two sisters had risen at four-thirty to take John to the airport from Walterboro, fifty miles northwest of Charleston. They brewed coffee, but John declined breakfast so early, insisting he would eat on the airplane. They left a little after five and reached the Charleston airport before six-thirty, sitting in the lobby chatting with John until he assured them he would be all right if they didn't wait to see the airplane off.

"I'll be fine, Aunt Marian," he had said. "I'll just sit here and read my book. You two go on. I'll be fine."

John always seemed to be reading a book.

So they slowly drove from the airport parking lot and turned onto the interstate, planning a stop at the Presbyterian retirement home to visit their younger sister Claudia Reaves.

Seven o'clock in the morning was a bit early to be popping in, but they didn't plan to stay long. Marian also wanted to visit her friend Mrs. Knight in Knightsville. The old woman's husband recently had died.

Jim Wilkes sat at the desk in the Eastern operations office counting the ticket coupons from Flight 212. He carefully stacked the first-class coupons in one pile, coach-class in another. With the same stamp he'd used at the counter in the lobby he imprinted "CHS 212 SEPT 11" on each coupon which was worth money until canceled.

His count complete, he turned to the computer terminal, called a CODACOM by Eastern employees. He typed in "September 11, 212" and waited. A form appeared on the screen and he began using the keyboard to enter information. He typed in data about how much fuel, baggage and air freight the DC-9 had aboard. Then he added the passenger information: seventy-one coach passengers, sixty-six bound for Charlotte, five continuing to Chicago; seven first-class passengers, five for Charlotte, two for Chicago; no non-ticketed children.

One Chicago passenger would need a wheelchair.

Wilkes bundled the ticket coupons into first-class and coach envelopes. He slipped the envelopes into a larger company mail container. The station's company mail bound for Miami would be collected in a large red bag and flung into the cargo hold of the last departing flight that night.

The telephone with a speaker where the dial should be that sits on the operations office desk is a radio link to Eastern aircraft. Wilkes turned to it now, waiting for the crew of 212 to call in with the information every departing flight relayed once off the ground.

"Charleston, 212," the call came a few seconds later. "On the hour. Zero five. Seventeen thousand."

Wilkes picked up the telephone receiver and pushed a button in the handle between the earpiece and mouthpiece.

"Thank you very much, 212. Good day," he replied.

The shorthand message from Captain Reeves meant the aircraft had left the Charleston gate on time at 7 A.M. It had taken off at 7:05 A.M. with 17,000 pounds of jet fuel aboard.

Wilkes rose, walked down the hall and into the area behind the ticket counter. It was deserted. The others had gone upstairs for coffee. Only the clicking of a teleprinter under the counter broke the silence. He glanced down at the machine. It was printing out the tickets for the passengers the computer listed for the 11 A.M. flight to Charlotte. When they finished coffee, the others would come down and tear the long string of tickets apart and stuff each one in an envelope to await the 11 A.M. rush hour.

CHAPTER SEVEN

7:07 A.M.

KAREN OSTREIM CLOSED her eyes. She groped for the release button, found it, reclined the seat and then snuggled deeper into the cushion, a beatific smile on her face framed by long blond hair. She felt suffused with a warm glow as her thoughts drifted—to Bruce, to his house trailer, to happy days and nights of her vacation spent there, to Charleston.

She hadn't particularly liked Charleston. Black people, so many black people. Everywhere. Their presence was alien to a farm girl born and raised on the endless plains of North Dakota. They *did* seem to smell different. She'd mentioned that in a letter sent back home to Edie Iverson, her best friend at the hospital. And Bruce teased her, playing to her fears. "Bruce says they may haul me off —scares me so I sit while he's working," she confided to Edie in the letter she dashed off one rainy afternoon while watching television in the trailer and waiting for Bruce to come home from work.

Bruce Thingstad. They met at a party at Taskar's Cooley outside Kenmare, North Dakota. The party had formed spontaneously. When the evening shift ended Karen and Jean Bodensteiner and some other nurses and nurses aides at Kenmare's tiny Deaconess Hospital headed for the cooley, a picnic area beside Lower Des Lacs Lake.

The shift ended at 11 P.M. It was midnight before they had a
fire going in the fireplace. They sat on the picnic tables talking,
steadily drinking the Budweiser and shouting at new arrivals to the
party. The firelight played on their faces, casting long shadows toward the lake and the trees. The ground was muddy from the winter snow runoff and an afternoon rain shower. Some of them, Budweiser cans in hand, had gone crashing through the trees and
bushes in the dark looking for wild flowers. The early May night
chill was a reminder of the winter just past.

Bruce and a friend came late. They sat on a table quietly drinking and talking and ignoring the din about them. Then Karen spotted them.

"What's your name?" She stood in front of Bruce, hands on
hips, feet planted wide apart, smiling, her attitude one of teasing
confrontation.

"Yes, you. What's your name?" she asked, fixing Bruce with
her gaze. He smiled bashfully and mumbled something.

"What's that?"

"Bruce."

"Hi, Bruce. Who are you?"

Karen Ostreim had come to the thirty-six-bed hospital at Kenmare nine months earlier, just after graduation from nursing
school at the University of North Dakota at Grand Forks. Big-
boned, plump, long blond hair, she had the infectious, open
personality of the Scandinavians who settled the plains at the Canadian border at the turn of the century. Her ready laugh was jubilant and booming. She quickly made friends and in less than a
year had a large circle of acquaintances in the small town. She
readily singled out a stranger and broke the ice, just as she did
with Bruce, who had come home on leave from the Charleston,
South Carolina, Naval Base.

Bruce sipped his beer and watched the jolly girl drift back toward the fire, stopping to throw an arm around someone and then
burst out laughing. The sound seemed to come from her toes. She
had several beers' head start.

Suddenly she strode back to the picnic table.

"Come on. What's your name? Where'd you come from?" She
laughed and Bruce chuckled.

He scooted over and patted the table beside him. They began to talk. He asked for a date.

Bruce picked Karen up at the hospital at the end of the day shift for their first date. They spent the rest of the afternoon prowling the narrow blacktop farm roads, Karen snapping Polaroid pictures of Bruce posing beside towering tractor tires, combines, gang plows and other farm implements that tilled the vast North Dakota farms. Bruce wanted to show them to some of his Southern farm boy friends in the Navy who were used to small tractors and twenty- or forty-acre farms. It was a strange first date, but it intrigued Karen.

Kenmare, North Dakota, sits twenty-five miles south of the Canadian border on the east slope of a narrow, shallow valley the Des Lacs River has carved from the flat prairie that stretches as far as the eye can see. The sluggish river has formed two natural lakes that stretch up the valley for more than twenty miles. Kenmare is on the east flank of the valley at the upper end of Lower Des Lacs Lake, a five-mile-long finger of water.

The town is a drab but conservatively prosperous community of about 2,000 people, drawing its wealth from the rich black soil and the short growing season that produces bountiful crops of small grains. Kenmare has no slums or ghettos. The frame houses with asbestos shingle siding are modest but well maintained. Power boats on trailers sit in many driveways. The farmers who drive into town each day come in late model sedans and pickup trucks that are paid for. America's expanding role as the world's producer of feed grains has assured Kenmare's prosperity.

The Kenmare business district—like that of many small towns—is laid out around a central square. Two bars, two cafes, a bank, drugstore, dress shop, J. C. Penney's, funeral home, newspaper office and hardware store face the square. From one corner of the square Kenmare visitors can gaze past the inevitable grain elevators and Soo Line railroad tracks a mile across the lake to the opposite valley slope and a resumption of the endless prairie.

Bruce Thingstad grew up in Kenmare and on the farms around it. From age eleven he worked summers, weekends and school vacations on the farms. He joined the Navy in 1967 and re-enlisted

in 1971, attracted by a cash bonus and an uneasy economy outside
the Navy.

Karen Ostreim grew up on a large farm outside Rolette, another
small farming community 100 miles east of Kenmare and fifteen
miles from the Turtle Mountain Indian Reservation. The third of
four children, she belonged to 4-H, played in the Rolette High
School band and graduated in 1969 as salutatorian of her small
class. Her mother was a registered nurse and Karen entered the
university at Grand Forks, determined to become a nurse, too.

The rural people of North Dakota still retain the neighborly in-
terdependence of pioneer times that is vanishing from much of
American life. As recently as the turn of the century the North
Dakota prairies remained a frontier beset by harsh winters,
drought, a short growing season and a remoteness that challenged
the fiercest spirit. The Norwegians, Danes, Swedes, Russians and
Germans who broke open the rich black soil survived only by
helping one another. The farmer was paid once a year when the
crops came in. The family that pitched in to help a neighbor raise
a barn or seed a field did so not only from neighborliness but also
from an underlying sense of self-preservation.

The people of North Dakota grew up close to the land and to
one another. The ties of one family to another through blood, marriage or shared adversity are complex but strong. The sense of in-
terdependence transcends personal relationships to embrace poli-
tics and economics, fostering a regional sense of oneness. There is
a genuine desire to serve among these rural people, a God-fearing
selflessness, a patriotic pioneer spirit that survived the American
cynicism following Vietnam.

Nursing was an attractive calling for a farm girl of Norwegian
lineage. It was an acceptable way to serve. Karen Ostreim emerged
from the University of North Dakota liberated enough to want a
career, liberated enough to invite a man to spend the night. But
she clung to traditional values and spoke wistfully of marriage,
children and family life within the close-knit fabric of a North Dakota town.

Karen Ostreim, Jean Bodensteiner and Marilyn Berg, brand-
new registered nurses, came to Kenmare Deaconess in the fall of
1973 from the university. They earned what seemed a grandiose

$3.50 an hour, took apartments on the third floor of the sagging Irvin Hotel beside the railroad tracks and grain elevators and became fast friends. Edie Iverson, a nurse's aide, was drawn into the circle.

Kenmare Deaconess is a thirty-six-bed hospital built of masonry block in the mid-1950s but equipped, in the eyes of the young nurses, as if it were operating two decades earlier. The patient census, even in the best of times, seldom topped twenty. The difficulty of attracting doctors to the small town dictated the work load. With one or two doctors practicing, the hospital staff would swell to six or more nurses and as many aides. Then a doctor would leave, the patients would be transferred to Minot forty-five miles away and layoffs would decimate the hospital staff.

Through late 1973 and into 1974 the hospital staff stood at full strength. But as the months passed and the new nurses settled into their career, they began to view their first jobs with a seasoned perspective. All but the most routine emergency cases went on to Minot. Twenty patients or less in the busiest times and half of those extended-care nursing patients. Outdated equipment. Resistance to new ideas.

"My God. Can you imagine? We don't even have oxygen piped into the rooms," someone would remark, perhaps for the hundredth time. In Grand Forks, the teaching hospitals had oxygen piped to outlets in each room.

"Here we have to wheel these big old heavy oxygen tanks up to the bed," someone else would respond.

Once Karen and Edie went to the basement to get a new oxygen cylinder. Somehow a valve jiggled open as they wheeled the tank down the hall. A loud "whoosh" filled the narrow space, sending both women leaping into the air. Karen hit the floor running. Then suddenly she stopped in midstride. Her booming laugh joined the racket.

"If it's going to blow up, Edie, running isn't going to do any good," she shouted. They closed the valve and giggled all the way upstairs.

Nursing schools teach nurses to spend time with their patients, a luxury most nurses in busy hospitals never have. But life at Deaconess was slow, even boring, and the young nurses had ample time. Karen discovered her forte: kibitzing with patients. She could get the most reluctant geriatric patient up to walk. She could yell right back at the cranky old farmer and bully him into a good mood. She became a favorite with the elderly long-term care patients.

"Where's Karen?" they asked when she was off duty.

In May Jean and Marilyn took jobs at the much larger Rolla hospital 100 miles to the east, not far from Rolette, where Karen grew up. They sought a more challenging hospital. They loaded a pickup truck with their possessions, like modern Okies heading for California. After Marilyn got off her last night shift, she and Karen went out drinking with a couple of fellows. They all came back at dawn wearing cowboy hats acquired somewhere, with an extra one for Jean, who had gone to bed rather than party. The beer drinking continued through the morning until they reached Rolla and moved into their new apartment.

After a visit, Karen returned to Kenmare and stayed on at Deaconess.

Bruce had two weeks of his leave remaining when he met Karen and carried her about photographing farm machinery. They seldom were apart after that. They went for long rides through the greening farmland, talking. They went to Kenmare's single movie theater sandwiched between the J. C. Penney's and the optometrist. They drank beer at Wayne's Bar, where a sign on the door warned: "Under 21 STOP." A few nights they went to the restaurant at Lake Shore Float, twelve miles up the lake, where they could eat, drink and dance. Bruce cooked steaks in the basement apartment Karen had rented when she moved out of the Irvin Hotel. They watched television. Bruce spent the night.

When Bruce returned to duty in Charleston they quickly learned the frustration of sustaining a love affair by telephone and letter. Sometimes the late night telephone calls would last an hour, ninety minutes, sometimes two hours.

The ringing telephone would drag Bruce to consciousness and he would groggily pick up the receiver.

"Hi. It's me. Whatcha doin'?" the bright voice would sing.

"What d'ya think I'm doing. I was sleeping." Duty for him began at seven-thirty each morning.

"I thought so." She would laugh.

"What's the matter? Can't you sleep?"

"Oh, not really. I just thought I'd call and see what you're doing."

Bruce returned to Kenmare for a long Fourth of July holiday just to see Karen. Then the letters and telephone calls resumed.

Karen talked of little else at work. But she was plagued by a vague uncertainty.

"I don't know, Edie. I don't know if I'm ready. But ya know what I mean? I think this is it."

In July Karen took a week of vacation and she and her college friend Karen Zacher drove to Spokane for the World's Fair. Then they went on across Washington to the Pacific Ocean, where late one afternoon as the setting sun turned the foam crimson they waded into the surf. Karen rolled up her pants and plunged in, grimacing over her shoulder and clowning as Karen Zacher snapped pictures with the Instamatic.

"I think I'm going to marry you," Bruce said matter-of-factly in a telephone call not long after that.

There was silence on the other end of the telephone.

"Oh?" she replied after a few seconds.

"Well, why not?" Bruce said.

"Oh, why not?" she replied.

In August Karen asked for her remaining two weeks of vacation and at the end of the month flew to Charleston to spend the time with Bruce. Edie drove her to Minot and stood beside the metal detector watching through the airport windows as Karen walked across the asphalt to board the North Central Airlines DC-9. In Chicago, Karen, who once flew to Minneapolis-St. Paul for her pediatric nursing training, bought a life insurance policy for the rest of the trip to Charleston and the return to Minot. She sometimes exhibited her stolid father's cautious approach to life.

For Karen, Charleston had been hot and muggy. She and Bruce went for a boat cruise past the harbor sights, including Fort Sumter. They drank beer at the air base. They went to the beach, where it rained and Bruce wanted to skinny-dip in the dark but Karen declined. They drank beer instead and Karen became drunk. They fought—lovers' quarrels. They made up and Bruce bought Karen a hairbrush and a bracelet and perfume and apologized. They talked more about marriage. Bruce was eager. Karen was reluctant at times. They went out for dinner. Bruce refused to let Karen pay for anything until she firmly insisted either she buy dinner or groceries.

"I've gotten bites all over me," she told Edie in her letter. "Must be some kind of bugs. Bruce has bites all over his butt—not me though—just a lot of hickies. On my butt. My stomach. Won't let him give me any that people can see."

The Eastern DC-9 gave a small lurch, tugging Karen's thoughts back to the present. She opened her eyes and stared at the ceiling. The hairbrush. Damn. She'd forgotten to pack the new hairbrush. She'd left it in the tiny bathroom.

CHAPTER EIGHT

7:08 A.M.

"FLAPS UP, PLEASE," First Officer James Daniels ordered.

"Up," Captain James Reeves barked, reaching deftly across the center control pedestal to raise the flap handle trigger and shove the metal bar full forward. The flaps, extended during takeoff to give each wing more aerodynamic lift, tucked themselves slowly into the wings.

Reeves reached above his head, craning his neck backwards slightly, and began flipping switches on the overhead panel, a thirty-inch-wide expanse of gauges, dials, switches and buttons reaching nearly three feet behind the two pilots, almost to the door of the crowded cockpit. Working from memory as much as the abbreviated checklist, he flipped the engine ignition switch to "off," the air conditioner automatic shutoff to "override" to prevent sudden loss of cabin pressurization should an engine fail and the "No Smoking" sign to "off." Reeves smiled, thinking of the passengers in the rear of each compartment anxiously awaiting that switch. Now, like a raggedly choreographed dance group, they were fumbling for cigarettes and lighters.

Through all this Daniels sat with his right hand gripping the control wheel between his legs, the left hand resting on the two throttle levers at the center control pedestal. His eyes constantly ranged over the instrument panel, pausing most often at the engine performance instruments, the airspeed indicator and the flight director, a grapefruit-sized orb. Hooked to a computer, the flight director constantly positioned a pair of green triangle-shaped guides that told Daniels how much to move the control wheel to make the DC-9 turn or climb properly.

Now the copilot's eyes began pausing more often at the altimeter on his side of the instrument panel, watching the large needle, like the sweep second hand on a watch, approach the number *5,* signifying 1,500 feet of altitude above the Charleston airport. As the altimeter needle reached the *4,* he caressed the throttle levers back slightly, concentrating as he did so on the EPR and RAT gauges, one for each engine, setting the EPRs at 196 and the RATs at 185. The DC-9 now was in maximum climb power, a small but important reduction from the thundering thrust that had turned heads a few seconds earlier as the jet boomed down the runway and into the air.

Reeves picked up the radio microphone, draped for convenience over the side window latch.

"Departure, Eastern 212," he said, depressing a small button.

"Eastern 212, Charleston approach control," a controller in the darkened radar room in the Charleston terminal building immediately replied. "Radar contact. Climb and maintain . . . ah . . . seven thousand."

"Awright. We'll go up to seven," Reeves replied, replacing the microphone and dialing "7000" into the altitude alert window on the instrument panel above the windshield. A buzzer would ring just before the airplane reached 7,000 feet, a reminder the controllers had temporarily forbidden ascent beyond that.

During this cockpit "cleanup," which had taken only ten seconds, Daniels had been holding the DC-9 in a graceful right turn to bring Eastern 212 around on a course toward Charlotte, 150 miles to the northwest. It was the turn that afforded Richard Arnold his rich view of the Charleston peninsula.

Eastern 212 took off on Runway 21, which put it on an initial compass heading of 210 degrees—south southeast. The flight plan stored in the FAA computer in Jacksonville, Florida, specified a route along a radio beam from Charleston called Victor 53 that

would take the airplane northwest for thirty-three miles, then
north northwest eighty-one miles to Columbia, South Carolina,
and then due north eighty-five miles to Charlotte.

So Daniels turned his control wheel to the right slightly, lowering the right wing, leading the forty-five-ton machine into a gentle
right turn. At Daniels' first movement of the wheel, the flight director computer sensed the pilot's desire to turn right. The green
guides, called command bars, promptly shifted a set amount to the
right. As the pilot turned the control wheel, a miniature airplane in
the face of the instrument inserted itself between the command
bars. Without having to look outside the airplane or refer to other
instruments, Daniels rolled Eastern 212 into a perfect turn with
just the correct amount of bank, so gently that had the stewardesses been up and about they would not have spilled a single drop
of coffee.

While still a student and before the first exhilarating solo flight,
the pilot is taught to use his eyes like a searchlight, constantly
scanning the instrument panel for the slightest hint of something
wrong, something abnormal. From the moment Daniels advanced
the throttles on the runway at Charleston both pilots' eyes had relentlessly searched the dozens of glass discs that stared at them.
Flight director, airspeed, altitude, vertical airspeed, engine gauges,
oil temperature and pressure, fuel quantity, fuel flow, hydraulic
pressure, even vibration of each engine, more than 200 readings
that the two pilots had to be capable of monitoring and interpreting.

As Daniels smoothly began the right turn, his eyes returned with
increasing frequency to the radio navigation instrument preset on
the ground to indicate reaching Victor 53, the airway that would
carry Eastern 212 away from Charleston. He watched the airplane
compass heading, displayed on a circular instrument hooked to a
magnetic compass, as it slowly crept up to 330 degrees. Then he
turned the control wheel slightly to the left, raising the right wing,
terminating Richard Arnold's view.

Captain Reeves maintained his own instrument scan, a bit more
relaxed, reflecting both his fatigue and his passive role as aircraft
commander and copilot during the leg to Charlotte. His eyes
strayed out the side window, where a translucent haze, the product
of thin ground fog and air pollution, hugged the forested plains

west of Charleston, dotted by housing developments, small towns and the patchwork quilt of farmers' fields. Summer still prevailed over autumn and the leaves of the trees hadn't begun to turn yet. As the airplane swung right Reeves glanced past Daniels to the east and the Atlantic Ocean disappearing into the horizon. A broken deck of clouds high above grew redder and redder in anticipation of the sunrise.

Reeves stretched his arms out in front of him, raising them slightly to avoid hitting the instrument panel, and flexed his back and shoulder muscles. Then he yawned, an open-mouthed delicious yawn that he might have stifled at a dinner party but in which he luxuriated within the privacy of his office, the airplane cockpit.

A raucous buzzer, like the signal for the end of a basketball game, pierced the cockpit. It would have startled a visitor in the aviators' domain, but neither pilot paid it any attention. Each had heard the sound thousands of times.

When Daniels drew back the throttles to climb power, he also lowered the airplane's nose slightly by pushing forward on the control wheel, lessening the rate of climb and increasing the airspeed. That and the wing flap retraction had substantially changed the aerodynamic forces acting on the airplane's control surfaces on the wings and tail, altering in turn the pressure Daniels had to exert on the control wheel to push it where he wanted. So the copilot squeezed a yellow button on the control wheel, which activated a wheel on the center control pedestal, which moved a control surface atop the DC-9's three-story-high T-shaped tail. The buzzer then sounded to let the pilots know the stabilizer trim had been changed.

It was a warning sound every DC-9 pilot has learned to ignore, so often is it repeated. It would raise alarm only if the buzzer began sounding rapidly, signifying a runaway stabilizer trim system, which could send the airplane into wild gyrations unless the trim system quickly were disabled with an emergency switch on the control pedestal.

A decade before, when Daniels was teaching young boys to fly two-seater Cessna 150 trainers a cable had snapped and the stabilizer trim system failed shortly after takeoff. The small airplane had no warning buzzer. But Daniels correctly diagnosed the cause of the airplane's frantic, frightening bobbing. He used his throttle and the controls that still functioned, barely keeping the airplane under control as he brought it down to an emergency landing in a street. No one was hurt. But he was shaken badly for days afterward. He slowly began to comprehend how nearly uncontrollable the aircraft had been; how much instinctive actions that resulted from several thousand hours of flight experience had taken over; how close he had come to dying.

"Eastern . . . ah . . . 212, climb and maintain one six thousand and . . . ah . . . turn right to a heading of about three six zero for traffic spacing, please." It was Charleston approach control, the controller's voice booming into the cockpit on two loudspeakers, one above each pilot's head.

Daniels turned the control wheel to the right ever so slightly and the right wing dipped, leading the aircraft into a gentle turn.

"O.K. We'll go up to sixteen, right to three sixty," Reeves said, acknowledging the instructions in the shorthand language of pilots and air traffic controllers. He reached up and dialed 16,000 in the altitude monitor, replacing the 7,000 put there a minute before.

The Eastern DC-9 was climbing much faster than the twin-engine propeller-driven Piper Navajo that had taken off before them. The controller was turning the DC-9 away slightly, not wanting to take a chance Eastern 212 might climb into the slower, smaller Navajo.

Daniels glanced at the airspeed indicator, watching the airspeed slowly increase until, as the needle neared 180 knots, he barked: "Slats up."

Reeves reached across the center control pedestal and shoved the slat handle forward beside the flap handle. On the leading edge of each wing the slats—extensions that had given the wing more aerodynamic lift—began to retract, converting the wing to its most efficient shape for the high altitude, high speed flight that was to come.

The stabilizer trim buzzer sounded loudly again. Daniels was squeezing the yellow button again to compensate for further control pressure change caused by the slats' retraction.

"Eastern 212, report passing seven thousand, please," the Charleston radar room instructed.

Reeves's eyes flicked over the lower of his two altimeters: 4,300 feet.

"Roger," he replied, clipping the word so that it was little more than a grunt. The controller's stratagem now was clear. The Navajo was en route to an assigned cruising altitude of 7,000 feet. Once Eastern 212 passed through 7,000 feet, the controller would be free to turn it back on course. There was no other traffic above that.

Reeves glanced out the right window at the ocean in the distance and the brilliant colored clouds.

"Hey. The sun is a comin' up," he shouted, a jubilant note in his voice, caressing the word "sun" with his tongue. A crescent sliver of orange fireball was peeking above the ocean horizon, its fierce intensity muted enough by the haze and clouds so that the two pilots could stare directly at it for a second or two without turning away momentarily blinded. Their day, which had begun in the middle of the night, was dawning at last.

Of the four Eastern 212 crew members, Jim Daniels had risen the earliest, at 3 A.M. He lived in Roswell, Georgia, a small village of old houses thirty-five miles from the airport. He and Kathy and their twin girls, who were five then, had moved from crowded southwest Atlanta in 1971 to the peaceful rural setting, seeking good schools free from the racial tensions in changing Atlanta.

Jim Reeves lived twelve minutes from the airport in early morning traffic, so he arose at three-thirty, showered, shaved and dressed in his black Eastern Airlines uniform. His wife, Jean, a large, plump woman six years older than her husband, rose with him as usual and prepared his Kellogg's Special K cereal and a cup of tea. She sat at the dining table as he hastily ate and rose to leave, carrying a small suitcase and his flight bag.

"Happy birthday, honey," he said at the door, giving her a kiss. It was September 11, Jean's fifty-fifth birthday.

Collette Watson, who six years earlier to the day had graduated from Eastern's stewardess school in Miami, rose about three forty-

five, quietly dressed and slipped from her suburban split-level house
five miles southeast of the Atlanta airport after kissing her husband, Mike, good-by.

Eugenia Kerth rose about the same time, dressed by the
dimness of the hall light in her condominium town house south of
the airport and, skipping breakfast, knelt over her husband, Jim,
lying on his back in their bed, and kissed his shoulder, her long
hair cascading over his face.

"See ya," she whispered. He mumbled something and she stole
from the room. Jim was preparing for final exams and in a week
would receive his associate of arts degree.

Jim Daniels parked his aging Toyota in the Eastern employees
parking lot and swung aboard the purple school bus that ferried
Eastern crews around the airport. He nodded at a stewardess,
spoke to a couple of Boeing 727 captains he vaguely knew and
started down the aisle as the driver sent the bus lurching forward.
Midway back sat Jim Reeves, the only DC-9 captain.

"Guess you're going the same place I am?" Daniels grinned,
dropping down beside Reeves.

"Yeah. I type-twoed it," the captain said.

"Me too," Daniels replied.

Neither pilot had known in advance who would share the cockpit on the coming two-day trip. Both had availed themselves of a
union contract provision allowing them to bid for the trip on short
notice when the originally scheduled pilots weren't available.

They stepped off the bus and entered a side door at the northwest corner of the terminal building that let them into the now silent Eastern passenger concourse. A few steps, and they turned
into an unlocked, unmarked door and deposited their suitcases and
flight bags on roughly built wooden racks. Then they turned down
a hallway and climbed a flight of stairs to the crew scheduling
office.

Each time a pilot comes to the airport for a flight, he first must
check in here. The crew schedulers sit with their computer consoles behind windows, like parimutuel dealers at a racetrack.
There are windows for Boeing 727 pilots, Lockheed L-1011

pilots, and McDonnell Douglas DC-9 pilots. Reeves and Daniels checked their mailboxes among the 1,500 Atlanta Eastern pilot boxes in the lounge and retraced their steps down the stairs to flight operations.

The flight operations office is long and narrow, the wooden suitcase racks at one end, the agent's counter at the other. A rotating carousel bulletin board in the middle of the floor holds weather reports; telephones along one wall connect directly to the Eastern Airlines dispatcher and weather offices at the headquarters in Miami; television monitors tell pilots at which gate they will find their airplanes. On one wall large weather maps received on a facsimile machine are displayed, giving a pilot an overall view of the weather he can expect in the region of his flight.

The Formica counter behind which the operations agents work has clips bolted to its surface. Under each clip an agent assembles all the documents for an upcoming flight.

"Got that ferry to Charleston . . . uh . . . what's the number?" Reeves asked.

"Yes, sir. Seventy-one sixteen. Right here," the rotund, balding man behind the counter said, tapping a clip. He wore the Eastern ground employee's uniform—blue pants, white shirt with a name tag on the pocket and a checkered tie.

Reeves leafed through the papers. There was a computer printout of pertinent information about the flight. Airplane No. 984; empty ferry flight to Charleston; route of flight; time en route; 17,000 pounds of jet fuel aboard; 5,000-pound burn-off. There was a dispatch release form which Reeves had to complete and sign, weather reports, a cargo and weight manifest, computer-generated instructions about conserving fuel.

Reeves turned to the weather carousel, studied it, and then glanced at the weather maps, which depicted a large high pressure area over much of the eastern United States, a sign of good weather. He walked to a nearby counter and began filling out the forms.

Daniels meanwhile had examined the weather charts, peered discreetly over Reeves's shoulder at some of the forms and then waited for the captain to finish. Then they studied the TV monitors and found that their bird awaited them at Gate 31, the far end of the concourse. They picked up the bags and began the long hike, exiting finally onto the humid, glaringly lighted concrete ramp area. Their DC-9, the numbers *984* visible on the side of the white nose, stood partially hidden in the shadows, its windows dark, its fuselage door open, the metal stairway extended, waiting. Daniels set his bags at the foot of the stairway, extracted a flashlight from his bag and began a slow, methodical inspection of the airplane's exterior, looking thoughtfully into the wheel wells, examining tires, brakes, hydraulic lines, instrument ports, control surfaces and the two jet engines at the rear of the fuselage, searching for anything out of the ordinary.

As Daniels finished and turned to climb the stairs to join Reeves in the cockpit, the two stewardesses approached across the concrete, their heels tapping loudly and the floodlights casting long shadows in front of their bodies.

"Good morning, ladies," Daniels said cheerily, standing aside politely, his bags in hand, as Collette Watson and Eugenia Kerth climbed the stairs.

A few minutes later the airplane thundered through the black night, the lights of rural Georgia and then South Carolina twinkling three miles below them, the two stewardesses curled up in the empty passenger seats asleep.

"Good morning, Mr. Wilkes, sir," Jim Reeves said fifty-five minutes later, striding into the Eastern operations office in Charleston, taking the flight documents tucked under a clip and handing over some completed forms Wilkes needed.

Daniels greeted Wilkes by name, too, when he came in a few minutes later after another walk-around inspection of the airplane and a bit of gossip with the blue-coveralled linemen who had begun heaving orange mail sacks into the DC-9's cargo holds. Their voices were nearly drowned out by the roar of the airplane's auxiliary power unit, which the pilots had fired up to supply air conditioning to the cabin while the stewardesses made coffee and prepared serving cups.

"Looks like ya got some of that old Carolina ground fog," Wilkes remarked idly as Reeves began unrolling the paper that had collected on a spool after passing through the weather teleprinter. The captain searched for the 6 A.M. Charlotte weather report.

"Yeah . . ." Reeves said, finding the report and translating the National Weather Service symbology. "Seems we do," he said more to himself. He looked up at Daniels and saw the copilot's face, a question mark.

"It's partial obscuration, one and one half miles, ground fog," the captain relayed. "The RVR is sixteen hundred to six thousand and—" Reeves studied the last notation. "And ground fog depth is ten feet."

He dropped the paper and watched it spool back up off the floor.

"Sittin' right there on the runway," Daniels said to no one in particular.

They chatted a few more minutes and then ambled back out to the cockpit while Wilkes went off to begin his ticket lift in the holding lounge.

Now, a mere 150 seconds after lifting off the Charleston runway, the airplane already was 4,000 feet high and five miles away from the airport. And the sun was coming up, signaling the end of that low period that besets the person who must stay up all night or rise in the darkest hours, spirits sagging in the long minutes before the dawn announces a new beginning.

Reeves stretched again and swallowed, feeling his ears pop and clear.

"Navajo six nine Lima, climb and maintain eight thousand," the loudspeakers in the cockpit ceiling boomed.

"O.K. We're out of three for eight," the Navajo's pilot replied.

Reeves smiled.

"You know, there was this colored gal . . . an' they didn't have many colored folks out in Arizona. She's gonna go out there. So she did," he said, beginning to chuckle.

"She got off this bus, ya know. As soon as she got off this bus she looked. She sees this old gal standing on the street corner almost as dark as she was.

"But her hair was as straight as a string. Went straight down her back."

Daniels began to chuckle too, partly to let the captain know his first officer was appreciative and partly in recollection. The joke sounded familiar.

"She looked and she walked over and she says, 'Who is you?' The old gal says, 'Well, I'm a Navajo.' 'Oh,' the colored gal says. 'You is? How's business? I's a Nigaho.'"

Daniels laughed, not a polite chuckle, but a hearty "Yuk. Yuk. Yuk."

It was time-honored cockpit ritual. The captain told the first joke. Once properly acknowledged, a good first officer then weighed in with his own.

"We got one boy," Daniels said, "in crew schedule. Saying about his wife. Says, well she's lazy, dirty around the house. You know, she never cleans anything up. Says everytime he wants to take a piss the sink is full of dishes."

Reeves burst out laughing.

"I can't tell a story," Daniels said self-consciously. "This old boy can tell it pretty good."

Even though they joked, neither pilot let his eyes wander from the incessant sweep of the instruments. The hand on Reeves's lower altimeter was nearing zero.

"Eastern 212's out of seven," Reeves said into the microphone. The Charleston controller had told the pilots to report reaching 7,000 feet.

"Eastern 212, roger. Proceed direct Fort Mill."

"Direct Fort Mill," Reeves responded. "Thank you."

"And, Eastern 212, contact Jacksonville Center on frequency one two seven point nine five. Good day."

Reeves reached down to the radio switches at the rear of the center control pedestal and dialed frequency 127.95 into the window of radio number two. He adjusted other switches so they could communicate on the new frequency and then picked up the microphone, glancing at the altimeter.

CHAPTER NINE

7:12 A.M.

HILLIARD, FLORIDA, is surrounded by jack pines, palmettos and dark swamps. Seven miles south of the Georgia state line, it is a tiny bump in the road whose single traffic light scarcely impedes the rushing automobiles ferrying tourists to and from Florida's warm, sandy beaches.

Decaying wooden frame houses set on concrete posts to keep them off the oozing swampland are scattered along both sides of the highway. Souvenir stands with homemade quilts hanging on clotheslines and signs that proclaim: "Oranges 2 bags for $1.00" are dotted along the road. The old black man sunning himself against the wall of the Majik Market and the white man with bulging stomach, close-cropped hair, beefy hands and a stubby cigar who emerges to fill a gas tank are pluperfect stereotypes of the Red-neck South. Time, like the stream of cars—windows closed to preserve their air conditioning—is passing Hilliard by.

A quarter mile down a side road, behind chain link fencing topped by six strands of barbed wire, sits a two-story building of yellow brick and bright blue corrugated metal siding surrounded by paved parking lots. A massive red and white antenna topped by flat microwave reflectors towers over the building. Entrance to the compound is through a single gate watched over from a glass-walled office by uniformed, armed guards. Small red, white and blue shields on the fence warn against trespassing upon U. S. Government property. A sign announces the Jacksonville, Florida, Air Route Traffic Control Center operated by the Federal Aviation Administration.

Inside the building in the permanent twilight of the control room, Bump Pate, a Hilliard area native who raises a few cattle on a small farm, roused himself from a sleepy slouch. He stood, stretching his arms above his head, emitting such a guttural yawn that Pete Coggins, who had just reported for duty, turned around, startled. Above and to the left of the radar screen a digital clock flashed the time: 7:08 A.M. In less than an hour Pate could sign off and go home to bed.

Pate sat down and idly fingered the switch button in his hand connected to the microphone on his headset.

"Jacksonville Center, Eastern 212. Climbing to sixteen," he heard in his earphone.

Pate glanced at the lower right corner of his radar screen, where a tiny triangle had appeared. Beside it the computer had printed several words. It was Eastern 212, which had taken off a few minutes earlier from Charleston en route to Charlotte.

"Eastern 212, roger. Climbing to one six thousand," Pate responded, squeezing his microphone button. He looked to the left of the radar screen at a small rectangular screen where the computer had printed, in the same electronic phosphorescent green, a list of airplanes approaching the Charleston Low Altitude Sector.

"And . . . ah . . ." He found the notation for Eastern 212.

"Squawk code one one zero zero and ident."

A few seconds later the radar target for Eastern 212 lit up brightly and then faded back. The pilot had dialed the code—1100 —into his transponder, then pushed a button labeled "Ident" that sent a burst of radio signals to the radar antenna. All airliners are equipped with transponders, devices which receive radar signals from the ground, amplify them, add data and then send it back. A transponder makes it easier for radar to track an airplane.

The Jacksonville Air Route Traffic Control Center—known simply as Jax Center—is one of twenty such complexes erected by the FAA across the United States in the early 1960s. Supreme traffic cops, the centers co-ordinate cross-country air traffic flow. For example, an airliner leaving Miami for New York begins under the jurisdiction of the Miami airport tower. Then Miami Departure Control, radar operators working in a darkened room in the terminal building, follows the jet as it turns northward and begins climbing.

Then it is transferred to Miami Center, which oversees traffic in Florida, the Caribbean and the Gulf of Mexico. Soon the airliner pushes into the airspace of Jax Center, then Atlanta Center, Washington Center, New York Center, New York Approach Control and finally LaGuardia Tower for landing and taxi instructions.

Throughout the flight the airliner is watched on radar along with dozens of other airplanes the controllers are handling simultaneously, airliners and private craft, all going in different directions. The controllers make certain each airplane is nestled in its own little cocoon of airspace so that two airplanes don't collide.

Modern airplanes, especially jets, fly so fast that even when visibility is unlimited—100-mile vistas—pilots are in effect nearly flying blind where seeing other airplanes is concerned. When weather is bad, when thick clouds blanket the earth from treetops upwards, pilots are truly blind, using only their instruments to keep from spinning out of control since they have no ground reference to keep them upright. Radio navigation equipment tells the pilot where he is. But only the controllers, their radar and the complex air traffic control system keep his airplane from hurtling into another.

Pilots fly under two sets of rules of the road—Visual Flight Rules, or VFR, and Instrument Flight Rules, or IFR. Under VFR a pilot must obey the airport tower during takeoff and landing, but most other times is free to fly where he wants, when he wants, with little restriction.

When bad weather restricts visibility, all pilots must fly IFR. Scheduled air carriers must always fly IFR, regardless of the weather. Under IFR pilots are told when to take off, what precise route to fly, when to climb and how fast, when to descend and when to begin entering the airport area for a landing. The pilot flying in the clouds—with nothing but an eerie whiteness outside his cockpit windows, sometimes even with the wing tips lost in the murk—must follow a controller's instructions explicitly. The controller has become his eyes. To deviate invites disaster.

But Eastern 212's flight was nothing as serious as all that. It was early in the morning and there was little traffic. The weather was fine—only a thin ground fog at Charlotte that would burn off with the first rays of the sun. The thirty-minute hop presented no air traffic control difficulties. Takeoff from Charleston under control of the airport tower, transfer to Charleston Departure Control, then Jax Center, Atlanta Center, Charlotte Approach Control and finally Charlotte Tower.

Bump Pate and Kay Alvarez were regulars in Crew F-6, known as F Troop, one of thirty-five twelve-man controller crews at Jax Center. F Troop was one of several crews that had drawn the midnight shift the morning of September 11, but only Pate and Alvarez had signed on at the log for F Troop a few minutes before midnight. The other ten controllers had been parceled out to other crews for day and night shifts during F Troop's midnight duty stint. Only a skeleton force is needed in the early morning hours.

Pate disliked midnight duty. But Alvarez relished it. She had become a full performance level controller or FPL just a few weeks before. On the midnight shift she was alone with a large section of airspace, completely in charge of its traffic. She liked the independence.

They passed the night quietly, working at adjacent radar screens. Pate took his break about one-thirty and ate a supper of tasteless meatloaf, green beans and coffee in the cafeteria. Alvarez took her thirty-minute break at three-thirty—breakfast, fried eggs sunny side up. The occasional airplane was a welcome relief as they walked about their positions, the coiled microphone cords following, stretching, yawning, fighting off sleep.

The Jax Center control room is the size of a high school gymnasium. The ceiling is two stories high, the floor covered with brown carpet and the lighting perpetually low, a never ending dusk. There are no windows, no pictures, no plants, no flowers. A glass-enclosed catwalk stretches across the middle of the room. It serves as a hallway connecting administrative portions of the facility, and as an observation deck for visitors. The windows are dirty from the hand prints—and nose prints—of Jax Center visitors who peer into the gloom, wide-eyed at the spectacle. It is an ant farm seen through glass, an animated cyclorama at Disneyland.

The room has four lines of radar screens, or "positions." Two lines are along either wall. Two more run down the middle of the room, back to back, like washing machines in a Laundromat. The result is two aisles with radar screens on either side. Plain government-issue metal desks protrude into the aisles at set intervals, and desk lamps cast a warm glow onto the crew supervisors who sit at the desks during each shift, one supervisor for every crew.

Each control room position is built around the radar screen, an eighteen-inch-diameter green glass eye set at an angle, like a child's easel. It is flanked by another small rectangular screen on which data about airplanes, weather and other information is printed by the computer. There are groups of switches to change the range of the radar screen, zooming in close for a detailed look at a bit of airspace or pulling back for a broad picture. The console into which the radar screen is built has a counter on which rests a keyboard. A controller uses it to talk to the Jax Center computer. A black ball, the size of a baseball, is set in the counter and the controller can rotate it and cause a little blip of light, a cursor, to move about the radar screen. By setting the cursor on some object on the screen, the target of an airplane, for example, and then typing commands into the keyboard, the controller can instruct the computer about the airplane. He may tell the computer the airplane is climbing to a new altitude, or changing course or altering speed. The computer flashes this news to other controllers at Jax Center or elsewhere who expect to handle the airplane.

The console extends above the controller, taller than a man, curving out over the controller for ease of reaching knobs and buttons. Banks of switches permit selection of radio frequencies into which the microphone is tied. Rows of buttons connect the controller by direct telephone line with other controllers in Jax Center or at departure and approach control at airports in the region. Softly lighted aeronautical maps of the airspace governed by each position top the consoles. They depict the airways, airports, radio navigation stations and restricted areas.

Near each position is a rack for plastic holders about the size of a blackboard eraser. A strip giving information about each approaching flight is inserted into the holders when received from a computer printer. As an airplane traverses a controller's airspace he makes notes on these flight data strips to show instructions given and complied with, requests and other information.

The Low Altitude East controllers working the midnight shift at Jax Center welcome Eastern 212 each morning. It is the harbinger of the end of the shift, the first airplane of an early morning rush that peaks about seven-thirty or seven-forty, just before the midnight shift goes home. A few minutes before seven Pete Coggins signed on to join Pate, and Jerry Lesiege joined Alvarez. They were the 7 to 3 P.M. swing shift on Low Altitude East, brought in to help with the morning rush.

Forty-five seconds after Eastern 212 lifted off the runway and began its slow right turn to the northwest, Bump Pate heard a click in his headset and then the voice of a Charleston radar room controller on the direct telephone lines.

"O.K.," the voice said. "Eastern 212 is a mile and a half southwest. He'll be climbing to seven and going."

Pate glanced at the flight strip that the computer had dutifully tapped out a few minutes earlier. Coggins, who sat by his side and had heard the Charleston report, already was penciling a "7" with a vertical arrow on the strip to indicate a climbing airplane cleared to 7,000 feet. In the rectangular screen, the notation beside EA212 said, "D1104"—takeoff at 11:04 Greenwich Mean Time or 7:04 A.M. EDT.

"Give him direct Fort Mill, direct Charlotte at one six thousand," Pate said to the Charleston controller, who would relay the instructions to the Eastern 212 pilots. The flight strip indicated Eastern 212 had requested 16,000 feet in the flight plan permanently stored in the computer.

"O.K. And let me know when you see him," the Charleston controller responded.

"W.P.," Pate said into his microphone, the initials with which he signed as a controller.

"K.M.," the Charleston controller replied, slurring the letters so that they sounded like the word "came."

All air traffic control conversations are recorded, and interchanges between controllers on phone lines are signed with initials, for the record.

Eastern 212's flight plan called for a dogleg path—along one airway to Columbia and then another to Charlotte. But if the pilot could obtain permission to fly direct from just outside Charleston to the Fort Mill radio navigation station fifteen miles south of Charlotte, he could save several miles, several minutes and several hundred gallons of jet fuel.

"Normally Eastern 212 will request direct Fort Mill every morning when they come over," Pate often explained to trainees. "So we just give it to them. You can even give it to them without their asking. If you can give it to them, then give it."

Coggins penciled in "D FML" on the strip. He tapped the keyboard, advising the computer that Eastern 212 was deviating from its assigned flight plan.

The two controllers turned their attention to other aircraft for a moment and then Pate sat back down in his chair, idly watching the phosphorescent green dots, numerals and letters slowly inching across the screen. His thoughts turned to his request, pending with Jax Center management, to move off the "boards" and into administrative work as an evaluation proficiency and development specialist, a member of the Jax Center training department. Pate had been an FAA controller eight years and before that a Navy air traffic controller. Lately he had been brooding about his future.

"Some guys just want to be controllers. And others have ambitions to move up the ladder to management," he would explain. "I enjoy controlling but you have a period when you're a better controller. But that doesn't last all your life.

"As you get older you lose something. It's bound to come. Everybody is going to run out of his peak. I still consider myself a good controller. But I don't think now I could handle the traffic I could six years ago."

So he had put in his bid to become an EPDS, a move that some veteran controllers would sneer at in their loathing of "management," but one which many controllers make as they contemplate middle age and begin to realize that, like aging quarterbacks, their reflexes, their toleration of constant pressure is beginning to wear ragged.

Pate's gaze strayed to the lower right quadrant of his radar screen. A target had appeared. He sat up and studied the data printed by the computer beside it. Eastern 212. The computer had picked up the transponder code and identified the aircraft. Pate reached up above his head and pushed a button labeled "CHSW."

"Ah . . . Eastern 212, radar contact," he said into the microphone.

"Roger, K.M.," came the reply from Charleston.

"W.P.," Pate answered.

Coggins was busy on another line, so Pate wrote an "R" on the strip, indicating radar contact with the airplane. In Charleston they now should be instructing Eastern 212 to change radio frequencies and contact Jax Center.

"Jacksonville Center, Eastern 212. Climbing to sixteen," the Eastern pilot called, just as expected.

Pate leaned forward and hit his microphone switch.

"Eastern 212, roger. Climbing to one six thousand. Squawk code one one zero zero and ident."

Bump Pate's decision to leave the boards in his mid-thirties and move into a minor administrative post wasn't unusual. Daily attendance at the control room floor burns men out in their prime. A normal retirement by a controller who has spent his career entirely on the boards is rare. Much more usual is an early medical discharge—ulcers, high blood pressure leading to cardiovascular disease, alcoholism or "nerves."

The air traffic controller is the fragile human link in a finely turned technology-based system so sensitive he must constantly hone his skills to the sharpest edge. Frequent split-second decisions can portend life or death as much as those made by the thoracic surgeon in the glaring light of the surgical theater. The controller in a busy facility like Jax Center can expect to spend his eight-hour shift concentrating on his task with the single-mindedness of a soldier pinned down by enemy gunfire, fighting for his life. Only at shift's end can the controller stand and walk away until the next day.

This intensely focused concentration is dictated by the constant stream of aircraft crossing each controller's airspace. Some are climbing, some descending, others cruising. Many are jets, some-

times with more than 200 people on board, gobbling up five or
more miles a minute, descending or climbing 1,500 feet a minute.
The controller must keep them apart. He must think in three-
dimensional terms while watching a two-dimensional radar screen.
He must anticipate where the dozen or more aircraft on his screen
will be in one, two or five minutes. He must see potential air traffic
conflicts before they begin. Two jet airliners fifteen miles apart at
one moment could, if bent on head-on collision, ram together sixty
seconds later, closing on one another at a rate of 1,200 feet per
second. Neither cockpit crew would be likely to see the other airplane until the final seconds—too late to take evasive action.

While concentrating on an aircraft separation problem at the
top of his radar screen, the controller must never allow concentration on the three or four other potential problems elsewhere on
the screen to slacken. In that moment of controller inattention
when two airliners come together with the force of an automobile
hitting a brick wall at 800 miles per hour; in that moment when he
turns the cargo airplane into the side of a cloud-hidden mountain;
in that moment when the airplane, too low, unnoticed, clips the
television station's transmitter tower and spins awkwardly earth-
ward, smashing a peaceful suburban garden, the controller knows
that he will live on—only to die a thousand future deaths reliving
his fatal error.

Thus stress is the air traffic controller's constant companion,
youth and its fast reflexes his only saving grace. As youth fades,
quickly for the controller, he lives increasingly by his wits. Lacking
the speed and agility once taken for granted, the aging quarterback
survives on his ability to read the defensemen's intentions.

Within this stress lies the genesis of the controller's neurosis, a
fear that the pressure is always increasing, that he won't be able to
cope with larger numbers of aircraft and ever more crowded airspace. There is a constant fear that the overloaded system—not
enough radar, not enough controllers, not enough runways—will
set him up for an accident for which he will take the blame, an accident that will maim his psyche for life. Every controller has
heard stories of colleagues who escaped anguished mental prisons
only through self-inflicted death.

Eastern 212's speed now was almost 300 miles an hour. Less

than five minutes after Bump Pate welcomed the DC-9 into the Charleston Low Altitude Sector, the little block of letters and numbers beside the radar target began flashing at him. The same target and flashing data block also had appeared on Kay Alvarez and Jerry Lesiege's radar screen a few paces down the aisle at the Columbia Low Altitude Sector. Lesiege bent closer to read the data block. Eastern 212. Altitude 15,300 feet. Transponder code 1100. Ground speed 325 knots. The flashing data block meant the computer automatically was transferring control from Charleston Low Altitude to Columbia Low Altitude.

Jerry Lesiege, like Bump Pate, began his aviation career in the Navy, just as the Korean War ended, as an airborne radio-radar operator. He spent two years at the University of Miami afterwards and then a brief, unhappy stint managing a dry cleaning shop. A friend urged him to apply at the FAA and six months later, in April 1959, he went to Boston Center. But Lesiege and his wife decided in 1962 to transfer to Florida, or at least somewhere in the warm South. After a long search, he located a Jax Center controller who wanted to swap jobs.

"We had to pay our own moving expenses. We had four kids at that time. One hell of a mess coming down in a small car and U-Haul truck. I think that was the coldest year they had ever recorded here in Jax dating back to the 1800s. My wife and I just looked at each other. 'This is Florida?' We were freezing."

Lesiege rotated the black ball—controllers call it the slew ball— wheeling the cursor, a bright dot of light, up to the Eastern 212 target. Then he tapped a key marked "enter" on the keyboard and the data block stopped flashing on the radar screen. The computer had asked Lesiege and Alvarez to accept control of Eastern 212. They had agreed. The airliner's safe flight through their block of airspace now was in their charge.

Pate had been watching for the data block to cease blinking.

"Eastern 212. Contact Jacksonville Center now on one two four point seven," he instructed. Lesiege and Alvarez handled their traffic on that frequency.

"Twenty-four seven. Good morning," the Eastern pilot promptly answered.

A few seconds later the pilot called the Columbia sector.

"Jax Center, Eastern . . . ah . . . 212. Coming up sixteen thousand."

Alvarez was busy sorting flight data strips. She glanced at Lesiege, who was handling radio communications. He was talking earnestly to someone in Atlanta Center on one of the direct telephone lines. She leaned over and studied the screen, searching for Eastern 212.

"Eastern 212, Jacksonville Center. One six thousand. Ident," she said. A target midway up the screen glowed brightly for a few seconds. She put a checkmark beside the airplane's assigned 16,000-foot altitude and wrote a neat *"R"* to show radio contact.

Kay Alvarez began at Jax Center as a key punch operator after finishing a nine-month business school course. The darkened control room and the life of the controller—mostly men who sat hunched over radar screens muttering into headsets—captivated her. But she couldn't meet the eyesight requirements. So she progressed upwards through the clerical ranks until one day word came of a relaxation in vision standards.

She was accepted, began a two-year on-the-job-training stint and only a few weeks earlier had become a FPL—full performance level controller.

"Well, you do run into discrimination here, just like anywhere," she told her friends. "Some of them have the attitude there is no room for a woman in controlling. It's some of the older guys who have been here twenty years or so. I think some of them resent it that a woman is making the same money that they are. A woman should be at home and raise children. But the young guys are fine."

To a pilot, the voice of a woman controller is as startling as the voice of a male telephone operator.

"When you tell a pilot to do something they sometimes will question you more than if you were a man telling them the same thing. But I notice that they listen because my voice is different. Then if there are a couple of woman pilots you're working, you can expect some man on the frequency to make a remark about women talking.

"Because it's a woman, an air carrier pilot who flies the same route will recognize your voice. Sometimes they'll ask approach control who you are. And sometimes approach control will know and tell them. And then they'll come up on the radio next time through and say your name. Sometimes they'll say, 'Hey, Kay. How are you this morning? Haven't talked to you in a long time.'"

Lesiege reached above his head and hit the black button cutting his phone connection to Atlanta Center. He had heard Eastern 212's call in one ear even while he listened to Atlanta with the other.

"Eastern 212. Jacksonville Center. Ident," he said, failing to note Alvarez' marks on the flight data strip.

"Awright," came the pilot's response, almost a growl.

The target blossomed, again.

Lesiege glanced at the rectangular screen beside the radar, where the computer updated weather information.

"Columbia altimeter, three zero one zero," he said.

"Right," answered Captain Reeves.

In the crowded, noisy cockpit the two Eastern pilots now should be peering into small windows in their respective altimeters and then rotating a knob to set the Columbia barometric pressure in their instruments. The Columbia pressure was one hundredth of an inch of mercury less than the barometric pressure in Charleston.

CHAPTER TEN

7:13 A.M.

JO JO WILLIS OPENED his left eye and peered out from under the bill of his cap at the tall, white stewardess in blue slacks and red vest who emerged from the galley, carrying a tray of coffee cups down the first-class aisle and into the coach section. He was slouched down in seat 3D, leaning up against the window, his chin cupped in his right hand. His outsized denim touring cap was pulled low on his Afro, hiding an acne-scarred forehead and shielding his eyes, permitting covert observation of the first-class cabin.

Cleve Willis sat upright in the aisle seat—3C—his eyes closed and his mouth open, breathing heavily. Sleep, turkey. Sleep, Jo Jo thought, straining to roll his eye far enough left to study his brother in profile. Jo Jo was the younger Willis. He had marked his twenty-third birthday the day before. Cleve had turned twenty-seven six days earlier.

The Willises were night people. They preferred to sleep until two or three in the afternoon and then prowl the streets of Charleston and North Charleston through the evening and into the early morning hours, making the rounds of the clubs, checking on their lieutenants, their runners and the junkies who sold their dope, collecting money, making the scene in Cleve's Cutlass or

Bland's Thunderbird or in one of the string of flashy cars they often rented for a day or two or a week at a time. Sometimes they meted out discipline. A few nights before, Jo Jo had taken a boy everyone called J.J. into Mary Ann's bathroom and pummeled him with short, sharp punches, grunting at each one, until J.J., shrieking with pain and fright, collapsed in a heap beside the toilet bleeding from the mouth, several teeth gone. "Don't mess with us, motherfucker," Jo Jo growled as he stepped from the bathroom and slammed the door.

Boarding a 7 A.M. airplane for New York City was contrary to the Willises' life-style. But National Airlines was on strike and they wanted to get to New York by afternoon to make their contact in Harlem with Cody and Didilly and still have time for the night life along Lenox Avenue. Cleve was particularly attracted by backroom crap games, an activity that had often consumed him during the five years he lived in Harlem after coming north from Greenville, South Carolina, and before his stretch in federal prison on a gun rap.

Rather than sleep the night before the flight, they had gone to Mary Ann's house in downtown Charleston, not too far from the Charleston Battery. Jo Jo, Mary Ann, Cleve and Cleve's new friend, Wanda, a prostitute he had taken up with the week before, were there. Bland had come along and then some others. They sat around talking, a mélange of rock, soul and jazz blaring from a stereo. There was pot and Cleve had some cocaine. Jo Jo smoked a roach and drank Robitussin—a narcotic cough syrup—mixed with beer. People drifted in and out all through the night, sometimes moving off to a bedroom, the tenor of the evening gradually subsiding as one after another sank into a drugged haze. Somehow Wanda had roused herself, coaxed Cleve and Jo Jo into the Volkswagen and driven them to the airport. Cleve purchased two tickets under the aliases of Williams, peeling bills off the thick roll in his pocket.

The aliases were to foil both the narcs and their own colleagues. Narcs monitoring airline reservations lists would spot at once the names Cleve and Jo Jo Willis and know what business took them to New York. The same airline reservation information in the hands of a dope dealer could lead to a ripoff attempt. So they bought their tickets under false names and stashed their guns at Mary Ann's.

Jo Jo turned to stare out the window. The pinkish tint of the clouds above the airplane was fading as the sun climbed higher. The sun had colored in orange the edges of a few puffs of scattered clouds. The vague dark greens and blues of the South Carolina forests were farther below. A haze hugged the ground in several places, hiding it. Jo Jo sat up and leaned over, pressing his nose against the window, looking below and slightly ahead of the airplane. The sun glinted off a large lake, backed up behind a dam across the Santee River, long narrow fingers of lake extending outward where the water had filled valleys. It was Lake Marion, sixty miles southeast of Columbia, South Carolina.

Columbia. Jo Jo had been living in Greenville, his hometown. Cleve was living in New York with Joy, a New York girl, a junkie and prostitute. Jo Jo was mulin' for a dope man named Mississippi, carrying his stuff, delivering it, collecting from Mississippi's dealers.

Columbia. Three years before. He had delivered a package for School Boy, who had gotten it from Mississippi, who had gotten it from New York. A hundred half loads. Good quality dope. Then the narcs came through the apartment door, led by a big, white cop. Mabry. Buford Mabry.

Jo Jo and Brewster Shell, who also was mulin' for Mississippi, were sitting on the couch trying to deal with some Columbia junkie who had heard they were in town. Suddenly the door crashed open.

"Police. With a warrant. Police with a warrant. Up against the wall. Move." Some of the narcs had their guns out and waved them about as they screamed their orders.

Jo Jo and Brewster and the junkie were slammed up against the wall while the other narcs rushed into the rear of the apartment and found Greg and Minnie. When they heard the commotion, Greg and Minnie stuffed most of the dope inside Minnie's panties before the cops burst into the back bedroom.

The narcs went through the apartment with a vengeance while Jo Jo, Brewster, Minnie, Greg and the junkie stood along one wall. They'd all played it cool with those white narcs.

"You can't search me. You're not allowed to search me," Minnie taunted them, daring the white cops to try and search a black woman.

"You let her alone, you hear? She's pregnant. You can't search her. You let her alone," Greg chimed in.

"Where's the dope? Where's your dope?" the narcs yelled back. "We know you've got that dope from Greenville. Where is it?"

Jo Jo remembered how cool he'd been about it. How he'd sassed the narcs.

"Man, I ain't got nothin' to do with this. I's jes' visitin' some friends. I don't know nothin' 'bout no dope," he answered loudly. "You motherfuckers ain't taking me to no jail on no bum rap. I ain't no dope man."

The narcs finally jerked up the couch cushions and found the guns—two automatics and a sawed-off shotgun. That got them excited. Then came the handcuffs and the narcs hustled them roughly down the stairs and into the unmarked cars and off to the county jail.

The jail matron found the dope in Minnie's panties. But Jo Jo had managed to beat the rap. Minnie wouldn't testify and the narcs only got Minnie.

"Coffee, sir?"

Jo Jo turned from the window at the sound of the voice. A stewardess extended a tray of paper cups. Jo Jo nodded his head and took one.

"Sugar or cream?"

"No."

Cleve still slept and the stewardess hesitated by his seat.

"Uh, should I wake your friend?" she asked, looking hopefully at Jo Jo.

"Let him sleep."

He took a sip from the cup and then held it at his chin, the steam bathing his face. Somehow, recalling Columbia reminded him of next week. He hadn't decided whether to show up or jump bail. Armed robbery. He and his friend Cobb had lured an old man between two houses on Gower Street in Greenville and relieved him of $180. But the old man knew who they were. Jo Jo had been short of bread then. He smiled. Now he and Cleve had nearly $20,000 between them. Cleve had $14,000 in his pockets and Jo Jo's $3,300 and Daffy's $3,300 were en route to New York by car. Cody would sell them at least an eighth of heroin and they would bring it back to Charleston and turn a $40,000 profit.

The airplane suddenly jerked. A bump. It jerked again. Jo Jo looked outside. Lake Marion was behind them now. Airplanes hit bumps in the road just like cars, he thought.

CHAPTER ELEVEN

7:15 A.M.

THE COCKPIT OF THE McDonnell Douglas DC-9 is noisy. The airplane's engines are aft on the tail, so knowledgeable passengers sit forward in the cabin, perhaps even buying a first-class ticket just to enjoy a quieter flight. It might thus seem that a DC-9 flight deck crew sitting in the tip of the nose would be even more removed from the noise, working in serene solitude, the silence broken only by the radio, conversation, the click of switches and an occasional warning claxon. Such is not the case, however.

The DC-9 cockpit is noisy not because of the two throbbing jet engines seventy feet aft, but due to the rush of air over the cockpit windows as the airplane's bullet nose slashes through the atmosphere. This noise is a high-pitched whistle, a steady whine that accelerates in pitch and intensity as the airplane's speed increases. It is a steady irritant like the buzz of a faulty fluorescent light only worse, a high frequency tone that won't go away. It is a potential irritant to some pilots, an ever present nuisance that fatigues and debilitates in subtle ways that no one has measured objectively. At the end of a long flight a pilot has only a dim awareness of the toll taken on mind and body by the noise.

As steady hands advanced the throttles on the Charleston runway, and Eastern 212 accelerated in thirty seconds to 150 miles an hour, the relentless whistle resumed. When Captain Reeves complained about his fatigue, First Officer Daniels in the next breath confessed his worries about the noise and the effect of working in an environment pressurized to 9,000 feet followed by rapid returns to the ground. Space exploration has shown that long periods in high altitude artificial environments subtly alter the body's metabolism. Could that happen to airline pilots?

Captain Reeves had a reputation as a cockpit whistler, aimless, tuneless whistling during a flight. He often would tug at an earlobe or pull at his upper lip and his small, neatly trimmed moustache. After the takeoff and cockpit cleanup and beginning of the climb, Jim Reeves whistled intermittently while his eyes kept up the rhythmic sweep—instruments, outside, instruments, outside. Jim Daniels concentrated on flying, maintaining a precise airspeed, an exact heading, the proper climb rate, faultless piloting that wouldn't invite a rebuke from a captain he knew only slightly and with whom he had flown just once before.

Daniels' eyes began returning with increasing frequency to the altimeter, which was creeping up on 10,000 feet. Federal Aviation Administration regulations prohibit flying faster than 250 knots while below 10,000 feet to preclude a jet flying at 350 knots in the same environment as a ninety-knot Cessna 150 trainer.

Daniels had been holding the airspeed at 225 knots. As the altimeter sweep hand crossed the zero, signifying 10,000 feet, he lowered the nose slightly and touched the red trim button once, then twice, sounding the raucous buzzer. Lowering the nose increased the airspeed but reduced the rate of climb. He had traded a fast climb for more speed over the ground. As the airspeed indicator needle crept up on 320 knots, the cockpit noise grew louder, the whistle more high-pitched, more annoying.

Reeves continued whistling. Daniels glanced curiously at the other pilot. Had the captain's whistling gone up a notch in pitch, too? A fleeting amused smile passed over the copilot's face.

A visitor to a DC-9 cockpit is surprised by the small windows and the restricted outside view they provide. It would seem that sitting in the nose of a jet airliner in flight would command an unprecedented panorama of the world outside. Such is not the case. There are three front windows, each about eighteen inches high and twenty-four inches wide. On each side are two windows, one of which will slide open, and above the head of each pilot another small opening that provides a limited view above the cockpit.

The seats have folding armrests and a deep slot is cut from the cushion of each so each pilot can pull his control wheel far back between his legs. The seats are adjustable fore and aft and up and down. When they are positioned so the pilot's feet can reach the rudder pedals, the outside view is further restricted by a ledge at the bottom of the front windows that extends outward over the instrument panel underneath.

This shelf is called the glare shield. Its edge is about two inches thick and switches and indicators are built into it so they are slightly below the pilot's line of sight. There are master caution and warning lights—two for each pilot—flight director control switches and the altitude alert system into which Reeves dialed each new assigned altitude. A pilot who wants to look directly forward and below the airplane would have to lift himself up in his seat and lean forward to see over the glare shield. Even then the area immediately below is obscured.

The side windows afford better visibility. But again a pilot who wants to look at the ground below the airplane must lean sideways and almost press his nose against the glass.

The seats are separated by the autopilot controls and the radio console, a flat surface studded with knobs and dials and switches to control the communications and navigation radios. The console extends forward toward the instrument panel and swells into a rounded hump from which protrude the engine throttles, the flaps, slats and speed brake handles and controls for aileron, rudder and elevator trim, cabin pressurization and fuel flow. The transponder is forward of these levers, set against the instrument panel base. The weather radar and two additional navigation radios are beside it.

The vertical instrument panel begins where the horizontal control pedestal ends, extending upward to below the glare shield, divided into three segments. The center panel above the control pedestal is filled with gauges that monitor the two jet engines—fuel flow, fuel pumps, oil quantity, pressure and temperature, engine pressure ratio, RAT readings and more. The airplane landing gear handle with a red knob is beside these gauges. Two red and white barber pole striped handles just beneath the glare shield discharge fire-fighting chemicals into either engine compartment if the loud fire alarm bell rings and the red warning lights come on.

To the right and left of the center instrument panel are nearly identical panels filled with the primary aircraft flight control instruments—one panel for each pilot. Each panel has a flight director, a gyroscopically controlled compass hooked to radio navigation equipment, a second radio navigation instrument, an airspeed indicator, vertical speed indicator, a clock and two altimeters—one that measures distance to the ground using radar beams and another that reads barometric pressure and converts it to altitude above sea level. The captain's panel also has a second barometric altimeter. In all, there are five instruments in the cockpit that measure altitude.

Immediately above the center front cockpit window is the annunciator panel—rows of black rectangles—ninety-eight in all—each the size of a postage stamp, that light up with warnings about aircraft systems. If the forward cargo door isn't latched properly, the words "FWD CARGO DOOR" will blink on in a rectangle in the lower right corner of the annunciator panel. It can flash more exotic messages. "L. OIL STRAINER CLOGGING" or "A/C CROSSTIE LOCK-OUT" or "L. ICE PROTECT TEMP HI." They seem cryptic, but a pilot needs only a quick upward flick of the eye to learn what is wrong.

Above the annunciator panel, stretching from just forward of the pilots' heads backwards for three feet is the overhead switch panel, an intricate assortment of dials, gauges, switches, buttons, knobs and handles. An emergency oxygen mask hangs behind each pilot's head. There are map lights, a wastebasket, oxygen bottles and even two small fold-down tables on which each pilot can write or clip navigation charts.

A locked door opens directly into the cockpit. A tall pilot must duck his head to avoid hitting the overhead switch panel as he eases into his seat. A third seat that folds up against the wall behind the captain can be lowered for an observer to sit between but slightly behind and above the pilots. In a shallow coat closet just inside the door Reeves and Daniels had hung their black uniform coats, placing their black caps on hooks above the coats.

The entire DC-9 cockpit is painted robin's-egg blue, an attempt to give it a light, spacious air, a seeming extension of the light and blue skies outside the small windows.

After Reeves contacted Jacksonville Center and dialed code 1100 into the transponder, neither pilot spoke. Reeves resumed whistling for a few minutes, then suddenly stopped.

"Boy, this trip you don't lay over as long in any one place," he said. "I like that." He felt the need to talk, to rouse himself, to sharpen his attention.

"Yeah. That's sure a nice trip I flew to Montego. I tell ya it gives ya that twelve hours and fifty-nine minutes instead of those trips messin' around six hours here and six hours there."

By FAA regulations and union contract Eastern pilots can fly only eighty hours per month—measured from the moment the airplane wheels leave the runway until they touch down again. However, a pilot may actually spend up to three times as many hours per month on duty or away from home—preparing for flights, handling paperwork after a flight, waiting on the taxiway at a busy airport for a delayed takeoff clearance or sitting in a motel room on the other side of the continent from wife and children awaiting the next flight. Many pilots prefer trips that quickly build their allotted time but don't keep them away from home for long periods. The flight from Atlanta to Charleston to O'Hare and Orlando on the first day and then from Orlando to Dallas-Fort Worth and back to Atlanta the next day was a good one, providing nearly ten hours of flight time.

Daniels glanced down at the radio console, checking that frequency 112.4, the Fort Mill radio navigation station to which they had been authorized to fly, had been set. Then he adjusted the radio volume until the Morse code identifying letters which the station broadcast in addition to its inaudible navigation signal boomed from the cockpit speakers. "Dot, dot, dash, dot. Dash, dash. Dot, dash, dot, dot." Over and over they spelled "F. M. L." Pilots always check the Morse code identifier to make certain they haven't inadvertently tuned to the wrong station.

"Well, a trip's all right if things don't get all balled up. Then things really don't make much sense at all," Daniels said, turning the radio volume back down.

"Yeah. That's right."

"Of course, now, Atlanta. Going through Atlanta all those times with all that traffic, all that shit goin' on, you always stay on the ragged edge with all that shit. It's just unbelievable," Daniels said, echoing a frequent pilot complaint about congested Atlanta, where everything is delayed—arrival, baggage, boarding and takeoff. A flight running on time when reaching Atlanta is often behind schedule by the time it is able to depart.

Reeves nodded his head as Daniels talked, murmuring, "Yeah. Yeah."

Daniels squeezed the pitch trim button once more, sounding the buzzer. He had been watching the altimeter needle creep up on 15,000 feet. He lowered the nose again to slow the climb rate even more, to the prescribed 500 feet per minute—the climb rate for the last thousand feet before reaching assigned altitude.

The copilot continued.

"Here you are getting behinder and behinder and behinder. And the more ya try to catch up the more screwed up ya get." He chuckled wryly, recalling a recent trip through Atlanta.

"Fifteen for sixteen," Reeves said, calling out passage through 15,000 feet. The thousand-foot call-out is the duty of the pilot not flying.

"So we said to ourselves, we said, 'We'll make it up in New Orleans,'" Daniels continued. "But by the time we got to New Orleans they were jammed up there. So it took an extra half hour to turn the airplane.

"When we got back there were only three people that made connections, three people whose trip was going to Minneapolis-St. Paul and Chicago. And one other person. A Piedmont gal . . . I mean a girl who was going to Piedmont. But she made it because the airplane was right next door to us. Had one engine running. Waited four minutes for her. Everybody else missed theirs."

"Yeah. It's kind of weird, isn't it?" Reeves replied.

"Well, when things start fillin' up, you know there's no way you can cover these people who have to make connections," Daniels said.

"No way. No way," Reeves said absently, half listening. His thoughts had turned to Atlanta and Jean's birthday. She was fifty-

five years old today, so that meant in nine more days he would
turn forty-nine. And November 27 they would be married twenty-
nine years.

Jean Staker had been twenty-six in the fall of 1945, an Okla-
homa farm girl working in Chicago. Her father died early in October and she took a leave to help her mother and younger sister cope
with the loose ends. They sold the livestock and the farm equipment and then drove to San Antonio, Texas, where her mother and
sister planned to live with an uncle.

It was six weeks before she was ready to return. V-J Day had
been celebrated three months before, but America still was a soci-
ety geared for war. Soldiers had first crack at airline flights, so she
left San Antonio by train.

As the train pulled out she watched with amusement as a young
soldier, laden with a duffel bag, ran breathlessly across the platform and, as the train gathered momentum, drew up beside the
vestibule in a final burst of speed, heaved his bag up and then
grabbed the handrail on the car and swung onto the steps. The old
porter sat him two rows back. Jean studied his flushed face as he
passed—very young, smooth, light skin, a small pug nose, an un-
ruly cowlick that swept up from his forehead. A pair of pilot wings
were pinned to his tunic.

The wheels clicking over the rails quickly lulled Jean Staker to
sleep. When she awoke, the young Army pilot sat beside her, smiling. He began at once to talk. His name was Jim Reeves. A fighter
pilot. Mustangs. A great airplane, that Mustang. Going home to
Milwaukee. To see his family. Then shipping out for China and
volunteer duty with the Flying Tigers. He had seen duty in Alaska.
He was twenty years old. He had tipped the porter to let him move
up two rows and sit beside the pretty woman who had fallen
asleep.

So they talked and shared their experiences and speculated
about the future through the long hours and into the night, sleeping in their seats, changing trains together in St. Louis, then on to
Chicago. He asked her to come to Milwaukee and spend the next
weekend—Thanksgiving weekend—with him and his family. She
accepted. They ate Thanksgiving dinner around the Reeves family
table. The next day he proposed marriage. She accepted. They

were married the following Tuesday by Reverend Lunger at the University Chapel of the Disciples of Christ Church in Chicago.

But Flying Tiger pilots had to be single. So Mr. and Mrs. Reeves were reassigned to Luke Army Air Field in Arizona, where Jim Reeves spent his honeymoon and the end of his military career trying to bridge the language barrier and teach Chinese soldiers to fly the Mustang.

Throughout an airline flight, in addition to the other cockpit noise, the radio speakers constantly bombard the pilots with sound. There sometimes are a dozen or more other aircraft on the same frequency to whom air traffic controllers are passing instructions. Skilled pilots easily chat with one another and fly their airplane while ignoring the radio chatter until the ear picks out a message meant for them, just as a mother ignores the noise of her children's play until a difference in sound alerts her to trouble.

"Eastern 212. Contact Jacksonville Center now on one two four point seven."

Reeves reached for the microphone.

"Twenty-four seven. Good morning."

He leaned to the right and looked into the radio frequency window in the number two radio, dialing in the new frequency.

"Jax Center, Eastern . . . ah . . . 212. Coming up sixteen thousand."

"Eastern 212, Jacksonville Center," a female voice replied. "One six thousand. Ident."

Reeves leaned forward across the throttles to the transponder. Reeves's thoughts returned to the conversation.

"Well, this is actually a decent trip except that gettin' up early in the morning," he said. He was really feeling it today.

"It's not too bad living up where I do now," Daniels said. He faced a much longer airport commute since moving from southwest Atlanta, but most of it was over expressways.

Reeves resumed whistling. Daniels continued.

"I have to get up about . . ."

The radio interrupted.

"Eastern 212. Jacksonville Center. Ident." It was a male voice this time.

Reeves frowned in irritation but patiently reached over and hit the ident button. "Right," he growled into the microphone.

"I have to get up about . . . hour and a half 'fore I'm due there at the airport," Daniels resumed.

The speaker sounded again.

"Columbia altimeter, three zero one zero," the male controller said.

"Right," Reeves snapped into the microphone.

A warning whistle sounded in the cockpit, a one-second single note, a whistle that except for its precise nature could have come from Reeves's mouth. Simultaneously on each pilot's instrument panel a square button that had lit up a minute before, illuminating the word "ALT," blinked out. It was the altitude alert. The lights had come on 750 feet below the assigned altitude of 16,000 feet. The whistle had sounded 250 feet below the assigned altitude and the lights had gone out. But the alert was unnecessary. Both men had been anticipating 16,000 feet. Daniels reached down to the autopilot console and shoved a lever forward, engaging the autopilot.

"When a trip goes out about eight or nine o'clock in the morning then I gotta get up about two hours early," Daniels said. "But even that ain't too bad."

"No. It's not," Reeves replied.

With his thumb Daniels turned a small wheel controlling how fast the autopilot permitted the airplane to climb. With his eyes on the altimeter, Daniels slowly reduced the autopilot climb rate so that it reached zero just as the altimeter hit 16,000 feet. Thus he let the mechanical pilot end the eleven-minute climb and commence level flight without a bump, more smoothly than a man's hands.

"But you've got to give yourself at least a half-hour cushion in case there's a wreck or something," he added.

"Yeah. Like an accident in your lane," Reeves said.

"Don't even have to be in your lane up there. Could be in another lane but they start gawking. Get everything all balled up."

"That sure is the truth, isn't it?" Reeves agreed.

Daniels smiled to himself with pleasure. A perfect level-out. If the girls are serving coffee, they didn't spill a drop, he thought. Flying. It never stopped challenging your skills. He loved it.

Jim Daniels, like Jim Reeves, learned to fly as a teen-ager in an old yellow fabric-covered Piper J-3 Cub. Five dollars here, five dollars there at the airport in Fort Myers, Florida, until one day the old charter pilot giving the lessons suggested that his student take his first solo. Federal regulations were looser then, so he'd been all alone at the airport when he took the J-3 up. His hands and then his legs trembled violently from excitement and fear as he brought the little airplane around the first time to line up for the final approach to the runway. He'd carefully brought it down closer and closer to the runway, raising the nose, slowing the airspeed, raising the nose, until the J-3 dropped onto the runway with a "whomp," fishtailing gently down the asphalt while Daniels rode the rudder pedals. He had never forgotten the exhilaration.

Jim Daniels had served in the military, too, a generation behind Jim Reeves. Tall, handsome, athletic, Daniels graduated from high school in Fort Myers in 1956 and went north to college in Georgia for eighteen months before returning home. He worked on the docks in the family seafood and poultry business, idled about Fort Myers, grew bored, joined the Air Force and became an aircraft mechanic assigned to a NATO base in Germany. His group handled special maintenance problems, often flying along with the crew to fix problems en route.

Sometimes a flight took them to Marseilles, and an enlightened aircraft commander would suggest they find some mechanical problem that would ground the airplane for several days while the mechanics fixed it. Daniels often recalled sitting on the wing of a "disabled" DC-3 at the Marseilles airport drinking a can of beer and admiring the bravado of a nearby Air France crew. He loved to tell the story.

"They were sitting there drinking two or three bottles of wine. Then they came out with a bottle of wine under each arm and a loaf of bread, and as the last man got aboard and shut the door the last of the four engines were turning over. As soon as the door closed, off they went. What a jaunty bunch they were."

Jim Daniels spent two years, six months and ten days in the Air Force. He came home shortly after his father's heart attack and ran the family business long enough to reaffirm his distaste for it. A friend who worked as a ticket agent for National Airlines urged him to make a career as a pilot. With a four-year bank loan and monthly payments of $108.33, he enrolled in the Valparaiso, Indiana, School of Aeronautics and earned commercial, instrument, multi-engine, ground instructor and flight instructor ratings. He met and married Kathy, worked briefly as an instructor for Valparaiso and then landed a job at Melbourne, Florida, as a flight instructor and charter pilot working for J. David Finger, an aviation pioneer who helped Lindbergh push *The Spirit of St. Louis* from the hangar on the morning of the famous flight.

Melbourne is south of Cape Canaveral, and Daniels soon was busy with charter flights to the fledgling spaceport. Walter Cronkite of CBS News flew in the right seat of a twin-engine Beech on one charter. Other times he piloted Jules Bergman, an ABC correspondent. Bergman had a commercial pilot's license and insisted on handling the controls. Such experiences made good cocktail party chatter.

"Bergman's not the world's greatest pilot. But he would always want to fly. And that would always strike terror into my heart. I would have to sit there and cross my fingers and cross my toes and cross my nose that he wouldn't do anything so absolutely stupid that I would have to snatch the controls away from him.

"Cronkite was a regular fellow but he never stopped talking. Maybe nervous. Never stopped talking."

Jim Reeves had begun whistling again. Daniels glanced at him. Some captains whistled. Some captains talked. Some captains hummed. He knew captains who drank too much, captains who were abusive, captains who were incompetent, captains who went by the book, captains with whom anything went. A good copilot made it his business to anticipate his captains' personalities.

Daniels broke the conversational lull.

"You see those things they put up at the counter there in Orlando where you take a picture of the passenger when he writes a check?" he asked.

"Take a picture of who?"

"The passenger. You know, for bad checks. They've had so damn many."

"Oh. Oh. Oh. Yeah. Yeah. You mean take a picture when they give ya a check?"

"Yeah. Every check they take a picture. So I asked the guy, 'Well, what good does that do?' "

"It scares the hell out of them."

"Well, no. Not really. He says actually not a damn bit is his problem. Said maybe once in a while, a couple of them."

"Yeah. A lot of 'em out there. Folks with bad checks."

Reeves resumed whistling.

Daniels' eyes continued to scan the instruments, paying particular attention now to the heading indicator and the needle that showed how closely the airplane was tracking the electronic navigation beam transmitted by the station at Fort Mill. If Eastern 212 stayed on the beam, the airplane would go directly to the station. To do that, Daniels had to keep the heading indicator navigation needle centered. But the autopilot did that automatically. If the copilot wanted to turn the airplane, he just reached down to the autopilot console and turned another knob. The gyroscopes and servos in the autopilot immediately would put the DC-9 into a gentle turn without the pilot touching the control wheel.

"I guess we'll find out this winter what the economy's doin'," Daniels said.

"Yeah. 'At's true," Reeves replied.

Through the summer of 1974, during the last agonizing weeks of the Nixon administration, inflation had been rampant. Now there was talk about an economic downturn in the winter, even an economic paradox: inflation coupled with recession.

"You know, it depends on whether the President stays with it or not," Daniels said.

"Well, what do ya think of old Ford givin' a pardon to Nixon?" Reeves asked.

"I was surprised," Daniels said.

"I was surprised, too, this early," Reeves said. "I figured he'd wait . . ."

Daniels interrupted.

"I didn't think . . . I thought he would let things ride. He's got some things goin' against him. The Nixon thing and the position he's taking on the draft. I'm very unhappy with the . . ."

Reeves interrupted, incensed at the idea of a presidential pardon for Vietnam deserters and draft dodgers, too.

"I'll tell ya what. If he gives amnesty to those so-and-sos up north in Canada he's gonna hear from me. He didn't hear from me on Nixon, but he will hear from me on that one."

"Yep. I'd . . . I would . . . say this." Daniels hesitated, choosing his words carefully. "I would say this. That if they want to come back to this country and take their lumps."

"Yeah. O.K. I'll go along with that," Reeves said.

"But to come back and say, 'Ha, ha, ha. See what I did,'" Daniels added.

"Yeah," Reeves said.

"I've got cousins and all 'at got killed in that shit in Vietnam. I didn't agree with that war."

"No, I didn't either," Reeves agreed.

Reeves had opposed the war near its end in the sense that other conservative, middle-class Americans had. He'd wanted the United States to extract itself from a hopeless situation. But he hadn't viewed Vietnam from a moralistic viewpoint. "I'm not a moralist," he would say. "I fight whether the war is right or wrong. We have it better in this country than any other people. It's not up to us to judge morally whether we're going to fight this or that war. If we did that we would have been taken over long ago."

But Reeves didn't feel it as necessary now to explain his feelings about the war as he had in earlier years.

Daniels made a small heading adjustment on the autopilot turn knob.

"A lot of things I didn't agree with. I went ahead and did it anyhow. I didn't agree with it. But I went ahead and did it," the copilot said.

"Yeah," Reeves replied.

"And not just because it was the thing to do," Daniels added.

"Nope . . . and let these guys in scot-free now?" Reeves said, the irritation he felt showing again in his voice. "No, sir, boy. I'll tell you Ford's goin' to hear from me."

"As far as I'm concerned, he's committed suicide," Daniels said.

"Yeah, he is," Reeves said. "And if he allows those guys to

come back he's *really* committed suicide. An he's on the verge of it right now. But he will have committed it if he lets them come in. 'Cause he's *really* gonna hear about that." Reeves emphasized the word really, stretching it out.

"That's right," Daniels said.

"I think he's trying to feel the public out," Reeves said. "And he's got more protest from what he did for Nixon than he expected. I think he figures he's gonna get a hell of a lot more if he goes strongly for amnesty for those guys." He paused. "Won't he?" the captain asked. Then he answered his own question. "I know he will."

Daniels folded his hands in his lap and watched the autopilot do its work. His eyes maintained the sweep of the instruments. He shook out a cigarette and lit it with a lighter, blowing the first puff of smoke at the side window.

"You know he was dead wrong in that appointing Rockefeller Vice-President," the copilot said. "Now the Republicans have got themselves in a position where they need to bring in an entirely different variety of Republican for '76."

Reeves tugged agitatedly at his earlobe.

"This guy. He's committed suicide. He is. And if he lets those damned boys come back, then he just committed suicide. I'll do everything I can to defeat him."

The captain glanced up at the overhead switch panel. The seat belt sign still was on in the passenger cabin. If conditions permit, the sign is turned off upon reaching cruising altitude. Reeves reached back and gave the toggle switch a push.

How could a President pardon deserters and draft dodgers?

CHAPTER TWELVE

7:18 A.M.

STEVE BOIREAU REACHED down and opened the clasp of the seat belt buckle with his left hand and pulled the webbed fiber belt loose with his right, heaving a sigh of relief. He wiggled his bottom deeper into the seat cushion and leaned back, closing his eyes.

Steve Boireau was big—well over six feet, 240 pounds, a large-boned man. He was wedged into the middle seat of a row of three on the right side of the coach cabin, midway back. You could expect a middle seat on standby.

He'd hovered about the Eastern counter in the holding lounge watching the hand on the clock draw steadily nearer 7 A.M. as passenger after passenger with confirmed reservations filed past the agent, across the lounge and out the door. Finally the stream diminished and then stopped, the agent beckoned and at last Steve emerged into the still, humid southern dawn, stepping briskly across the asphalt past the workers in blue coveralls, one of whom had his headphones on talking to the pilot, waiting for the engine-starting ritual. He would make it to Boston by early afternoon and be in his office in Lexington by 1 P.M., time left for some work. The nervousness about getting a seat, the prospect of waiting at the airport four more hours until the next flight, were gone. Steve Boireau smiled contentedly. Life treated him well now.

Glenn. What pleasure his son now gave. What pride he felt as the marine recruits, ramrod straight in their blue and red dress uniforms, arms and legs flashing in unison in the sun, marched across the parade ground. During the pomp and circumstance of boot camp graduation how intense the parental pride had grown, how remote the unease, the alienation, the anxiety Steve felt at times as his son passed through adolescence, coping with the usual travails, and enduring in addition unhappy parents who resorted finally to divorce.

Four months earlier Glenn walked into Steve's office and announced his enlistment in the marines. Steve had been a marine in Korea, decorated with a purple heart when a bullet shattered his wrist. Glenn had been out of high school a year, moving through a succession of odd jobs after a three-week fling at higher education at Lowell Tech. On his own he enlisted in the marines. But Steve reacted to the news with indifference, failing at the crucial moment to comprehend the significance of his son's action, Glenn's need for fatherly approval. Loren, one of Steve's salesmen who had been with the agency for fifteen years, a man as close to Steve as any, had gently berated him afterwards. "My gosh, Steve. Couldn't you have said, 'Wonderful!' or been a little more jubilant about it? Don't you see the compliment he's paid you?"

The marines had changed the father–son relationship. They began corresponding—letters to Steve and Eileen at home, letters just to Steve at the office. Boot camp graduation neared. Loren coaxed. "Gee, Steve, he'd probably really love to see you there." Eileen urged him, too. So he flew down Sunday and spent Monday tramping about the Parris Island training center, losing himself in the memories. He attended graduation the next day with Lonnie, Glenn's mother, with whom he now got along well, and then called Eileen at home to share his emotional awakening, the exhilaration of a father who discovers himself in his son.

"Coffee, sir?"

Steve opened his eyes and turned toward the aisle and the voice. A stewardess offered coffee to the man in the window seat, who reached across Steve for the proffered cup.

"Coffee, sir?"

"Yes. Thank you," Steve said. He held the cup with one hand and opened the fold-down table with the other, resting the cup on the tray, leaning back and closing his eyes again.

The trip to Charleston and boot camp graduation was only, what, the second time he and Eileen had been apart since marrying? A few weeks before, Eileen had gone to New Jersey by herself to visit a sister with a new baby. She had urged Steve to make the trip to Parris Island. She, too, had realized what it would mean to Glenn—and Steve.

Curious. After meeting someone and falling in love you reach back into your memory and try to picture the very first moment you met and what your thoughts were in that instant, not knowing then, of course, that some undefined chemistry would bring you together permanently, alter your lives.

After the divorce Steve moved into a singles apartment complex. Glenn chose to live with Lonnie. Glenn's sister, Michelle, lived with Steve, washing his clothes, cooking, taking care of her father.

He was lounging about the pool one weekend with some neighbors when a statuesque woman with ivory skin and a quick giggle, perhaps in her late twenties, joined them. Eileen was her name. The group's conversation drifted to restaurants they had known and loved. When one particular restaurant was mentioned, Eileen, in all innocence, said, "I'd like to go there some time." And Steve, before he quite realized that he had opened his mouth, asked: "Would you like to go with me?" They often chuckled about that later. It seemed such a come-on from Eileen, who hadn't meant it that way at all.

They dated regularly and the children began to accept Eileen. Even Gertrude tolerated Eileen, in her own jealous way. After the divorce, the old bulldog lived with Glenn and his mother. But she visited Steve, climbing up on the bed to sleep the day away—except when Eileen appeared. As Eileen sat on the couch in the living room, Gertrude would creakily jump from the bed, pad into the living room and climb into the easy chair, facing the couch. There she would sit, fixing Eileen with a baleful eye. Only when Eileen rose to leave would Gertrude abandon her chaperone's post and throw herself on the bed to resume napping. After they were mar-

ried, Gertrude permitted Eileen less supervision. Eileen cried when
Steve finally had to take Gertrude to the vet's and have her put to
sleep. The old bulldog could be both a child and a parent.

Children. Steve found himself wanting children, a second family, another chance. He would do it right this time. Though he
would be old—in his sixties—when they finished high school, the
prospect of beginning a new family delighted rather than dis-
mayed. Now he was ready. Twenty years late, perhaps, but now
mature, established, certain of his path through life. And he had
Eileen. She wanted children, too, though she would be in her fifties
when they were grown.

They sought an adoption agency and began the paperwork and
the interviews, the interminable answering of questions. They were
accepted at length. They wanted two children. But no children
were available, of course. Please wait. Be patient. Meanwhile, they
would enjoy each other. Weekends on Cape Cod. Fishing in New
Hampshire.

They fished in Crystal Lake, not far from Gilmanton Iron
Works, New Hampshire. The first time Eileen ever fished, she
hooked a large bass on the fifth cast. He was incredulous. She
giggled with glee. Then they both roared.

They drove from the tiny village up toward Guinea Pond, at the
foot of Guinea Ridge, each mile taking Steve farther back into his
childhood. They stopped at the old Boireau summer home. No one
was there. They peered into the windows.

Steve had spent summers there growing up, playing with the
Jordan boys across the road. As an adolescent Steve attended Belmont Hill School in Belmont, a Boston suburb. Mr. Hamilton, the
school headmaster, a friend of Steve's parents, bought the small,
run-down farm next door to the Boireau summer home. When
Steve's father died two decades before, his mother offered Steve
the house by Guinea Pond. And Steve, just starting out in the real
estate business, unsure if he could support the house, declined.
How chagrined he felt in later years.

They returned to the car and drove down the road toward Gilmanton. On an impulse Steve turned into the Hamilton driveway.
The elderly couple was home. Soon Steve and Eileen sat in the

Hamilton living room gazing at Guinea Pond, which really was a lake, a striking view through a large picture window. They talked of the school, Steve's love of basketball then, and of his classmates, doctors and lawyers and successful businessmen now. Belmont Hill Academy was a good preparatory school.

Bass fishing wasn't as good in Guinea Pond as it once had been, Charlie Hamilton said. Camp Leo across the lake had closed its property to the smelt fishermen in the spring. So more smelt were reaching the lake, providing the bass ample natural food. The bass weren't interested in a fisherman's bait.

They told of their adoption plans and Steve spoke with affection of a return to the rural life he remembered. A good place to raise children. Teach them self-reliance, responsibility. Would Charlie consider selling some of his land? Perhaps ten acres with some lake front. They would build a small house. Perhaps an A-frame, a chalet.

Perhaps he would sell a few acres for old times' sake, for the friendship he had known with Steve's parents, for the memories of Steve and the Hamilton children growing up at Guinea Pond and the next generation of youngsters. At least Mr. Hamilton hadn't said no outright. He'd promised to think about it. Afterwards in the car Eileen excitedly began to decorate their new country home in her mind.

Steve Boireau opened his eyes and sat up, gazing out the window at a few puffs of clouds below. His coffee had cooled, untouched.

Actually, the best thing that had happened to him was the hip operation. Eileen had been mostly responsible for that, too. She'd steadily coaxed him, convincing him he should consider an artificial hip replacement, drawing on her professional knowledge as a nurse to reassure him.

With each passing year his hip—severely damaged nearly twenty years before in a head-on automobile collision—had grown worse. Sleepless nights. A worsening limp. He needed a cane often. He popped Darvon pills by the handful for the pain. But the operation changed everything. The pain slowly left. The limp disappeared. His temper, the irritability born of constant pain that his staff gingerly tolerated for years, began to wane. He felt better. He slept better.

What a difference Eileen had made. How proud he was of Glenn. His son was driving back to Boston with Lonnie, to spend his furlough at home. How nice to have Glenn around. How much fun rediscovering his new son.

CHAPTER THIRTEEN

7:20 A.M.

THE ATLANTA CENTER computer was down. Again. The tiny clocks at the top of each radar screen no longer flashed the seconds and minutes. Each clock had stopped at 11:20:40 GMT—7:20:40 A.M. Eastern Daylight time. At mid-screen in large letters the computer had printed a succinct notation: DISPLAY FROZEN.

At Sector 28 in the darkened control room, Horace Hicks sighed loudly and slapped his pencil down in irritation. Throughout the southeastern United States airplanes hurtled onward. But at radar screens in the Atlanta Air Route Traffic Control Center in Hampton, Georgia, thirty miles south of Atlanta, the radar targets just sat there—fat, dumb and happy.

"Well, here we go again," he muttered to Lyle Williams and Dave Brock, groping under the console with his right foot for the radar scope release button. He found it, gave it a push and then pulled the entire console outward—radar scope, counter and all. He gently pushed the radar screen downward from its near vertical position until it lay flat. Then he shoved the console inward again, locking it in place with a snap. Up and down the control room aisle controllers at other radar scopes were doing the same.

"Get the shrimp boats," Brock ordered Williams, scooting closer to the counter in the tall swivel stool with a high back and armrests. Williams was a trainee, Brock's responsibility. It was his second day of a six-week on-the-job-training session covering the manual controller's duties. Brock anxiously watched Williams to see if he would need help.

Williams reached to the left of the radar screen and retrieved a handful of shrimp boats—thin pieces of translucent orange plexiglass, about half the size of a postage stamp. Referring to the vertical row of flight data strips nestled in the rack in plastic holders, he began writing with a grease pencil on each shrimp boat the call sign of each airplane they had been handling. As he completed each shrimp boat he shoved it along the counter to Hicks.

After lowering the radar screen, Hicks pushed a button in the upper corner of the console that converted the radar display from the frozen, now useless computer-controlled mode to the old-fashioned "broadband" coverage that he had come to know so well after sixteen years in Atlanta Center.

The half dozen computer radar targets, each with its neat data block, vanished. In their place appeared the familiar phosphorescent green radar sweep, rotating around the screen once each six seconds, like the second hand on a watch gone berserk. At every pass, the sweep illuminated each target on the screen. Instead of neat tiny triangles, the radar revealed larger targets—each target a series of parallel slanted lines. The sweep's movement corresponded to the rotation of the radar antenna, which in the case of Sector 28 was located forty miles north of Charlotte, North Carolina.

With the computer data blocks gone, Hicks now quickly had to identify each aircraft and make certain the momentary lapse had not precipitated any traffic conflicts.

"Delta 608, ident, please," he said, squeezing the microphone button in his fist. A few seconds later a target glowed brightly when the sweep passed over it. Hicks took a shrimp boat on which Williams had written "DL608" and placed it beside the target. Quickly he ran down the list of aircraft flight data strips, confirming the location of each with a radio call for a transponder ident, and placing a shrimp boat beside it. By the time he had finished, the first aircraft, Delta 608, had pulled away from its plastic chip. Hicks made the rounds of the scope, pushing each shrimp boat up beside its target.

"How long, Lord? How long? When will it end?" he asked in mock exasperation. But his tone was partly serious.

In the history of air traffic control, the 1970s will be the era of the computer. Atlanta Center's computer had finally become fully operational only a few months before. Eventually, all major air traffic control facilities—centers and airport towers throughout the country—would monitor all traffic by computer controlled radar. But the Atlanta computer, like many others, sometimes "bombed" —temporarily ceased working. Although the controllers marveled at the computer's versatility, its amazing ability to feed as much information as might be needed about a traffic situation, they nevertheless viewed the machine with a certain cynical suspicion. It was a tool that couldn't be completely trusted. At least not yet.

Hicks had spent much of his midnight shift working several sectors combined into one, using the broadband radar display because the computer had been off for maintenance. It had come on a few minutes after Brock and Williams plugged in at 7 A.M. for the swing shift to help Hicks with the flurry of morning traffic into Charlotte. It had worked fine. And then, a dead clock and that damned electronic message: DISPLAY FROZEN. It had come just as a flock of jets were bearing down on Charlotte Approach Control, just as Atlanta Center's Fort Mill Sector had to meld them all into a stream, adjusting their airspeeds downward, turning them, descending them to lower altitudes so they formed a neat procession with just the right spacing between each airplane.

Controllers, like policemen and firemen, are an outspoken lot. They have definite views about how their jobs should be performed, the shortcomings of those who supervise them and the lack of equipment, manpower and adequate pay. Talking to a reporter, without the knowledge or permission of FAA superiors, speaking in small groups, in their homes, a motel room, bars or at the local Professional Air Traffic Controllers Association office, they speak freely. Names aren't mentioned. They are storytellers because every day at work generates a tale. Some experiences

stand out sufficiently to be repeated, and they become local folk
legend. Though precise details may blur with time, each tale pre-
serves its lesson.

They sit in uncomfortable plastic chairs in a small carpeted
office. It is late, after the night shift.

"I'm an outdoorsman. Just getting out releases the pressure for
me. In the winter I enjoy just cutting wood. At certain times you
can feel the pressure on the job. Especially when your outbounds
are taking off from Atlanta. Here they come. You know what time
each day that'll be, and you can see everybody getting just a little
bit edgy and the tension builds up. You actually feel it. I don't
think I smoke more. We pick at each other a lot at work. That's a
way I relieve tension. Kid people—in a friendly way. Just little
things about people you pick on. The other person understands
you're kidding.

"When you start getting a little nervous your leg goes to jumping. I think most everybody does that. You look real close at times
and you'll see a lot of legs jumping."

FAA officials insist that air traffic controllers can't purposely
slow down air traffic flow; that supervisors would spot an obstruc-
tive controller and replace him; that supervisory controllers could
step in and take over; that the trying periods in the late 1960s and
early 1970s when controller "job actions" forced changes in the
air traffic system and gave birth to the Professional Air Traffic
Controllers Association won't happen again. The room rocks with
hoots of derisive laughter when such assertions are repeated.

"Following the rules and regulations right to the letter is in itself
a very effective slowdown. In Chicago at O'Hare and New York
and San Francisco and busier places the only reason the aircraft
get there as quickly as they do is that guys chop corners. They
break rules. I guarantee you they'd run a two-hour delay everyday
at O'Hare if they adhered strictly to FAA's rules and regulations.

"But they start getting pressure from the top. The user starts
bitching about the delay and someone knows a congressman and
what have you and the pressure starts feeding back down the line
to the guy on the boards. And he's coming up for a new GS rating
that'll mean more pay. And so a supervisor comes up and says,

'Well, you've been running aircraft a little too far apart.' So the guy starts chopping corners."

The rules and regulations spell out the minimum distance the controller must maintain between aircraft in given situations.

"I think any controller that tries to operate on basic minimum separations is walking the tightrope. At the center, for example, we can have as little as three miles separation within forty miles of the radar antenna site. That's in the book. But nobody in his right mind will do that. My limit is ten miles. Any time I run them less than ten miles it's a special situation.

"The odds are too heavy against you. Too many things can happen. Your attention gets diverted from this position and you're watching two airplanes up here and a guy you've told to slow down to two hundred and fifty knots doesn't do it. And while your attention is up here you look back and he's up the other one's ass.

"I give myself five miles for the FAA and five miles for me and the wife and kids."

One man leans forward earnestly. His stomach reflects a healthy appetite. A few minutes before he lit a large cigar amid catcalls. "Hey, man, don't light that thing here." He gestures grandly with the cigar, spilling ashes on the floor.

"I think the book strictly refers to minimum separation. It doesn't speak to maximum separation. We had a controller criticized because he had too much separation. How can you have too much separation when safety is concerned?

"The whole thing is interpretative. You're a controller sitting there running five or six miles for years and you feel comfortable with that. Then you become a supervisor and you're standing over me and I've been running eight or nine miles for years and I think that's what's safe. So you're going to be all over my ass every day because I don't run them like you did.

"It's all a matter of personal opinion. That's what we're talking about. Everybody in the business is pure personal opinion. And some of the top boys who make the rules haven't been on the boards in twenty years and the fastest thing they ever controlled was a DC-3."

Every controller has his story of an incident, near misses, an injustice. Each story mirrors a frustration.

"We had a dignitary coming into Atlanta one day, landing at Dobbins Air Force Base. This particular dignitary is the one who has a press plane that flies ahead of him so the press can all be there waiting with their goodies."

He winks. Everyone laughs. They know the story. It is becoming one of those local controller legends.

"So *Air Force One* is thirty miles northeast of Athens, Georgia, and his press plane is seven miles ahead of him. They're coming di-rect as they always do. And I mean di-rect, so we're moving everybody out of the way." The storyteller rises and hops forward, waving his arms, imitating a farmer's wife shooing chickens from her path.

"So we have all these outbounds off of Atlanta on one side coming one direction, climbing, and then we have the press plane and *Air Force One* coming the other direction. And there's an Eastern that's off course from another sector and they're vectoring him inbound to Atlanta. And there's a slight conflict between this Eastern and the press plane. This doesn't involve *Air Force One* at all. He's fine.

"But there's this problem with Eastern and the press plane. The controller doesn't want to turn the Eastern to the right because it would conflict with the Atlanta outbounds. And he can't turn him left because of *Air Force One*. So the controller tells the press plane to make a left three-sixty-degree turn for traffic separation that will delay him enough to clear things out.

"The press plane pilot rogers the turn and then he just keeps on trucking. He doesn't turn. So they go a little further and the controller is sitting there about to piss his pants and finally says to the press plane, 'Are you making that three-sixty?' So the press plane pilot says, 'Center, I got to be on the ground at Dobbins at so-and-so time. I've got a White House security man in the jump seat and you're supposed to contact Major So-in-so." And he keeps right on trucking.

"No telling how many people on that Eastern and how many on the press plane, and *Air Force One* in the middle of all that shit. So they had to dump the Eastern quick to get him down lower and then turn him. Any other pilot should've lost his damned license."

Another controller is young, stylishly dressed, platform shoes, handlebar moustache. He's been an FPL for eighteen months.

"There are times when you come off your sector and your palms are sweaty. Fear. My blood pressure is unusually low. But I'm working an inbound rush and I get up tight. It goes up. A half hour after I get off the boards it's still up. Things just pile up and there is no way out even though you're doing the best you can. I don't know what it's doing to my body."

An older controller, contemplating retirement after nearly twenty years on the boards, speaks:

"I personally believe that a man who has been there ten to fifteen years, he gets to the point where he gets, well, not careless, but he's gotten so damn used to it something is going to get by. He's just not as attentive as he should be. He lets a situation ride and says, 'Well, shit. They'll make it.' And they do. But it scares the hell out of me."

The smoke is thick. The room has grown warm. But no one seems to notice. There is a point at which an FPL's skills begin to go downhill, announces one too young to have reached that point yet.

"After you're turned loose as an FPL there are three to five years while you're getting as good as you're going to be. And then you level off for a few years and then it's downhill.

"You get shot at by too many cannons. You see too many things that couldn't be prevented or could be prevented but nobody took the trouble to prevent them. The pressure. Some guys take it all home. We have a case in our area now. The guy is slowly going bananas."

Another older controller eyeing retirement hikes himself up on the edge of his chair.

"I'm working next to a guy who's been an FPL for a year. The situation he faces tonight I've faced a thousand times. He'll run the chance with it. I won't. Because there's one chance it won't work. Now, whether being cautious like that is going downhill to you youngsters, I don't know. Now, there's no way you'll get me to admit I'm half shot. But you do it all these years and sit there eight hours at a stretch all tensed up and that's work.

"My background is climbing up and down oil well rigs in West

Texas. And I know what hard work is. But I've never been as tired as I am after I've worked that radar scope for eight hours."

A young controller is nodding in vehement agreement.

"How often do you wake up at the boards and keep grabbing at your brain. Keep forcing yourself to look at something. That's what our job is. You sit there and you can't afford to wander. You're always forcing yourself to be aware. You're telling yourself to be attentive."

Another man, who has quietly listened, speaks finally, a slow drawl.

"We now have a restriction that we can't work more than six days in a row. But at one time I worked seventeen days in a row when the FAA was shorthanded because of poor planning."

A brief game of oneupmanship begins.

"I worked thirty-four days in a row once. About ten years ago. And it was always balls to the wall. We didn't eat lunch. You sometimes had to wait fifteen or twenty minutes just to go take a piss. You just couldn't get away."

The controller lives in fear of a "deal," a situation in which airplanes come too close.

Each controller works at his own pace. So, too, do groups of controllers, even whole facilities. Some crews are conservative, some crews are "hot rods."

"So one day I had this kid as a trainee and he'd been emulating those hot rods who'd been training him. And we have a Gulfstream southbound at thirty-five thousand for Orlando. And an Eastern northbound off from Orlando and climbing to twenty-nine thousand. The Eastern is being handled by the low altitude sector but we're going to have him handed off to us at twenty-three thousand feet, the bottom of our high altitude sector.

"So this hot rod dumps the Gulfstream from thirty-five thousand all the way down to twenty-four without looking to see what's coming from below. And that's wrong. But this fellow is being trained. So when do you stop him and when do you let him go to teach a lesson?

"Well anyway, sure enough in a minute they hand off the Eastern and this trainee immediately gives the Eastern a clearance to continue climbing to twenty-nine thousand. So here's one coming down from thirty-five and one going up to twenty-nine and they're head-on. Naturally, something doesn't compute in my mind. But the hot rod is just sitting there. These guys are head-on and seventy-five miles apart and the intersection point is perfect.

"So I say, 'You'd better turn the Eastern right to a heading of zero two zero to separate them so we can get the Eastern up.' And he says, 'Yeah.' But he just sits there. I say, 'You'd better do something pretty soon. Those guys are moving fast.' He says, 'I could turn the Gulfstream.' I say, 'You can turn either one of them but you'd better do something.' All the time he's bullshitting these airplanes are still head-on, closing.

"So finally he says to Eastern to turn right fifteen degrees. Eastern says, 'Roger.' But Eastern isn't going to snap it over in a hard turn and spill coffee on someone's lap. He banks around making a nice slow turn. And the intersection is still perfect. I can see it's going to be a deal. It's not going to be a collision, but it's going to be a deal right now.

"So I told the kid that fifteen degrees wasn't enough. You're going to have to turn the Gulfstream. So he gives the Gulfstream a left turn. A LEFT TURN! Right in front of the Eastern. So I grab his shoulder and take over.

"I told the Gulfstream to ignore that turn and give me a fast rate of descent and traffic at twelve o'clock, twenty miles climbing out of twenty-seven thousand for twenty-nine, in a turn to the right. The Gulfstream said, 'Roger.' And I told the Eastern to continue his turn and turn another twenty degrees. And all of this from me came out in a continuous transmission and the Eastern realized something was wrong and turned it faster. And I gave the Gulfstream a ten-degree right turn and they passed four miles and thirteen hundred feet altitude separation.

"I didn't have a deal because the altitude separation didn't go below a thousand feet."

Another controller, another story.

"I had a trainee and we had three airplanes in our sector. But I looked down the aisle there at the next bunch and I could see they were going like gangbusters. So I expanded the range of my scope to watch them and they had nineteen airplanes. So my trainee and I are watching this. They have three aircraft at thirty-three thousand feet all coming together over Augusta. One from the South-east. One's coming from Macon and another one from somewhere. All at thirty-three thousand feet. And we're watching this to see what they're going to do.

"Then all of a sudden the computer fails. Wham! Display Frozen. Oh, shit. I'm not thinking it for myself but for those poor guys next door. Because they have a trainee sitting on the scope and a guy monitoring him. So I leave my trainee to watch my three airplanes and I stretch my cord out and go over to help them. I pop a scope down and haul out the shrimp boats.

"There was a panic situation for about ten minutes. The kid who was working the radar panicked. Wanted to get out. I'm trying to help him. Brought in another couple guys to help him. It was a Delta 727 and a Falcon that were the problem. I had to grab that kid on the scope and tell him to turn the Delta to a zero nine zero heading and climb the Falcon. They were about four miles apart when I told him to turn the Delta.

"The third airplane had squeaked through the center of it all somehow. By the time we reidentified him he had snuck ten miles into Atlanta Center's airspace.

"So we had a deal. Nothing was said. But a Delta 727 almost knocked a Falcon Fan Jet out of the sky."

The loudspeaker on the console overhang boomed above the three controllers sitting at the Fort Mill sector in Atlanta Center.

"Fort Mill. Five oh six. Hand-off."

It was Jax Center, calling with an aircraft hand-off.

Horace Hicks was busy talking to an aircraft. Lyle Williams was speaking into his microphone, co-ordinating a hand-off from another Atlanta Center sector west of the Fort Mill sector. Dave Brock studied the blips on the radar screen, checking the shrimp boats against flight data strips.

"Fort Mill. Five oh six line. Hand-off."

It was Jax Center again, patiently insistent.

Williams reached up and punched a button, cutting his line with the Knoxville Sector. He hit another button, silencing the speaker and tying his headset into the 506 line between Jax and Atlanta centers.

"Fort Mill," he said.

"At Longtown is Eastern 212 at one six thousand," Jax Center said. It was Jerry Lesiege, although Williams didn't know that. Names weren't important.

Williams had been expecting Eastern 212. A shrimp boat was ready. He leaned to the right, studying the radar screen at the point where Longtown Intersection was located. The intersection doesn't correspond to a landmark but is a point at which the 169-degree radio navigation beam of Fort Mill VOR forty miles to the northwest intersects Victor Airway 155 running northeast from Augusta, Georgia, to Raleigh-Durham, North Carolina. It is marked on controllers' radar screens and can be found by a pilot using his cockpit navigation equipment.

Williams could see the slanted lines of a transponder-equipped aircraft target about four miles southeast of Longtown. He reached over and placed the shrimp boat beside the target.

"Eastern 212. Radar contact," he replied. "My control for lower?" Eastern 212 was about ten miles inside Jax Center's airspace and technically still Jax's airplane. Williams sought verbal authorization for Atlanta to assume control early.

"Yeah. Yours for lower," Lesiege replied.

"W.S.," Williams said, signing the conversation for the tapes. He drew a small, neat box with the red-tipped end of his pencil and placed a downward arrow beside the box on Eastern 212's flight data strip. It told Hicks that Jax Center had no conflicting traffic at altitudes below Eastern 212 if Atlanta wanted to start the DC-9 down from 16,000 feet at once.

Williams reached up to cut the line. But Lesiege wasn't through.

"Also, can you see . . . ah . . . just northwest of Blythewood, ten miles. That's Eastern 590 at one three thousand."

Blythewood is another intersection, sixteen miles southwest of Longtown. Eastern 590 was en route to Charlotte, part of the morning rush.

Williams peered at the radar screen, fingering the shrimp boat for Eastern 590.

"O.K. Eastern 590. Radar contact."

"He's released also," Lesiege said.

"W.S.," Williams said again. He reached up and punched the 506 button, cutting the connection. He set the shrimp boat beside the target and searched the rack for Eastern 590's strip. Finding it, he made a small red box with a downward arrow on the strip and then leaned back in his chair, letting out a gusty sigh. The damned computer.

CHAPTER FOURTEEN

7:21 A.M.

AFTER STEPHEN W. LANE, who was eighty-five years old, had been ignominiously carried up the DC-9's steps in the curious high-backed chair and strapped into seat 1D, his daughter bent and kissed him, murmuring her farewell. Collette Watson, the senior stewardess, supervised the old man's seating, standing in the aisle slightly behind the first row of seats.

The daughter rose and exited into the aisle and then back a step, so that the airplane galley wall partially shielded her from the view of her father. Clenching her right fist and pointing the thumb upward in the classic thumbs-up sign, she rocked it toward her mouth several times while she shook her head vehemently. Pursing her lips in exaggerated movement she silently mouthed instructions to the stewardess. "No alcohol. No alcohol," her lips silently said.

Collette's eyes darted to the old man. He was gazing out the window at the baggage loading. Collette had handled every conceivable problem. Puking passengers, drunk passengers, frightened passengers, angry passengers. Engine failures, emergency landings, sick children, demanding, thoughtless businessmen. Amorous businessmen, amorous pilots. She liked the gentle old man. Goodness. Would he be asking for a drink at seven in the morning? What would she say if he did?

Steve Lane hadn't asked for a drink. His wizened frame sank into the spacious first-class seat, lost in its roominess, and his thoughts receded into the past as old men's thoughts do when there is little to ponder in the emptiness of the present.

Steve Lane had been twenty-six on that July 2 morning in 1915, a Saturday. He worked at the Western Electric plant in Cicero, had worked there eight years, in fact, and although he didn't know it then, of course, would spend his whole working life at Western Electric, forty-six years in all, rising to department chief. He was still single in 1915, not unusual for a man of his age. Men married later then. He rose early, well before 6 A.M., and boarded a street-car for the jouncing ride into downtown Chicago and the pier on the Chicago River at the foot of the Clark Street bridge.

Each July the Western Electric employees went by excursion boat to the sand dunes of the Indiana shore south and east of Chicago across Lake Michigan. Five boats were chartered for the 7,000 ticket holders—the *Theodore Roosevelt, Petroskey, Racine, Rochester* and *Eastland*. Thick crowds swarmed the pier when Steve Lane swung off the streetcar. A ragtime band played and strains of music drifted down from other bands on some of the boats. A festive air prevailed despite the mist and an intermittent light drizzle. Men wore straw boaters and white shirts and suspenders under their coats. The women wore white and pastel summer frocks that reached to their ankles below the tops of their high buttoned shoes. Broadbrimmed floppy bonnets decorated with lace and plumes and artificial flowers were tied in place with bright scarves atop piled-up knots of hair. Scrubbed children dashed amid the grown-ups and anxious mothers called to them, warning to be careful, not to become lost.

The five boats were to sail at staggered times through the morning, the *Eastland* first at seven-thirty. Picnickers, wanting to get to the Indiana dunes as early as possible and stay as long as possible and thus get maximum enjoyment from a one-dollar excursion ticket, began lining up two abreast at the *Eastland*'s gangway a full hour before the sailing. A few minutes after seven the boat already was filled. The crewmen, who had counted aboard more than 2,500 people, pulled away the gangway. At one point earlier they paused to urge the passengers to move further into the ship, to go below or above but not to mill about the deck by the gangway and impede the loading.

The Chicago River pier by the Clark Street bridge was high, and to board the *Eastland* passengers had to walk down rather than up the gangway. Midway through the boarding, the ship sank lower and engineers in the bowels of the ship began pumping water out of the starboard ballast tanks, the tanks on the pier side of the ship, to raise the gangway entrance and lessen the incline, which had become precariously steep.

Presently the ship's complement of passengers reached its limit and the crew removed the gangway. It was at the moment the crew pulled away the gangway that Steve Lane arrived beside the *Eastland*. He had paused to buy himself a beverage for the picnic and thus missed boarding the ship. But he too wanted to reach the Indiana shore early. The chasm between the pier edge and the gangway port was six, perhaps eight feet wide. The port was three feet lower than the pier. Certainly it could be leaped by an athletic, if somewhat foolish young man. Steve Lane turned to a stevedore on the pier and gave him a coin, enlisting his aid. Then he stepped back, ran headlong at the edge of the pier and leaped for the opening in the *Eastland*'s railing, a perfectly timed shove from the young stevedore carrying him neatly across the gap and down into the gangway port, where two passengers still standing there caught him. It was at that moment that the *Eastland,* amid frantic screaming that suddenly burst from the throats of hundreds of passengers, slowly rolled to port—away from the pier—listing more and more steeply until finally it capsized.

What happened was this:

The *Eastland* had a reputation as a "crank" vessel, particularly unstable in shallow water. To accommodate the shallow water beside the Chicago River pier, ballast tanks were emptied so the *Eastland* rode higher. But that, in turn, made her more unstable. It was a routine risk assumed frequently by the crew.

Once in 1904, when returning to Chicago from a Lake Michigan excursion, lightly loaded ballast tanks caused the *Eastland* to list sharply, sending frightened passengers to the rail, thus worsening the list. Crewmen finally resorted to fire hoses to drive passengers back from the rail and belowdecks to distribute their weight more evenly and lessen the list. The *Eastland*'s instability tended to disappear after she got into deep water and the ballast tanks were filled. The danger was in port.

So on that morning, the ballast tanks were partially filled, as was the custom in the Chicago River. But even more water had been pumped out of the starboard tanks to raise the entrance port and lessen the downward slope of the gangway. Earlier during the loading the *Eastland* had listed to port and then righted herself. Concerned engineers began filling some port ballast tanks, leaving the starboard tanks as they were because of the sloping gangway. In addition, they opened valves that admitted river water into the open hold, an effort to make the vessel more stable by increasing the mass at its keel.

Now the gangway was pulled away, a mooring rope at the *Eastland*'s bows was cast off, the engines were running in preparation for departure, a bell sounded to signal a tugboat out in the river and the tug began to move up to assist the *Eastland* into the main channel. A throng of curious passengers on the upper decks rushed to the port rail to watch. The ship began to list to port again. The water being admitted to the hold, its movement unrestrained by tanks, shifted its mass, making the boat more unstable. The list increased. All at once all the factors came together—a ship of unstable design, lightened ballast tanks, free, shifting water in the hold, a shallow river, passengers rushing to one rail, a cast-off mooring line. The *Eastland* listed more sharply and then even more sharply and in the next moment gracefully rolled over on its side and sank within seconds to the bottom of the Chicago River. It lay with its keel six feet from the pier. Eight feet of its hull, including the starboard propeller shaft, protruded above the water.

The final list to port began just at the moment Steve Lane landed in the starboard gangway entrance, his heart beating double time, his veins filled with the adrenaline his body had marshaled in anticipation of the daring leap. Pandemonium broke loose. Deck chairs and picnic baskets and bassinets and boxes and crates slid clattering down the sloping deck, mingled with a screaming, shouting mass of humanity, men, women, children, all scrambling for something to grab onto. The men beside Steve Lane who had steadied him a moment before were gone. Glass tinkled as chairs and people crashed through windows. There was a rumbling and hissing as water thundered into portholes and down passageways and flooded the engine room. Everywhere there was screaming, wailing and crying as 2,500 frightened, startled holiday makers pitched into the river or were immersed and entombed.

Steve Lane lunged at the railing and grabbed the polished wood with an intense grip whose strength later amazed him. He dangled there, ducking his head against the debris that seemed to fly everywhere. The roll stopped and then the sickening, sinking sensation began and abruptly ceased. He hung by his hands from the rail, his feet dangling just a few feet above the dark river water, which was filled with dozens of bobbing heads, waving arms, picnic baskets, deck chairs, clothes and wooden crates.

"Help me. Help me," a woman below screamed over and over, her bonnet still intact. A wicker basket floated by, a picnic basket, no, he thought, his mind rebelling, a feeling of nausea sweeping him, not a picnic hamper. It was a baby's crib, slowly filling with water, its helpless occupant lying on his back wailing with fear and anger. The water below was a seething, turbulent pool of humanity, more and more heads bobbing up, people climbing upon one another, women being dragged beneath the water by others who bobbed up and grabbed their hair. Panic was everywhere. A man hanging from the railing dropped with a splash into the water, his failing hands no longer able to sustain the grip. Others nearby grabbed him, climbed up on him as if, newly arrived, he possessed more buoyancy. He sank from sight. The screaming continued. A man lunged upward, attempting to grab Steve Lane's legs and pull himself from the water. If he succeeded, they both would fall into the water. Above the din he could hear the bells of the firemen. Help was coming.

For the rest of his life Steve Lane would remember the piteous screaming, but the memories of his own actions in the next moments remained unclear. With a final desperate surge of strength, a realization his life hung in the balance, he pulled himself up and over the railing, scrambling onto what now was the top of the ship but moments before had been the side of the starboard hull. His new perch was slimy and slippery. He sought a place to rest, to consider his situation. Suddenly he lost his balance, his foot hit a particularly treacherous patch of slime and he plummeted down the hull, into the narrow strip of black water between the *Eastland*'s keel and the pier. He struck the water in mid-scream and sank beneath the surface, down, down until his shoes touched the river bottom ooze. Then up he came through the murkiness, his head popped into the light. He was treading water, still alive. At the top of the pier firemen in their red helmets with the long bill in the back stared in horror at the specter of chaos and mass death below.

"Help. Help. Throw me a life preserver. Throw a life preserver," Steve Lane screamed, again and again. No one seemed to hear. The firemen and other rescuers on the pier moved in slow motion. They appeared to take up their duties with elaborate casualness from Steve Lane's vantage, though, in fact, of course, they raced with such frantic effort that they often tripped up one another. A round doughnut-shaped life ring sailed down and landed beside Steve Lane. He lunged, caught it and held on, bobbing up and down.

The *Eastland* sank until the starboard propeller shaft was just above the water, horizontal, the giant screw at its end rising up like some bizarre marine animal. Rescuers aboard a tugboat that nosed up against the *Eastland* cut a hole in the hull with oxyacetylene torches and lifted out passengers, nearly unconscious with fear in the putrid air. Firemen on the pier rigged lines to begin bringing to shore several hundred survivors huddled on the hull. Rescuers wept openly as they performed their tasks.

Steve Lane somehow found himself sitting on the propeller shaft with the white life ring around his neck and one shoulder. Others stood beside him. One man at the end of the shaft was standing beside the screw blade that was nearly as tall as he, like a man leaning on a lamppost.

At that moment a Chicago *Tribune* photographer took a picture of the frightened passengers, including the little group stranded on the propeller shaft. It became one of the most famous *Eastland* disaster pictures, along with a photograph of a weeping fireman clutching the lifeless body of a young girl, reprinted thousands of times in succeeding years each time an anniversary article recalled the horror of that day.

The memories haunted Steve Lane all his life. The babies, the helpless babies. One man in the water striking another on the head with an object so he could gain a hold. The other man sinking out of sight, never to reappear.

They placed the death toll at 812. More died in later weeks of injuries. The *Eastland* was sold to the U. S. Navy for $42,000 and renamed the *Wilmette*. The Navy shortened her hull, corrected the instability problem and turned her into a naval training gunboat. Thirty-one years later, after Steve Lane had become an important man at Western Electric, the *Wilmette* was towed down the Chicago River, past Clark Street, and cut into scrap.

One fall day twelve years after the *Eastland* disaster, at the height of Prohibition, workmen dredging the site for a construction project brought up a gold bracelet, a child's locket, a purse containing eighty cents and two bottles of beer. They opened the bottles, lustily consumed the contents and proclaimed the beer's unspoiled quality after so many years.

Collette Watson left the galley and started for the rear with another tray of steaming coffee cups. She paused and smiled at the old man in 1D, who gazed at her from sunken eyes. Their eyes met. He still had a light there. They hadn't exchanged a word but she liked him. She smiled more broadly. He hadn't once mentioned a drink.

"Everything all right?" she asked cheerily.

CHAPTER FIFTEEN

7:22 A.M.

"HEY. THE FOG. You can't even see the numbers now."

Pete Hogan turned from the console in the Charlotte control tower's glass-walled cab atop the terminal building and stared at the end of Runway 5, where Al Hare's voice guided him. Hare was right. The billow of fog that had hung just off the end of the airport's main runway since they came on duty fifteen minutes before had moved closer. The large white numbers—a zero and a five —and the broad white stripes marking the runway threshold and the airplane touchdown zone receded into the white gossamer curtain.

"Yeah. Movin' in some, isn't it?" Hogan replied. He stepped around Hare, trailing a coiled headset cord, and studied the small rectangular instrument window at mid-console that presented a digital readout of the runway visual range. The two RVR towers beside the runway touchdown zone, clearly visible a few minutes ago, now were dim, dark shapes.

Down in the National Weather Service office Robert Green based the official weather observations on an RVR reading taken from a moving paper strip chart over which a pen scratched as the fog advanced and retreated. But a computer also monitored RVR signals and once each fifty-one seconds averaged the readings and

displayed the result in a window. It was this computer RVR value
that Pete Hogan moved down the tower console to examine.

"Would you believe thirty-eight?" he replied jauntily to Hare's
quizzically arched eyebrows. "A big three, eight, zero, zero."

"Uh huh," Hare grunted. He frowned.

An RVR readout of 3,800 feet. The reading had a special
meaning for Hogan and Hare, and for the other controllers in the
radar room at the bottom of the tower cab stairs. It was a porten-
tous warning to the dozen or more pilots whose machines at that
moment converged on Charlotte, a monition to hundreds of passengers in those airplanes had they known and possessed sufficient
aviation sophistication to understand. In fact, that RVR reading of
3,800 feet had assumed importance a decade before, when the
business and political leaders of Charlotte, pondering the future of
their city, rightly concluded that long-term economic growth de-
pended on a thriving, well-equipped airport with good airline connections.

Consultants were hired, surveys commissioned, maps drawn,
meetings held, growth rates projected, opinions sampled, first
drafts and second drafts and working drafts submitted, reports
written, reaction sampled, support gauged, public attitudes
molded, deals consummated. Charlotte, it was concluded, must
have a second north–south runway, parallel to the present
north–south runway, a Cat II runway on which jumbo jets could
land in the worst weather. It would be a runway as fine as any in
Atlanta. One day Charlotte would awaken and like Atlanta become a boomtown, another jewel in the crown of the New South.
The airport was a key. So in 1969 voters approved a $4 million
bond issue and then two years later a second $6.25 million issue.

From their lofty glass-enclosed perch the Douglas airport controllers watched eagerly as the survey crews sighted through
transits, waved signal flags and pounded stakes. The new runway
eventually would mean a new tower. Then came the great earth-
moving machines—bulldozers, loaders, dump trucks, water
sprayers, rollers—felling the trees, cutting and filling, laying the red
clay open, filling the air with a fine orange dust. The new runway
would parallel the present north–south runway nearly a mile to the
west. Its southern end would extend through the Runway 5 ap-

proach lights that reached southwestward 2,000 feet from the Runway 5 threshold.

Thus, on May 20, 1974, the Runway 5 approach lights at Douglas Municipal Airport were turned off. The horizontal bars of bulbs mounted on pylons that guided anxious pilots straight into the runway at night and through fog, rain, haze, snow and thick clouds came down as bulldozers advanced. It was a compromise with safety, to be sure, but tribute gladly paid to the conqueror progress. Weather teleprinters, pilots' chart services and airline operations documents thereafter noted the decommissioned approach lights. The dispatch papers handed Captain Reeves in Atlanta made note of the situation. He already knew about the absence of approach lights but made a fresh mental note.

Airline and charter pilots were particularly unfortunate because the approach light decommissioning reduced the adverse weather situations in which Runway 5's instrument landing system could guide them safely to the touchdown zone. The ILS did as much as the high-flying jet airplane to bring all-weather operations to the airline industry. It consists of two radio navigation signals received separately but displayed on the same instrument—the flight director in the case of most airliners, such as Eastern's DC-9s.

One radio signal gives the pilot lateral guidance to the runway. Ten miles or more out he can line himself up on the runway by intercepting a radio beam and keeping a vertical needle centered on a horizontal scale. It is the same principle by which First Officer Daniels and the autopilot kept Eastern 212 flying direct to the Fort Mill navigation station.

The second radio signal gives vertical guidance. By keeping a second, horizontal needle centered on a vertical scale, the pilot flies his airplane down a radio beam to the touchdown. If the needle falls below centerpoint, the airplane is high. The pilot retards the throttles slightly to command less power from the engines and steepen the rate of descent. If the needle is above center, the airplane is low. The pilot advances the throttles, calling forth more engine power.

Ten miles out and 5,000 feet high an accomplished pilot who centers both needles, puts them "in the doughnut," can ride his airplane down through soupy weather like a marble rolling down a pipe until he reaches decision height—usually 200 feet above the ground. If the approach lights and the runway are in sight then, the pilot lands. If they aren't, if the airport ceiling is even lower, the throttles are rammed forward and an immediate climb back to safety begins, followed by another try or a diversion to another airport.

In the sophisticated airliner cockpit, autopilots, flight directors and other electronic aids perform most of the work. Pilots take over at the end. There now are even automatic landing systems, frequently found in the jumbo jets, that can accomplish a landing without assistance from the pilot. But the pilot who harbors pride in his skillful hands or perhaps has a suspicion of relying too much on technology often turns off the gadgets and flies the approach himself.

Despite cockpits filled with electronic equipment and the precision with which it can bring an airliner to the runway, sometimes an ILS landing ends in sudden disaster. The man-machine synergism breaks down. In July 1973 a Delta Air Lines DC-9 crew inadvertently switched the sophisticated flight directors to the wrong operating mode during an ILS approach through bad weather at Logan International Airport in Boston. An already erratic approach caused by other weather and air traffic control problems suddenly grew more so as the copilot, who was flying, followed the flight director's control commands without realizing they were wrong. The DC-9 crashed into a sea wall and all eighty-three passengers and six crew members died.

With the Charlotte approach lights in operation, an airline pilot could descend on the ILS to a decision height of 200 feet above the ground if he had an RVR visibility of only 2,400 feet. But with the lights gone, the minimum landing conditions changed—4,000 feet RVR visibility and a 250-foot decision height. In good weather, the lack of approach lights made little difference. With the morning fog still billowing up from the Catawba River and descending more densely now on the runway, the missing approach lights relayed a plain message to Hogan and Hare: Close Runway 5. Switch the incoming traffic to some other runway.

"Actually we can't really close a runway or close the airport because of weather," Hogan had once patiently explained to a non-aviation friend who had raised the question. "To start with, I don't have the authority. If the airport is completely socked in and some pilot wants to make an approach, I'll clear him to the approach on whatever runway. If he lands or doesn't land is his decision.

"Of course if it's clearly below minimums and he violates the regs by landing, we can write him up. But a runway or an airport isn't officially closed. It's closed in the sense that they can't get in. It's the pilot's neck, not mine."

Hogan walked back around Hare and pushed down a button on the console, opening a line between him and Hare and Dennis Hunter, one of the controllers sitting in front of the glass screens in the darkened radar room one floor down.

"Hey, Denny."

"Yeah."

"RVR's down. Thirty-eight hundred."

"Uh huh. I noticed." The radar room had a RVR readout instrument, too.

Hogan and Hare swiveled their heads about, inspecting the fog in all quadrants. Visibility was 1,500 feet out towards Runway 5. The fog seemed to be advancing relentlessly. The water tower one and one half miles away to the north, visible when they signed on, still stood out. They looked south, then southeast, past the approach end of Runway 36.

"It's like a slice out of a pie," Hare murmured.

Indeed it was. With the airport at the center, a great aviation weather god with a giant knife had sliced out a wedge of fog. They could see three, maybe four miles in places past the end of Runway 36. Billows of fog perhaps 100 or 200 feet high protruded from above some of the trees. But they didn't tower up in obscuring masses like those on the other side of the airport.

"How about three six?" Hogan said into his microphone. "Any problem with three six?"

"Yeah. Sure, that's fine," Hunter said. He would have to begin vectoring the inbound airplanes toward Runway 36 instead of Runway 5.

Although Hare, the trainee, performed the duties of the local controller position, it was Hogan, the instructor, who had decision responsibility.

"O.K. three six," he said. "But if anybody wants to try an ILS on five, we'll let them."

"O.K."

Pilots who approach busy airports can tune their radios to a special frequency and hear the Automatic Terminal Information Service broadcast. For Charlotte, the ATIS frequency is 110.6 megahertz. A tape-recorded message about weather, runways and special instructions repeats itself over and over. The tower cab controllers update it at least hourly, more often as conditions change.

A few minutes later, pilots approaching Charlotte heard a new ATIS message: "This is Charlotte Douglas Airport information Uniform. Charlotte weather, sky partially obscured, ceiling 4,000 broken, 12,000 broken, visibility one and one-half, ground fog, temperature 67, wind 360 degrees at five, altimeter 3016. VOR Runway 36 approaches in use. Landing and departing Runway 36. All arriving aircraft make initial contact with Charlotte approach east on 124.0; approach west on 120.5. Runway 5 approach lights decommissioned. Inform the controller on initial contact that you have information Uniform."

The ATIS message didn't say it, of course, because the pilots listening understood from experience. But the message clearly implied that the only Charlotte ILS runway was closed. So the pilots now had no choice but to use the less desirable VOR instrument approach system available on Runway 36.

The FAA bureaucrats who sit behind metal or mahogany desks in their glass and marble edifice at 800 Independence Avenue Southwest in Washington have terms for the two categories of instrument approaches. An ILS approach is a precision approach. The VOR approach, which requires more visibility and higher clouds, is a non-precision approach. The FAA officials will argue that the two categories of approaches are equally safe. Experienced pilots and years of aviation accident statistics indicate otherwise.

But busy pilots and controllers have no time in the heat of the moment to ponder such esoteric points. The decision was made.

The morning rush at Charlotte would use the less precise VOR approach to Runway 36 because the Runway 5 ILS had no approach lights to lead the pilots through the fog to the rubber-scorched concrete. The RVR had fallen too low.

CHAPTER SIXTEEN

7:23 A.M.

JOHN PINHEIRO HAD a secret wife.

At least, she was a secret from some people. His mother and Charlene's parents didn't know the engaged couple had married eight months before in a justice of the peace's office on Commonwealth Avenue in Boston while John was home on leave. Next year, after John's discharge from the Navy, they would kneel at an altar and receive the blessing of a priest. But meanwhile, why upset their parents? The secrecy added to the adventure.

Louie knew, too. He was a sailor, attached to the *Yellowstone* like his brother. When John returned from Boston he came to Louie's berth and elatedly broke the news. He couldn't resist confiding this latest daring escapade.

The Navy knew of the marriage, too. They paid extra each payday. Mike Gagnon knew, of course.

John Pinheiro stole a glance at Mike, who sat in the aisle seat of a row of three on the left in the rear of the coach cabin smoking section. He was watching the slender stewardess. Her name was Eugenia. He had heard it on the intercom when the other stewardess made the announcements.

On the ground in Charleston she had hooked one foot in the little step hole in the side of the seat directly across the aisle and

pulled herself up to place a coat in the overhead rack. Her skirt
rode up, revealing stockinged thighs. They stared unabashedly,
with the frank lust that is endemic to all young men, not just
sailors. She sensed their stare. When she lowered herself back to
the floor she turned and smiled at them. Silly boys, the icy smile
said, stewardesses wear panty hose, too. Their eyes followed her
up the aisle. Mike let out a small whistle.

"How'd ya like to get into that?"

"Yeah."

Girls filled their thoughts, lessening the boredom of life on a destroyer tender that never went to sea. In the taxi to the airport
John had been struck with their impulsive act. He and Mike were
skipping the *Yellowstone*'s decommissioning ceremony to catch
the 7 A.M. flight and not the 11:35 flight so as to arrive at Logan
at 11:57 in the morning instead of 3:37 in the afternoon.

"We're risking court-martial to be with our women five hours
early," he told Mike in tones heavy with mock melodrama.

"Leavin' early to get a little?" somebody had said. It was Cody
or Sterkey who'd nodded knowingly.

Mike was going home to see Cathy, to Lawrence, Massachusetts, where he had been a high school baseball star. Everybody knew their wedding date because Mike spoke of it so often:
third Sunday in June, nine more months.

All summer the sailors had stripped the old *Yellowstone,* preparing her for mothballs. Air conditioners, machine shop lathes,
desks, beds, everything went ashore. In the last weeks they moved
into barracks beside the pier. Duty sections 1, 2, 3, 4 and 6 received liberty that ended at 8:45 A.M. Wednesday with the call to
quarters to begin the decommissioning ceremony. Then by ten-
thirty, the ceremony over, they would pile into the personnel
offices on the docks and receive their orders. Many of the *Yellowstone* sailors would report to the U.S.S. *Fulton,* a submarine tender
tied up at State Pier in New London, Connecticut. For the New
Englanders, the new assignment meant weekends at home

The idea of disappearing early struck them Tuesday. A yeoman
in the personnel office had shown John the orders—row upon row
of boxes filled with alphabetized manila envelopes.

They weighed the risks.

"Look, if they take muster Wednesday morning and we're not there . . ."

"Yeah, but don't you see? If you have your orders you're O.K. You're legal."

"But what if they take muster?"

"Don't matter. If you've got your orders it's legal. You've got your orders, right? And you have to obey your orders, right?"

Duty section 5 didn't get liberty but had to spend Tuesday night aboard the *Yellowstone* cleaning up loose ends. Tuesday morning the old chief, short a hand in section 5, reached out in the Navy's arbitrary manner and picked Louie.

"Report at nineteen hundred hours."

"Yes, sir."

After supper, while Louie dressed for duty, John and Mike burst into the room in a boisterous mood. After carefully closing the door, each drew out his envelope and extracted the official documents complete with the authorizing signature on the bottom. The yeoman had acceded to their persuasion.

"Come on. Go with us. Just ask him. He'll give you yours, too. We'll be in Boston tomorrow morning."

Louie shrugged plaintively.

"Duty. I'm in section five."

"Well, find somebody to stand in for you. You can find some guy that'll do that."

"Sure. If I pay him twenty-five or thirty dollars."

"Well, come on. What's wrong with that?"

"Shit, man. You mean twenty-five dollars to get home five hours early? That's five dollars an hour. I'm not crazy."

"We're goin' to the Little Nashville. Right now. You can see Julie."

It was the ultimate inducement. The sailors often hung out at the Little Nashville. Louie liked to sip beer and talk to Julie, the barmaid.

"Nah. I'll stay."

The Little Nashville is on Dorchester Road in North Charleston, a fifteen-minute drive from the Navy base. It sits pressed against the street in a run-down neighborhood of small factories, fast food chains and service stations. There are three beer joints

side by side, fitted into what once must have been a small factory—
Little Nashville, Gaslight Lounge and Sportsman Club. A dirt
parking lot pocked with chuckholes that fill with water at each
rain and a small sign with movable letters mounted on a trailer are
by the curb. Cheap signs painted on plywood facades with peeling
paint, ringed with rows of incandescent light bulbs, set off each entrance.

Inside, Little Nashville has a bar against one wall in the front of
a long room. Beside the bar, set off by a partition, are pinball machines and pool tables, over which hang plastic imitation Tiffany
lampshades. Beyond the partition are rows of tables and chairs
and a bandstand at the far end. The trusses that hold the building
together are visible above, painted black, along with the automatic
sprinkler system installed during the room's former incarnation.
The windows are boarded up to give Little Nashville a perpetual
intimate gloom.

Julie was gone. The gum-popping girl who brought their beers
shrugged her shoulders elaborately when asked about her. Happy
Hour was over. A mug of beer had jumped from twenty cents to
sixty-five cents. They each took a heavy draught and rose, leaving
the glasses behind, heading for a pool table. Mike racked the balls
and handed a cue to John.

"You break."

He bent over, thrusting the cue fore and aft over the bridge his
thumb made, then sent the white cue ball cracking into the racked
balls. They scattered, but nothing dropped into a pocket.

"Too bad," Mike said, taking the cue.

John sighed. While Mike circled the table for his shot, John
walked to the bar, where he could look around the partition at the
tables ringing the dance floor. There were several men at one
table, two couples, but no single girls.

"Nothing," John reported back. They listlessly pursued the balls
with the cue, draining their mugs and ordering another round.

Ordinarily, the bar would have been filled. But Tuesday was the
one night when a country and western band didn't appear. Little
Nashville wasn't known as a sailor hangout. Gagnon and the Pin-
heiros considered it a red-neck bar. More than once they'd been
harassed by young men with thick drawls at adjacent pool tables

who would "accidentally" bump into one of the sailors. They made fun of the New England accents, the way they said the word beer. They made remarks about sailors. Sometimes a purposely careless cue stick might strike someone. The tormentors didn't seem to want actually to pick a fight, just to assert themselves, reassure their vanities. The sailors tolerated the locals. Their absence on this night was both a relief and a vague disappointment.

The door opened and two girls entered, dressed in cutoff jeans and halters. Their hair fell below their shoulders, down bare backs. Each carried a lighted cigarette. The jeans were faded and tight. One girl had a series of bright patches stitched over her buttocks.

John nudged Mike.

"Check it out. Check it out."

Mike hurriedly took his shot and then casually strolled to the bar to look around the partition and watch them take a seat.

"Not bad. Not bad," he announced. "I get the tall one."

The door opened and two bearded men entered and stood, their eyes adjusting to the dark, surveying the room. Then one waved and started toward the rear. The sailors heard laughter. John rushed his shot, sending the ball glancing off the edge of his cue stick. Then he, too, casually walked to the bar to look around the partition. The men were standing by the girls' table. They laughed at something the tall girl said. The men sat down. He returned to the pool table and Mike's questioning expression.

"Forget it."

The sailors came to the Little Nashville because of the pool, the cheap beer and the girls, easy pickups, one night stands looking for drinks, dinner, a night with no great expectations for the morning. John, who prided himself as a master of the art of seduction, had scored there. So had the others.

John had always gotten the girls. It was his Latin good looks, a certain obsequious charm. He sought and won the prettiest girls. He had first dated Charlene in junior high school. They went steady, then broke up. When he enlisted in the Navy and friends gave a farewell party, Charlene came. They hadn't seen each other for some time. He corresponded with her during boot camp and became engaged when he came home on leave. Charlene hadn't moved to Charleston when they married. John led the sailor's double love life unfettered. He went home to Boston once a month.

The sailors at the pool table bought a third round, began a second pool game, bought a fourth round. They looked up eagerly each time the door opened. Other men came in, sailors, then rednecks, then more sailors. Girls entered, too. Then came their dates. They finished the second pool game.

"Let's go to the Flying Dutchman," John said.

They exited into the damp night and crossed the rocky parking lot toward the Flying Dutchman two blocks down the street. A week before a police cruiser had pulled them over after they drove away from Little Nashville. The officer had asked for their military IDs.

"Why do we have to show our military IDs? What's wrong with a regular driver's license?" John demanded from the back seat. He had begun his beer drinking in the barracks as they came off duty, paying forty cents a can for beer in Navy-supplied vending machines. John ignored the nudges and sotto voce admonishments. He leaned forward in the seat.

"What's wrong with my regular driver's license? This is discrimination. You're discriminating against sailors."

He'd been fingering his wallet.

"Here. Here's my driver's license. That's all I'm going to give you. You can't discriminate against sailors."

In the end, the officer's partner joined him at the car window, John was ordered out, searched and escorted back to the cruiser. He was under arrest. Drunk and disorderly. You can bail your friend out tomorrow.

Tonight the Flying Dutchman was dead, too. They drank more beer, sitting at a table staring about the room. There were long periods of silence—and no girls. Their last evening in Charleston was a dud.

They rose early and walked down the pier to the *Yellowstone* to find Louie and say good-by to others they knew in duty section 5. Stripped bare, the old *Yellowstone,* built thirty years before, exhibited her age more frankly, seemed much more a derelict. She was unfriendly. It was hard to comprehend that they had lived aboard her in comfort, if amid mild boredom, for so many months.

Louie was gone, driving a pickup truck loaded with mattresses and bedsprings to a warehouse. They chatted with Sterkey, who told of the duty section spreading sheets to sleep on the hard deck. It was so hot below without air conditioning.

"Tell Louie we'll see him tonight," John said. They walked to the taxi stand.

"I hope they don't take muster," John said.

"Well, we've got our orders," Mike replied. "What can they do?"

"Oh, they could tell the *Fulton*. Send us up before the Ex-O's Mast."

"Yeah. Big deal. What'll be the worst we get? Five days' restriction? We're not the only ones."

They felt more confident after passing through the security check at the airport.

The stewardess was coming down the aisle, holding a tray. Their eyes ranged expertly over her body.

"Coffee, sir?"

CHAPTER SEVENTEEN

7:23:30 A.M.

FIRST OFFICER JAMES M. DANIELS' altimeter was off by 100 feet. It indicated an altitude 100 feet lower than the readings on the two altimeters on the instrument panel in front of Captain James Reeves.

The two pilots hadn't discussed the difference. But Daniels, taking another chapter from that unwritten book on the care and feeding of airline captains by aspiring first officers, terminated the climb from the Charleston airport and leveled the DC-9 so that his altimeter read 15,900 feet altitude and Captain Reeves's two altimeters read 16,000 feet.

Daniels' reasoning was simple. A conscientious pilot insists on flying his aircraft precisely at the altitude assigned, not twenty-five feet high or fifty feet low, but right on the money. Nothing might potentially irritate Captain Reeves more than sitting in the captain's seat, acting as copilot, watching his airplane cruise to Charlotte 100 feet off the assigned altitude. So Daniels extended a small courtesy to his captain, a mark, he felt, of his professionalism.

But if Captain Reeves appreciated it, he made no mention. Reeves was an opinionated man. His thoughts had turned to one of his passions, aroused by their conversation.

"Ya noticed old Kennedy got booed out. They wouldn't even let him talk," Reeves said. "Splattered him with eggs and tomatoes up there. 'At son of a bitch."

A few days before, Senator Edward M. Kennedy had gone home to Boston, a city whose liberal facade cloaks passionate intolerance, to appear at a rally protesting forced school busing to achieve racial balance. He was shouted down and forced to retreat under a barrage of verbal abuse and fruit and vegetables.

"Well, that do-gooder shit is backfiring on all those people now," Daniels answered, his eyes continuing the rhythmic sweep of the instruments.

"Yes, sir," Reeves agreed. The captain was vehemently opposed to the meddling in the fabric of American life by well-intentioned liberals whose solutions only became part of the problem.

"I think it is backfiring. I really honest to God believe it is," Daniels added in a deliberate tone.

"That's right. It's about time," Reeves responded.

Daniels continued. "Because I think if there's any good comes out of it, it'll be fantastic. You know, I can't do the things now that I used to do on less money. And I'm at the point now where my children are starting to want a lot more . . ." He paused. "A lot more of the things they should have at that age. I have two daughters that need everything at the same time . . ." His voice trailed off and Reeves began whistling.

Daniels resumed. "So, hell, the Democrats, I don't know what the hell they're gonna do. I can't . . . they're gonna run Kennedy. That's what."

"Yeah."

"'Cause they're gonna bring, I got the feelin' they're gonna bring somebody, somebody's gonna bring Chappaquiddick up and use that as well . . ."

"Oh yeah. Oh yeah," Reeves interrupted.

". . . whether they're right or wrong," Daniels continued.

"Yeah. They're gonna bring that up. Kennedy's shot down now. I mean, hell, if they run him they just got beat no matter who the Republicans run. Whoever he is," the captain said.

"Well . . ."

"I think he's thinkin' about runnin'," Reeves added.

"These politicians have backed themselves in a corner on this damn contribution crap and rightly so. 'Cause we're sufferin' today because of it," Daniels said.

"Boy, they don't like that busin' up there. God damn 'at busin'," Reeves said.

"And that tickles the shit out of me," Daniels said with a gleeful chuckle.

"Boy, they really got old Kennedy up there," Reeves said, relishing again the news accounts. "Throwed eggs at 'im. Tomatoes. Wouldn't let 'im talk."

While the captain spoke, Daniels interrupted his instrument scan to reach down into his leather flight bag on the floor at the right side of his seat. He felt about and came up with a thick loose-leaf binder filled with airport approach charts. The charts, printed on thin paper, are slightly larger than a paperback book. There is a sheaf of charts for each airport—the bigger the airport, the more charts. In the case of Charlotte, there were seven.

Daniels extracted the Charlotte charts and laid them on the small writing table to his right, which he raised up and snapped into place. The copilot studied the top chart, seeking the Automatic Terminal Information Service frequency. He found it, 110.6 megahertz, the same frequency as the radio navigation station located on the airport grounds.

Daniels reached down to the second navigation radio switches and dialed in the Charlotte frequency. The other radio, set to the Fort Mill navigation station, still guided the autopilot.

The radio speakers continued to blare the intermittent conversations between other aircraft and Jax Center controllers. So as not to interrupt this and chance missing instructions for Eastern 212, Daniels reached back and retrieved his earphones, hanging on the nozzle of an oxygen bottle, and carefully placed them on his head, adjusting the earpieces to fit comfortably. Then he moved a switch and turned a volume knob and the earphones filled with the Charlotte ATIS in mid-broadcast.

"VOR Runway three six approaches in use. Landing and departing Runway three six. All arriving aircraft make initial contact with Charlotte approach east on one two four point zero . . ."

Daniels turned the volume knob down without waiting for the

rest of the broadcast. He leafed through the Charlotte approach charts and placed the one labeled "VOR Rwy 36" on top.

Then Daniels returned to the instruments. His eyes stopped at his altimeter, 15,900 feet. Then they flicked to the captain's lower altimeter, 16,000 feet, and then the captain's upper altimeter, 16,010 feet.

The captain's lower altimeter is the most sophisticated in the cockpit. It is hooked to the airplane's air data computer, an electronics-filled box that senses atmospheric pressure outside the fuselage through special ports. The computer compensates for perturbations caused by aircraft altitude and speed, feeding corrected atmospheric pressure signals to the captain's lower altimeter, the flight director, the autopilot and other DC-9 systems that need precise atmospheric pressure readings.

Altimeters are merely sophisticated barometers. As an airplane ascends, the atmospheric pressure decreases. An altimeter, instead of registering declining inches of mercury, reports increasing altitude. If an airplane descends, atmospheric pressure increases and the altimeter reports lessening altitude.

The captain's lower or number two altimeter is hooked to the transponder, which relays its readings to ground radar antennas so that controllers can see an altitude print-out on their screens. Controllers in Jax Center were reading 16,000 feet for Eastern 212 because that was what Captain Reeves's lower altimeter reported. The altitude alert system also is connected to this altimeter, and the one-second warning beep when the airplane reached 15,750 feet was triggered by it. Although it is the most sophisticated altimeter in the cockpit, its position at the bottom of the instrument panel made it difficult for Daniels to see, particularly if his left hand rested on the engine throttles.

Higher on the instrument panel is the captain's number one altimeter, just to the right of the flight director. It is connected by tubes to a fuselage port. Signals from the air data computer are fed into this altimeter to help correct pressure perturbations caused by the port or tubing. A small window in the altimeter face displays the letters "CORR," which confirm receipt of computer signals. A switch on the altimeter permits the captain to break the computer connection and obtain "raw" atmospheric pressure data from the fuselage port.

On the right instrument panel, in the same position as the captain's number one altimeter, is the first officer's single altimeter. It is not corrected by computer signals, but takes atmospheric pressure directly from another fuselage port.

This was the altimeter that read 100 feet lower than the other two. The disparity was probably the result of differences between air data computer signals and raw atmospheric pressure. It could have been caused in part by an error in Daniels' altimeter, a need for servicing. But on the ground in Atlanta when the pilots checked their altimeters, the difference was less than forty feet, just within the tolerance permitted by a chart in their operations manual. Now at 16,000 feet, the 100-foot difference still was just within tolerance. The limits increased with altitude to a permissible 205-foot difference when flying at 35,000 feet.

It is common for pilots to misread and misset altimeters. With much less frequency, fortunately, such misreadings and missettings cause accidents. In 1971 the FAA commissioned a study of altimeter-related airline accidents. Of 1,400 U.S. and foreign air carrier accidents during the study period in the 1960s, 18 per cent or 262 accidents were identified in which deviation from proper altitude played a role. But there were only four clear cases of altimeter misreading and eight cases of a pilot missetting an altimeter.

However, in dozens of other accidents, investigators sifting wreckage and reconstructing a flight reached inconclusive findings. Why did pilots, who surely had no desire to destroy themselves or their passengers, allow their aircraft to stray from the proper altitude? The suspicion is that perhaps a misread or misset altimeter led to the crash, which then obliterated the conclusive evidence. As a result, although the FAA study found only 1 per cent of the accidents directly attributable to altimeter misreading or missetting, many safety experts are convinced these are but the tip of the iceberg, and the true number is far greater.

The most clear-cut reports of altimeter misreadings and missettings stem from those that were discovered in the nick of time, that didn't result in accidents, in which pilots admitted a mistake.

For example, on a moonless night in 1967, a DC-8 over the Pacific Ocean inbound to Los Angeles began its descent. The copilot was flying, the captain calling out altitudes. The captain called 30,000 feet, then called out leaving 20,000 feet. As the aircraft neared 10,000 feet, both captain and copilot were distracted by radio communications. Then, as the altimeter neared sea level, the captain, thinking they were approaching 10,000 feet, reminded the copilot to level out and reduce his airspeed to 250 knots, the speed limit below 10,000 feet. The copilot leveled out at what he thought was 10,000 feet and only then did all three pilots look outside and see the black waves 100 feet below. Each pilot had misread the altimeter by 10,000 feet. The airplane was equipped with a three-pointer altimeter. One hand, like the hand on a clock, read hundreds of feet, a second hand read thousands of feet and a third hand read tens of thousands. The DC-8 crew hadn't noticed that the tiny tens of thousands hand was at zero instead of one.

An airliner crew a few years ago thought it was flying at 29,000 feet, with clearance to descend through bad weather to 24,000 feet and then 11,000 feet. The first officer radioed air traffic controllers each time, reporting passage through 24,000 feet, 23,000 feet and 17,000 feet. As they passed through 12,000 feet, he called out the thousand-foot warning to the captain for aircraft level-out at the assigned 11,000 feet. The airplane still was in the clouds and just as the captain began to stop the descent, the first officer saw trees and shouted a warning. The captain climbed the airplane upward so violently that a stewardess in the aisle was thrown to her knees. All three pilots had misread the altimeter by 10,000 feet at different times, beginning during the climb to the 29,000-foot cruising altitude and continuing during the descent. At the time they thought they were at 29,000 feet, the airplane actually was cruising at 19,000 feet.

Airline industry and government files are filled with similar accounts.

The barometric pressure varies from airport to airport, so pilots must constantly update their altimeters with the current pressure so the altimeter reading will reflect local meteorological conditions. An altimeter set to read correctly in Atlanta, where the atmospheric pressure one day might be 30.12 inches of mercury, would be 100 feet off in Charleston if the atmospheric pressure that day was 30.02 inches.

When the Jax Center controller passed along the "Columbia altimeter" to Reeves and Daniels during one transmission, he was giving them the local barometric pressure nearest Eastern 212's position. It only differed one hundredth of an inch of mercury—ten feet on the altimeters—but both pilots immediately reached out of long habit for knobs on the side of each altimeter and made the tiny correction, reading it in small windows on each altimeter.

This constant resetting of local barometric pressure is another cause of altimeter accident. Sometimes pilots set the wrong value. In the United States, local pressure is passed along to pilots expressed in inches of mercury. Abroad, it often is stated in millibars, another barometric pressure scale. Captain Reeves's lower altimeter had windows for setting both scales.

During a DC-8 approach into Palma, Majorca, the air traffic controller relayed a pressure setting of 996 millibars. The U.S. crew set 29.96 inches of mercury, thinking the 996 value wasn't in millibars. Clear weather prevented a disaster.

During an approach into Nairobi, Kenya, an altimeter was set to 938 millibars instead of the correct 839. The airliner prematurely touched down on an open hilltop nine miles from the airport, recovered and made a successful landing at Nairobi. The altimeter was off 3,000 feet because the first officer had mentally transposed the pressure setting numbers.

Like every pilot, Reeves and Daniels had misread altimeters—sometimes by 10,000 feet, sometimes by 1,000 feet. They had misset barometric pressures. But like most pilots, they caught the errors within seconds or minutes, long before they were of any consequence. Being professional pilots, men who strove for as near perfection in their work as possible, each mentally berated himself every time such an error occurred and tried to relive the circumstances that led to it, to pinpoint what had allowed such a small, but potentially fatal mistake to happen. They seldom found a satisfactory answer. Such mental exercises rarely lead to a specific conclusion. The value each time lay in the anxiety the incident produced and the subsequent vows of increased vigilance.

Jim Reeves and Jim Daniels were fortunate that their DC-9

wasn't equipped with the old three-pointer altimeters that had nearly caused the DC-8 pilots to fly into the Pacific Ocean.

Reeves's lower altimeter, the most modern, also was the least ambiguous, the altimeter least likely to be misread. It is called a counter-drum-pointer altimeter and works like this:

A hand, like the sweep-second hand on a watch, revolves around the dial, numbered from zero to nine, indicating hundreds of feet. In the middle of the dial, in a horizontal window, digital numbers report thousands of feet and tens of thousands of feet. The thousands window works like that portion of the odometer in an automobile that measures tenths of miles. It is a continuous scale so that if the airplane is at 4,500 feet, the scale is midway between the four and five with both numbers visible. The tens of thousands window works like a digital clock. When the airplane, climbing, passes through 20,000 feet, the 1 in the window disappears and the 2 takes its place with a snap. This feature precludes a 10,000-foot reading error. Below 10,000 feet, instead of a zero in this window, a cross-hatched cover blanks it out. Below 1,000 feet another cross-hatched cover blanks out the thousands window. Thus 10,000- and 1,000-foot reading errors are difficult.

Unfortunately, this altimeter, the best in the cockpit, is low on the panel, where the captain's eyes might not return to it as frequently and where the copilot has to strain to see it. It is not considered a primary altimeter for use during the final stages of a landing.

The other two altimeters, the primary altimeters, are more ambiguous in altitude presentation, more likely to be misread. Called drum-pointer altimeters, each has a sweep hand measuring hundreds of feet, like the captain's lower altimeter. In a single window on the right side of the face, a continuous counter, like that on the automobile odometer, measures thousands of feet, up to 50,000 feet. During a climb, for example, the drum steadily rotates as each 1,000 feet passes. Between 3,000 and 4,000 feet the 3 and 4 appear. Then the 3 disappears and the 5 emerges as the climb continues. Next, the 4 recedes and the 6 appears.

Thus, at an altitude of 6,700 feet, for example, the sweep hand points to the 7, signifying 700 feet. In the window, the index mark is between the 6 and 7, closer to the 6. A pilot quickly glancing at the instrument must pause and mentally ask whether the altimeter reads 6,700 feet or 7,700 feet. There is less ambiguity when the index mark is closer to one drum number than another, but the possibility of transposing the reading and making a 1,000-foot error still exists. The drum-pointer altimeters are an improvement over the old three-pointer altimeter. But, unfortunately for the pilots of Eastern 212, these altimeters lack the "fail-safe" sophistication of the captain's lower altimeter.

Neither Reeves nor Daniels consciously pondered the difference between the altimeter faces. They had earned their pilot's wings on the old two- and three-pointer altimeters. Both pilots had thousands of hours in airliner cockpits with a variety of altimeters, including the most modern. If asked, each would have expressed a preference for Reeves's lower altimeter, the counter-drum-pointer instrument. But neither had any serious reservations about the other two altimeters, both drum-pointer instruments. Neither man expected to misread an altimeter. They were careful, conscientious pilots.

While Daniels monitored the ATIS broadcast, the speakers continued to chatter. When the copilot finished, he shoved the earphones back on his head so he could hear, but didn't take them off. A radio message then arrived for him and Reeves.

"Eastern 212, contact Atlanta Center one two seven point one five," a controller ordered amid a burst of static.

Reeves picked up the microphone.

"One two seven one five . . . ah . . . 212. Good day," he answered.

The captain reached down and dialed the new frequency into the second communications radio, leaving the old frequency in place. In case of difficulty making the new contact, he could return to the former controller for help.

"Eastern 212 with you at sixteen," he announced into the microphone.

"Eastern 212, Atlanta Center, roger," came the immediate reply. "Ah . . . descend and maintain eight thousand. Squawk . . . ah . . . three four two four and the altimeter's three zero one four at Charlotte."

"O.K. We're squawking three four two four and down to eight," Reeves crisply responded.

While the pilot's conversation continued, several things occurred in quick succession.

Reeves leaned forward and dialed code 3424 into the transponder and hit the ident button. Then he set the Charlotte altimeter setting in first his upper and then his lower altimeter.

"Busin' to me, I . . . ah . . . nobody likes it. So why the hell do we have to do it? Huh?" Reeves asked, reaching out to the glare shield and spinning a knob, resetting the altitude alert from 16,000 feet to 8,000 feet. The ALT warning lights now would flash on at 8,750 feet, the warning beep at 8,250 feet.

"Why don't we stop at ten?" Reeves suggested. If they leveled out at 10,000 feet they could maintain their cruise speed of 320 knots for a minute or two longer before reducing to the 250-knot speed limit below 10,000 feet. That could put them in Charlotte a couple of minutes earlier.

While Reeves performed his chores, Daniels had reached down to the autopilot console and thumbed the pitch control wheel forward, ordering the autopilot to put the airplane into a gentle descent. Then he grasped the two throttles with his left hand and slowly drew them back. The airspeed began at once to increase slightly, climbing to 355 knots. The vertical speed indicator needle hesitated a few seconds and then dipped downward, registering a descent of 1,000 feet per minute. Daniels rested his hand on the throttle levers and presently drew them back even more, carefully watching the EPR gauges, pulling back until the EPR stood at 140. Then the copilot shoved one earphone back in place and turned up the volume to hear the Charlotte ATIS again.

Reeves leaned back and reached up to the overhead panel, flicking on the seat belt sign he had turned off a few minutes before. Then he reached farther back and to the right and hit the switches for the two boost pumps in each of the two main fuel tanks, a precaution that would assure continued fuel flow to the engines if a pump failed.

"Guess I'm pretty stupid about why we have to have this busin'," Reeves said sardonically.

Daniels turned next to the cabin pressurization. All during the flight the DC-9 had been pressurized to Charleston's altitude, even though the airplane flew three miles high. By varying a cockpit control, pilots can specify the altitude in their controlled environment. Because Eastern 212 had to climb only to 16,000 feet, they had left the cabin pressure at Charleston's altitude, just above sea level.

The copilot reached overhead and turned a knob, setting the Charlotte airport elevation, 749 feet, in a window. Then he turned another knob, setting the Charlotte barometric pressure just relayed by the Atlanta controller—30.14. Finally he turned a third knob, beginning a slow increase in the cabin pressure, equivalent to an airplane climbing 300 feet a minute, to bring the cabin pressure up from sea level to the Charlotte elevation. When the stewardesses opened the door in Charlotte there would be no difference between atmospheric pressure outside and cabin pressure. Passengers would experience no discomfort.

Daniels accomplished all this with little conscious deliberation. Then he spoke.

"That busin' cost me a lot of money." But it was worth it, he thought. Thank goodness he had moved his family from southwest Atlanta to Roswell. True, a more expensive home, more commuting. But a nicer environment. Worth it just to escape problems like racial troubles in the schools.

"Plain point is I don't know anybody that likes busin'," Reeves said. "Even blacks don't seem to like it. Why the hell do they fool with that? Nobody wants it. Nobody likes it. But we still have to do it."

Reeves reached above his head to the airplane's third communications radio, the radio used to talk with the Eastern Airlines ground station personnel. He dialed in the Charlotte frequency, 130.45 megahertz.

"I'm goin' to get some numbers," he announced.

Daniels pushed a yellow button on the control wheel. A small whistling whoop sounded, the autopilot disconnect warning. Daniels had disconnected the autopilot and would fly the airplane manually during the rapid descent into the Charlotte area. Charlotte was still sixty miles away. But they would be there in ten minutes.

Reeves leaned over and looked out the side window. There was a layer of scattered fleecy clouds a few thousand feet below. Through the clouds he could see dark greens and browns of farmland and swamps and forests. The snaking finger of another dammed river was off to the left. The low sun glinted off the water. It was a beautiful morning.

Daniels concentrated on the flight director, now using the green command bars to position the downward angle of the nose just right for the descent, holding the compass heading to keep the navigation needle centered, keeping the wings level.

Yes, sir. Getting out of Ben Hill and moving to Roswell had been a good move.

"All that shit is gettin' pretty bad over there in the Ben Hill area," he said. He looked at the vertical speed indicator. The descent rate had increased to 2,500 feet per minute.

Eastern 212 was plummeting back to earth.

CHAPTER EIGHTEEN

7:24 A.M.

JOHN MERRIMAN BEGAN at CBS in 1942 as an eighteen-year-old page. He had spent all his career as a journalist there. A writer, editor and producer, he worked with them all—Murrow, Lowell Thomas, Sevareid, Cronkite. He produced CBS Radio's "The World Tonight," an evening news program anchored by Harry Reasoner. He and Reasoner became closer later, when Reasoner regularly substituted for Cronkite on the Evening News, where Merriman had risen to news editor, an important, influential position.

Merriman and Reasoner played word games, tirelessly searching for the hackneyed phrase, the journalistic cliché, the reporter's metaphor. A piece of wire service copy from Washington crossed Merriman's desk in which the writer spoke of congressmen leaping legislative hurdles to pass a bill. "Pictures of the hurdles, please," John scrawled across the margin and routed it to Reasoner. When Reasoner created a stir at CBS by leaving to join ABC as an anchor man for that network's evening news program, the two men maintained their friendship.

There are important broadcast journalists scattered among the three networks who see each other frequently socially. They play poker together, eat together, drink together. More than once at the

height of Spiro Agnew's attacks on the "liberal Eastern media"
they chuckled wryly. If Agnew only knew of their social connections. They were careful not to permit such friendships to interfere
with the competitive journalistic spirit or their judgment of the
news.

They met for lunch regularly on Fifty-seventh Street at Le Biarritz, a French restaurant. "John, you're both a gourmet and a
gourmand," his colleagues chided him. He freely admitted to both
charges. He loved junk food, piling his paper plate high and returning for seconds and thirds at the table of potato chips and cold
cuts brought into the studio on election nights. But he knew the
finest restaurants in major cities throughout the world. He had
traveled everywhere, on his own and with Cronkite. Going to
Athens? Ask John Merriman about the best restaurant, the best
hotel. Going to Brussels? Ask John.

"What you have here," he lectured his luncheon companions at
Le Biarritz, gazing at the red velvet decor, "is a French restaurant
rare in New York. What you get here is what any bourgeois
French businessman expects from the place where he eats lunch
every day." Merriman, Reasoner and Charlie West, a Cronkite
writer, ate there, often haggling rather than splitting the bill
evenly, John insisting he pay less because he hadn't had a drink or
his entrée cost less.

But he loaned money generously, even foolishly, dipping into
his ample income. He had no wife or children. He came back from
space shots in Florida laden with bags of oranges and grapefruits,
which he passed around the studio in comradely, thoughtful gener-
osity.

When Reasoner moved to ABC they exchanged their journalistic clichés and metaphors by letter and telephone.

"Dear Harry. Enjoyed your editorial on the Stanton-Staggers
business very much. However, did note you mentioned that law-
men and the press lived in reasonable amnity; actually it's Reasonable Amityville—on Long Island a stone's throw from Freeport.

"Bob Blum says UPI was the only one to note that Veep
Agnew arrived in Seoul in a Light Drizzle. I wouldn't go up in one
of those Air Korea planes for a million bucks.

"Hope to have lunch with you soon, as soon as I recover from being belted in the back of the neck by a Stinging Rebuke. Best, John."

One day he gleefully telephoned Reasoner. A wire service writer describing the saga of Watergate wrote that a pall hung over Washington because of the latest revelation.

"Did your guys get a picture of that pall?" he asked his friend. "Ours missed it. The pall made it too dark."

John Merriman pushed the button in the armrest and reclined his seat. He settled down more deeply and closed his eyes. Perhaps he would doze.

It was less than five weeks since Watergate reached its inexorable close—Richard Nixon's resignation. The resignation marked the end of a difficult period of stress—long hours, lunch and dinner in the studio, special programs, broadcasting the Evening News and then turning around to put together more special coverage, constant deadline pressure. The Evening News moved to CBS's Washington studios at midsummer for the House Judiciary Committee hearings and just stayed on as the drama played itself to a close. Day after day they maintained the pace. Into the studio by 10 A.M., back to the hotel at midnight. The memory of one day merged with another. Finally on August 8 Nixon announced his intention to step down, the first President ever to do so.

When in Washington, the Evening News staff takes over two small rooms, ordinarily used for storage, just off the larger newsroom-studio combination on the second floor of the red brick CBS building on M Street. In one room, equipped with soundproofing on the walls and ceiling and a soundproof door, Cronkite, Merriman and two or three writers worked at two battered tables shoved back to back and a small desk. Wire service copy came to them, the producers hurried in and out, the script girls bustled about. The writers crafted the script Cronkite would read to report the news events and tie together the film stories.

John Merriman studied the voiceover scripts for the August 8 broadcast. It was late afternoon. Dan Rather had the White House story. He reported that Nixon had decided to resign as early as Monday after release of the transcript of a White House tape directly linking Nixon to Watergate. During a cruise on the Potomac aboard the presidential yacht the Nixon daughters had

urged against it. Some of the family was in tears at dinner the
night before. Nixon was working on a resignation speech. White
House aides were saying privately that "It is over."

Merriman hadn't edited Rather's copy before the film story was
prepared. But if in his judgment its focus was wrong, a fact was
questionable, its tone was not quite correct, he could initiate discussions with Cronkite and the Evening News producers regarding
changes. John Merriman was the conscience of the CBS Evening
News.

He read other scripts. A report from Phil Jones on the activities
of Vice-President Gerald Ford that day. The Vice-President had
met for one hour and ten minutes with the President, then sum-
moned Secretary of State Henry Kissinger for a two-hour meeting.
As President, Ford was expected to retain the Nixon Cabinet.
Melvin Laird was front-runner for Vice-President.

From Capitol Hill Bruce Morton discussed concern among
congressmen about whether Nixon's expected resignation would
include a confession of guilt, whether impeachment should be pursued. House leaders seemed to be lining up against immunity from
prosecution for Nixon.

Roger Mudd reported on similar sentiments among senators. In
political terms, Mudd reported, Congress appeared not to be vin-
dictive. However, the President would not be permitted to get beyond the law.

Connie Chung had spoken with somber spectators clustered
outside the White House gates. Terry Drinkwater had gone to
Yorba Linda, California, the Nixon birthplace. The local newspaper planned to drop reference in the newspaper's masthead to
"Yorba Linda, birthplace of President Nixon."

In Grand Rapids, Michigan, Ike Pappas had a report about the
Vice-President's hometown. And from New York Gary Shepard
reported that wholesale prices had risen 3.7 per cent nationally in
the last month for a projected annual wholesale inflation rate approaching 20 per cent.

Merriman had more direct jurisdiction over the Cronkite script
written by the others in the small room. There was the all-impor-
tant opening in which Cronkite summarized the day's program, the
script tying the film stories together, the stock market report—the

Dow Jones was down twelve points—a brief report on continuing fighting on Cyprus. He edited them carefully, sometimes rolling paper into his typewriter and rewriting something.

"This can't go on. Look what it's doing to my stocks," he grumbled to Hinda Glasser, a script girl, as he edited the stock market copy. She hoped to leave at week's end for a vacation.

"Oh, John," she moaned. "What if he doesn't resign? I can't walk away from this story."

John reassured her. "The son of a bitch is going to have to resign. It's going to be resolved today. You'll get your vacation."

By 6 P.M. Cronkite was at his desk reading the script, timing each section with a stopwatch. The script girls dictated finished scripts and changes to others in New York so those who directed the program and worried with video switching could follow its progress. The writers tinkered with last minute stories, discussing possible changes. Cronkite insisted on the Evening News being up to the minute. Sometimes prepared stories were scrapped and a late-breaking story substituted. Often they wrote and rewrote and substituted stories even as Cronkite was on the air. They never stopped considering possible deletions and insertions until the sign-off.

At six-fifteen Cronkite took a small mirror from a desk drawer and carefully combed his hair. A woman with tubes of makeup and tissues arrived. A styrofoam cup of hot tea with a lemon slice appeared by his elbow. He stepped out into the large studio-newsroom and sat at a metal desk with a piece of brown velvet taped over its top. The other shabby desks, piles of old newspapers, coffee cups, typewriters, chairs, editors and technicians standing about gave the room a down-at-the-heels look, a commonness in sharp contrast with the small island of matched colors, backdrops, brown velvet, makeup, combed hair and straightened tie seen on the television monitors.

At the Teleprompter, technicians busily taped sheets of script together into a continuous strip for display on a screen beside the camera into which Cronkite looked and recited the script seemingly from memory. The script girls took their positions at desks beside the anchor man and the producer, telephone lines open to New York, the phones cradled on their shoulders. They would

relay any last minute changes. Merriman sat down at his desk next
to Cronkite.

"Five minutes," the floor manager shouted. It was like a group
of midgets driving a car. One person pushed in the clutch. Another
shifted the gears, not knowing if the clutch had been engaged.
Someone else moved the steering wheel. Another person looked
out the window, shouting instructions. Each did his job, confident
the others were doing theirs. Through teamwork the car moved
down the road, the program got on the air.

"One minute . . . Thirty seconds . . . Ten seconds." The red
camera light came on.

"Good evening," Cronkite said to the camera.

"President Nixon reportedly will announce his resignation tonight, and Vice-President Ford will become the nation's thirty-
eighth President tomorrow. That word comes unofficially from
aides and associates of both men but not from the two men themselves. And the swiftly moving events of this busy day in Washington tend to confirm it."

Merriman followed the script, smoking a cigarette European
style, pinching it between thumb and forefinger. He helped Cronkite keep the script in order, making last minute checks, stepping
into a nearby room filled with wire service teleprinters, watching
for late developments.

A few minutes into the newscast a call came from one of the reporters at the White House. A strange thing was happening. The
large group of newsmen gathered there had been locked into the
briefing room. A guard stood at the door. Someone wrote a script
reporting this development. Merriman read it, decided to rewrite
it.

He hurriedly turned to a typewriter, his fingers flying over the
keys. He stopped to stare at the wall, take a drag on another cigarette, mentally compose a sentence. His fingers flew again. Then he
searched for a hole, a place to delete something and insert a
twenty-five-second story. A commercial began. Sixty seconds.
Cronkite turned toward them and they conferred. Put it after the
commercial. Cronkite took the script addition and turned back into
position. The camera light came on.

"There's been a mysterious move at the White House tonight,"

Cronkite told the camera. "In advance of the President's TV speech, members of the White House press corps have been locked in the briefing room there. A policeman is guarding the door and he won't let any of the newsmen out. No explanation for all of this."

Then Cronkite moved smoothly to the introduction of Eric Sevareid's taped commentary. Another telephone call. Merriman turned to the typewriter again. The program was almost over but still time for a final script revision.

Sevareid was finishing. "Ten seconds," the floor manager called.

". . . no free country has lived with that for more than a couple of years and retained free, democratic rule," Sevareid concluded.

Cronkite's camera light came on.

"After twenty-three minutes of incarceration, newsmen at the White House are now free again to leave their briefing room.

"Our continuing CBS News coverage of this historic night will resume immediately after this broadcast. This is Walter Cronkite, CBS News. And I'll be back in a couple of minutes."

They would break for commercials and then continue the live coverage leading up to the President's resignation speech and then beyond. Now the end to a long tiring story was in sight. It was at once exhilarating and depressing. They were firsthand witnesses to dramatic political history in the making. But it was a tragedy they reported, the sad story of a man who lied to protect his associates and eventually toppled his government. It was as if they looked through a mirror into another world.

John Merriman felt the knees of the man behind him through the seat back. Damned cramped seats and narrow aisles.

Eileen had convinced him to go home to Walterboro and see his mother, Julia Bell Merriman, a grand old southern lady. Eileen worked for NBC, part of the network's election news unit. She had to work late during the weekend rehearsing for the New York primary election and then again primary night. They wouldn't be able to see one another. In Walterboro he had watched the primary coverage on television and then his mother and Aunt Marian rose early and drove him to the Charleston airport.

John would take a taxi from LaGuardia into Manhattan, get his things together and then pick up Eileen at NBC for the four-day weekend in Camden, Maine. Eileen had suggested Camden. Not a place he would pick, a small uninteresting fishing town. But she had read an article about it somewhere.

They had to settle their future, decide if marriage was what they wanted. They had been regularly seeing a psychiatrist—together. The dual sessions were a form of marriage counseling—expensive marriage counseling. John paid the fees. The psychiatrist charged double his usual rate when he saw two people at once.

It was nearly four years ago that they met—at a Universalist Church service. Now they maintained separate apartments, but Eileen spent much of her time at his. Should they marry? A big step for a bachelor of fifty. They got on well. Vacationed together in the Caribbean each winter. She had helped share the pressures of work, relieve the stress of Watergate, the constant assessing and reassessing of the Cronkite news coverage, making certain it was fair and as accurate as possible. They must document everything they said. Sometimes they bent over backwards so far to be fair that they treated others unfairly. How often he unburdened himself on that score to Eileen.

What raging fights they had. Eileen was British, raised in a family that detested "scenes." She let her resentments fester, build up to an explosive point. She was getting over that. The shrink was helping them both.

He smiled. He hadn't been able to get her on the telephone. She didn't know when he would arrive. Every night she had been in the NBC studios away from her desk. If you didn't know the extension where someone worked temporarily, it was impossible to find him through switchboards at NBC. He would just walk in and surprise her. A CBS spy in the camp of the enemy. He could picture her smile of happiness, her little cry of pleasure.

CHAPTER NINETEEN

7:24:10 A.M.

' "Hey, Charlotte. Five ninety. Take your numbers please.
Over."

Bob Beal turned in his padded swivel chair with armrests and
looked at the digital clock beside the radio console. It was 11:23
GMT—7:23 A.M. Eastern Daylight time.

"Charlotte, 352 in range. How about some numbers?" the pilot
of a second aircraft barked over the speaker box atop the console.
"All right. All right. I'm coming," Beal muttered, reaching to a
rectangular panel filled with buttons and punching one that
selected the radio channel on which he talked with the pilots of
Eastern Airlines' arriving and departing flights at Charlotte's
Douglas Municipal Airport. He picked up a telephone and pressed
a switch in the handle that hooked him into the Eastern ground
station radio transmitter.

"Good morning, astronauts," he said in a nasal southern drawl.
"The Charlotte pressure is five forty, that's five four zero. Got an
altimeter of thirty sixteen, that's three zero one six."

"Eastern 352 gets twenty-nine . . . ah . . . thirty-four," a pilot
aboard an airplane replied.

"Thirty-four is exact," Beal replied. "And your fuel is seventeen
and twenty-two. And what was the other flight out there?"

"Eastern 398 has three zero one five on the read-back . . ." The transmission was cut off by a high-pitched squeal, the kind when two radio transmitters on the same frequency broadcast at the same time.

Beal frowned. No Eastern flight 398 ever came into Charlotte. And the read-back was wrong for Charlotte. Must be some spill-over on the same frequency from another Eastern ground station somewhere else. He was right. It was Eastern 398 en route from Raleigh-Durham to Washington beginning its letdown 200 miles to the north and requesting Washington's in-range numbers. Atmospheric conditions, antenna positions and timing were just right to receive the single transmission in Charlotte.

"Hey, Charlotte, 590 is . . . ah . . . twenty-nine thirty-four."

"Five ninety, that's exact," Beal said. "And I say, I believe you crew change here. So we'll see you at Gate Two with the brake set."

"O.K."

Beal reached for the pad of ground communications record forms and began filling them out, one for each aircraft. The morning rush at Charlotte had begun.

Beal, who was nearing his twentieth anniversary with Eastern, had arrived a few minutes ago. He was alone in the Eastern control center on the second floor of the airport terminal building two doors down the hall from the National Weather Service office and just around the corner from the radar room door. The second member of the control center day shift would report to work any minute.

The control center is in a corner room of the terminal building where two walls of windows look out on the graveled roof of the long, narrow Eastern concourse stretching away from the main building. Through the windows he could see below the stout tractors used to move airplanes and baggage carts, and pickups and stairways and fuel trucks, the station wagons and baggage carts, and the ramp service workers in their blue coveralls and earmuffs hanging around their necks busily preparing for the flock of morning arrivals, the shuffling of passengers between connecting flights. Charlotte has no jetways that move up to the airplane's open door. So arriving aircraft park several yards away from the concourse doors and extend their own stairways. The parking spaces marked by yellow stripes were vacant now. Soon they would be filled by big jets, DC-9s and Boeing 727s.

The control center is carpeted in blue. The two-position console is set in a corner of the room so the operators have the best possible view of the scene below through the windows. Looking out beyond the Eastern concourse toward the end of Runway 5, Beal could see a fog bank rolling in, obscuring the numbers painted on the concrete, shrouding the RVR towers and the red and white corrugated metal building that houses the instrument landing system transmitters.

Beal's job is to communicate with arriving and departing aircraft, to pass up the altimeter and fuel information to the inbound airplanes and obtain the gate departure and takeoff times of the departing flights. Beal's console and desk top are covered with glass underneath which lists of procedures, telephone numbers, radio frequencies and the like are kept for ready reference. Atop the console sit speakers which broadcast radio communications and an altimeter, a three-pointer model like those in many airliner cockpits.

To the left of Beal's console is a Codeacom, like the one in Charleston Jim Wilkes used to enter data about Eastern 212 into the central computer. Beal could use the computer keyboard to call up information about any arriving flight—type and amount of baggage, fuel requirements, passenger count, special services required, takeoff time, estimated time of arrival, unusual problems. As each flight departed he entered the pertinent information into the computer.

The other console, to the left of the Codeacom, has a control panel for the Eastern television monitors in the terminal building. By using a control board the operator can change displays on the television screens at the ticket counters and in the waiting lounges reporting arrival times, gate numbers, delays and other information. The in-range man passes along information to his companion, who constantly updates the television screens.

As one after another of the inbound aircraft called for their in-range numbers, Beal's attention centered on the altimeter mounted in a wooden case on the console. Its presence was a legacy of

Eddie Rickenbacker, the World War I fighter pilot ace who became the founding father of Eastern Airlines, regularly flying company aircraft on the airline's routes.

In 1940 during an approach and landing in Atlanta, Rickenbacker misread an altimeter by 1,000 feet and crashed an Eastern Airlines airplane. The altimeter was set to read feet above sea level, the traditional practice then, as now. Chagrined, quite naturally, he set his best pilots searching for a procedure to prevent such mistakes. They came up with the dual altimeter system still in use by Eastern and American airlines in the United States, and by some foreign airlines.

The idea was simple. When an airliner crew begins its letdown for an approach and landing, they set an altimeter to read altitude above the airport, not altitude above sea level. Thus, in Atlanta, where the airport elevation is 1,000 feet, the field elevation altimeter reads zero as the airplane's landing gear settles onto the runway at the end of the flight. The other altimeter reads 1,000 feet. A pilot always knows his altitude above the airport and above sea level. If the airport elevation is 749 feet, the case at Charlotte, for example, ordinarily a pilot must subtract 749 feet from his altimeter reading of, say, 2,400 feet above sea level, to know he is 1,651 feet above the airport. Under Rickenbacker's system he reads 1,651 feet from the field elevation altimeter. So the dual altimeter system is standard procedure at Eastern Airlines, a procedure that has endured throughout aviation's immense growth in the three decades since it was inaugurated.

The pilots calling Bob Beal that morning for "the numbers" were seeking altimeter setting information to set two of their three altimeters to read altitude above Charlotte and not altitude above sea level. This field elevation reading would be set into the captain's number one or upper altimeter and the copilot's altimeter. The field elevation altimeters then become the primary altimeters for the letdown and approach and landing. They tell the Eastern pilots how high they are above the Charlotte runways.

When pilots are given an "altimeter setting," like the one for Columbia passed up by Jax Center to Eastern 212, it assures that an altimeter set to it will accurately read altitude above sea level in that vicinity. That setting is obtained from actual barometric pressure at the ground weather station involved—Columbia in this case —and corrected to reflect standard conditions at sea level. An altimeter on the ground at Columbia set to that corrected value will not read zero feet altitude, but will indicate the Columbia elevation, 210 feet above sea level.

Shortly after reporting on duty, Beal popped his head in the door of the National Weather Service office and asked the observer, Bob Green, for the station pressure. Green read his mercury barometer and called the value across the room—29.34 inches of mercury. He earlier had corrected that to a sea level value, allowing for Charlotte's altitude, arriving at a Charlotte altimeter setting of 30.16.

Beal returned to his console and turned a knob on the altimeter, setting the altitude hands to zero. He looked into the little window on the face of the altimeter—called the Kollsman window—and read the value there, 29.34 inches of mercury. He knew that his altimeter agreed with the precision barometer in the Weather Service office. Thus any altimeter set so that 29.34 appeared in the Kollsman window would read zero feet on the runways at Charlotte. A pilot inbound need only set 29.34 in his altimeter's Kollsman window and he would be ready for the descent. But Eastern Airlines procedures made it more complicated than that. They required confirming read-back of values so Beal and the pilots could be certain no mistake in altimeter setting had been made, a mistake that could conceivably cause a fatal crash.

When Beal set his altimeter hands to zero, separate small indices on the altimeter face moved independently of the hands, pointing to other numbers on the face. They read 540 feet altitude. This was another means of expressing station pressure, a value called pressure altitude—540 feet on this morning. When Eastern 590 and then Eastern 352 had called, requesting in-range numbers, Beal replied, "Good morning, astronauts. The Charlotte pressure is five forty, that's five four zero."

In each airplane the pilot not flying had reached to the knob on his upper altimeter and twirled it so the indices on the face—exactly like those on Beal's altimeter—read 540 feet. The altimeter hands moved at the same time, no longer indicating the airplane's

altitude above sea level. The value in the Kollsman window also
changed.

Then Eastern 352 had been first with the read-back. The pilot
looked into the Kollsman window and saw a new value of 29.34 in
the window.

"Eastern 352 gets twenty-nine . . . ah . . . thirty-four," the
pilot had radioed back, squinting at the small numbers in the
window.

Perfect. He had been given the field pressure in one value which
he set into his altimeter, then he read it back in another value correctly without any idea what that second value should be. Therefore, the reasoning of Eastern's management went, he must have
set his altimeter correctly. No one had taken any shortcuts. Haste
or carelessness hadn't intervened to introduce a potentially fatal
error.

Eastern procedures in the manual Beal and his colleagues used
specified that each inbound aircraft go through the numbers ritual
exactly. But at busy stations throughout the Eastern system, harried pilots listening on the same frequency as other inbound pilots
hear the pressure altitude setting read up—the setting for the two
indices—and they hear the resulting setting in the Kollsman window read back down to the ground. As a result, some Eastern
pilots take a shortcut. They simply set the value they know must
appear in the Kollsman window and don't bother further. Unless
an altimeter is defective or a pilot has heard the Kollsman setting
wrong, the altimeter will read altitude above the airport just as if
the pilot had followed the stipulated procedure.

A more conscientious pilot could take the shortcut, but check
his Kollsman window setting against the value shown by the indices on the altimeter face. If they both agree with what he's heard
on the radio, everything is set properly.

Beal knew Eastern procedures called for a full exchange of in-
range numbers with each flight. But he, like others in the Eastern
system, permitted the shortcut. The work was completed faster.
He trusted the inbound pilots to hear the settings correctly and adjust their altimeters properly. After all, they were professional
pilots.

"Ah, Charlotte, this is 212," Beal's speaker crackled. Another party heard from. "We got twenty-nine thirty-four."

"Two twelve, that's exact," Beal replied, picking up the telephone and pushing the button. The crew of 212 apparently had been monitoring the frequency, heard the pressure elevation of 540 feet, set the indices and read 29.34 in the Kollsman window. Of course, they'd also heard the 29.34 value in the radio traffic too. Mentally he shrugged his shoulders. Maybe the 212 pilots hadn't set their altimeters, just mouthed back the numbers expected of them. But Bob Beal wasn't a policeman.

"And, 212, your fuel is twenty and twenty," Beal added. Eastern 212 needed 20,000 pounds of fuel in Charlotte for the trip to O'Hare. Weight restrictions meant the aircraft also couldn't take on more than 20,000 pounds. If the captain felt otherwise he'd have to discuss it with the dispatch office.

"We'll take twenty," the 212 pilot replied.

"Oh, that's all right," Beal said. "And we'll see you at Gate Five with the brakes set."

"All righty," the pilot said.

He began filling out a form on Eastern 212, a record of the conversation. Eastern required that they retain the forms for thirty days.

CHAPTER TWENTY

7:24:50 A.M.

SOMETIMES AIRLINE PILOTS aren't as rested as they should be when they slide into their seats and pull out the pre-flight checklists.

For example, Eastern Airlines crews based in Atlanta sometimes fly an Atlanta–Seattle–Atlanta sequence of flights that leaves Atlanta at night, arrives in Seattle in the early morning and returns to Atlanta the following evening. During the day in Seattle the pilots are free. They are expected to rest. In the winter, however, some pilots spend the day strenuously schussing down the nearby ski slopes. At day's end they return to their motel rooms, snatch a few hours of sleep and then take the controls of their airliner filled with passengers.

These pilots may or may not be prepared to conduct the flight with optimum efficiency and safety. Each pilot is different. Age, emotional health, work load, personal problems, temperament and many other factors all play a role. One pilot could be all that a nervous passenger might ask even though he spent the day perfecting his parallel turns down the steepest ski trails. Another man could be a catastrophe waiting for the unique set of circumstances to come together. Intuitively it seems that the pilots shouldn't go skiing. But no one can say with scientific precision that it's unsafe

—no one at Eastern Airlines, the Federal Aviation Administration, the National Transportation Safety Board or the Air Line Pilots Association.

Airline pilot fatigue is but one small corner of a vast gray area in the air transport industry called human factors—the human element of flying airplanes, the man–machine interaction. No one can assess the skiing pilots' fitness qualitatively or quantitatively because the human factors in flying have been systematically ignored or given short shrift since early in the industry's relatively short history—as early as Orville and Wilbur Wright's historic flight. In fact, two years before the Wrights' flight at Kitty Hawk in 1903, Wilbur Wright wrote a colleague: "For some years I have been afflicted with the belief that flight is possible to man. My disease has increased in severity and I feel that it will soon cost me an increased amount of money, if not my life." Wright's fatalistic attitude toward aviation safety endures in some quarters to this day. It was prescient of a yet-to-be-born industry's penchant for developing technology with man as an appendage, not an integrated component.

There are startling examples. The National Transportation Safety Board investigates airline accidents impartially, issuing reports and recommendations for changes in procedures, air traffic control, whatever needs correction. The NTSB members are political appointees, in the past often appointed without technical expertise. They approve before issuance all accident investigation findings of the NTSB's staff of professional aviation accident investigators, among the finest in the world.

For years the board has steadfastly refused to allow its staff to delve into the psychological questions each airline accident raises: What was the psychological condition of the pilots at the time? Did they have marital or sexual or monetary problems? Did those pilots in that cockpit get along? What was the quality as well as the quantity of their rest? How were they motivated? The list of questions is immense, ranging from issues as diverse as the design of altimeter hands to whether cockpit noise caused by poor windshield design increases pilot fatigue.

There is agreement among several safety experts who investigated a Texas International crash of a Convair 600 in Arkansas in

1973 that the captain probably committed suicide, carrying his copilot and passengers to death. The NTSB assiduously avoided that question.

The first jumbo jet to crash, an Eastern Airlines Lockheed L-1011, went down in the Everglades west of Miami one night late in 1972 because the crew, distracted by the problem of determining whether the nosewheel had been extended, failed to notice the autopilot had disconnected and the airplane had begun a gradual descent. Several points at which the autopilot interfaced with the pilots had been designed poorly, leading to the inadvertent autopilot disconnection. The pilots, in turn, had grown too accustomed to relying on the autopilot to handle the airplane without close supervision. Many Eastern pilots who knew the crew members believe a factor in the accident might have been the animosity between the captain and the flight engineer. The captain was known for his quick, violent temper. An autopsy revealed a brain tumor.

The FAA also pays scant attention to the human factors question. Its tiny staff of psychologists ponders such things, but these human factors experts are shuffled to one side in the agency's organizational chart with little chance for significant input into policy decisions.

The Air Line Pilots Association—the pilots' union—has recently begun to pay more attention to human factors, even hiring an expert consultant.

There are experts scattered through the industry, the regulators and the investigators, who worry about human factors, who chafe at their neglect. They are a loose-knit cadre with no official ties, convinced that aviation accident rates will begin to show improvement only when proper attention is paid to the pilots who fly multimillion-dollar machines carrying hundreds of people and the subtle ways in which these men, their machines, the weather and the air traffic control system interact.

These human factor advocates speak candidly, passionately, if assured anonymity. Their unwillingness to speak openly is a mark of insecurity, a reflection of the conviction that at least for now more can be done behind the scenes. For some, to speak their minds publicly might cost them their jobs. They are pilots, ALPA officials, NTSB investigators and airline officials.

"The pilot must have the gift to be wary. We would have an ideal situation with today's modern airplanes with reliable engines and instruments if we still had pilots who used to fly the old buckets of bolts that might fail at any minute. Then they could not afford *not* to be suspicious of everything and everyone—including that other man in the cockpit." The speaker is an NTSB investigator who flew fighters in World War II, has taught airline pilots to fly. His desk is neat, organized, like the cockpits he once commanded.

"You have to stress the caliber of the man, the quality of the man, his character. The young man they hire now will someday be a captain. You must look at his character above all else.

"Spend ten minutes in the jump seat in a cockpit and you have a feel at once for the atmosphere. Whether it is a good team, whether the captain's authority is recognized and respected, whether there is a good co-operative spirit. Or you can come into the cockpit and within a few minutes see that it's just some people thrown together. You sense the tension, disrespect or animosity.

"A team of two or three pilots may not be compatible. Cases of incompatibility could be dealt with by proper scheduling. But the air carriers won't talk about it. If it is the first time the pilots have flown together or the first time in a long time, there is a period of coming to terms with one another in a subtle way. The good captain steps in and lays down the rules immediately so there is no uncertainty. Even with a crew he has never met before.

"There is a certain amount of talent in the cockpit. Talent in the captain. Talent in the first officer. If they work well together the total talent is more than the sum of the two. If it doesn't click, the talent of each is lessened."

Washington. The late afternoon sun streams into the office of an ALPA official, who is an airline captain.

"Oh, sure. There obviously are times when personality conflicts get into it. But I see a lot of adaptation on the part of individuals not to let social interactions get in the way of flying.

"It's far better now than when I started twenty years ago. Then we really had hard-ass captains and I think if there ever was a

time when people thought they were little gods in the cockpit that
was the time.

"I always said this about the captain. If he was going to be a
belligerent bastard I wouldn't mind sitting there and letting him
screw up just a little, especially if it would embarrass him and
teach him something. But if it gets to the point where it's a safety
situation, then my neck is on the line, too. I'm not going to sit
back."

At Eastern Airlines headquarters in Miami, an old captain, past
the mandatory flight retirement age of sixty, a veteran of pilot
training, has advice about how to handle the captain.

"When you get a new captain, do it by the book and then you
can't be criticized. If he wants to do it some other way, he's got to
tell you. Go to standard operating procedures and if the captain
has some objection, let him tell you. I used to think when I was a
copilot that I should take a course on mind reading because you
never know what the guy wants you to do."

He chuckles at the memory and waves away a passing fly.

"Our safety expert here recommends that once you get down to
a certain altitude that you have a sterile cockpit. No talk below
three thousand feet and on takeoff nothing but commands and the
like until you climb to three thousand feet."

It is morning in Washington. One of those small offices in the
building at 800 Independence Avenue Southwest. The light is soft.
Sitting behind the desk is another NTSB accident investigator who
grumbles unhappily that more attention isn't given human factors.

"Riding jump seat as we often do, just to observe, I have been
struck by the differences between cockpit atmospheres. One has an
authoritarian captain. Another is relaxed, happy. Who's to say
which is safer. We aren't allowed to study that.

"I was in a DC-9 headed down south one day to Win-
ston-Salem or Charlotte or some place like that. Turned out the
captain and I had been military pilots in the same service at the
same time. We began playing that old game of who do you know
and kind of got swept up in it. I became conscious that we were
talking a little more than was appropriate, but it was a beautiful
clear day.

"So they cleared him to land Runway one two and he let down

and as we swung around I looked at our heading and I could see he was lining up on Runway one six. And I was debating how long to let it go before interrupting him. You know, I was just a guest in the cockpit. Then the tower politely told him he seemed to be lining up on one six and didn't he still want Runway one two? So he swung around and no problem.

"But here was one more little distraction which permitted an error. What if it had combined with several other small errors. Imagine the cockpit voice recording on that flight if there had been an accident."

Like the air traffic controllers, the NTSB investigators each have their tales. Another investigator who once flew for the military and now occupies one of those small cubicles in the NTSB suites recalls one flight.

"I flew on the jump seat from here to Dallas with one crew and I heard nothing but fishing. Except for the checklist and the air traffic control instructions and the repeats from the time we took off until well into the approach I heard nothing but fishing. They had all fished together and they pointed out every goddamned crick and pond and reservoir between Washington, D.C. and Dallas, and told me what they had caught in each one and when. And the autopilot just sitting there truckin' down the road.

"You know, Eddie Rickenbacker wouldn't even let Eastern pilots have autopilots for the longest time. He wanted hands-on flying all the time."

It's nighttime in an Atlanta suburb. An Eastern flight engineer on the Boeing 727 has put the children to bed. His wife is out. Once he dreamed of becoming a captain. But cutbacks and layoffs and stymied industry growth have relegated him to the third spot in the cockpit, seemingly forever. He never gets to handle the 727's control wheel, to fly the airplane. There are hundreds like him. He is jaded, his remarks sincere but doubtlessly colored by his dissatisfaction with a stagnant career.

"We have a staff of captains who are check captains. They ride on a line flight with a captain to evaluate him. A check captain is afraid to bust another captain for improficiency because it builds an inner fear that if they do this it's going to set a precedent.

They're afraid that if somebody gets mad at them, when they have a checkride someone will bust *them*.

"One of the most prevalent attitudes among the captain force is the idea that a captain cannot make a mistake. If I had to point my finger at the one thing that should change it would be more equality in the cockpit. The first officer and the second officer are professionals, they have good judgment, a contribution to make. The captain must have command, but he should be a co-ordinator of the cockpit activities, not a god.

"If a captain doesn't like you, you're in trouble. If a captain wants to get you he can force you into a mistake. He asks you to do one thing. And then he asks for another before you've finished that. Then, do this. No, do that. The captain just sits there and tries to distract you and yells at you and harasses you until you make a mistake and you're nailed. That doesn't contribute to safety.

"I knew a captain who threw copilots off his trips if he felt their hair was too long. There was one wacko captain who carried a big revolver in his flight bag. He would take it out during cruise and pound its butt on the control pedestal to make his points.

"I honestly think every airline pilot should have an annual psychological profile run, just like a physical exam. But airline management won't touch that idea. The union won't touch it. That'd be dynamite. The public should demand it. I think everyone would be amazed at what regular psychological screening would turn up."

The old Eastern captain in Miami has given many a checkride.

"One of the company's problems is you'll go out and ride with the guy and he'll do everything right by the book. The next day when he's back on his own he'll do it like he damn well pleases. Most check pilots are pretty hard-nosed. They know what they're looking for and if they don't see it in a guy they'll raise hell. I've trained a hell of a lot of check pilots. I know they're conscientious about this.

"Now, take steep turns. You don't do them except in an emergency. But you gotta know them. So you're giving a check and a pilot can't hold his altitude in a steep turn. So you suspend the check and you practice. He does two or three and they're getting better and you say, 'O.K. This one is for the book.' That's how you do it.

"But some check pilots will just mark down 'satisfactory.' You don't know how many times the pilot had to practice. Sometimes the check pilot will write 'continues to improve.' To me that means he wasn't worth a shit to begin with and I had to work to bring him up to standards.

"But, for example, there was a crash of a DC-6 where one engine went into reverse and they went into Elizabeth, New Jersey. Well, that pilot in his proficiency checks had a problem with steep turns. The check pilot had written that down and those records got into the lawsuits. So that kind of put all the airlines off from putting anything specific down.

"You almost have to keep two sets of books. It shouldn't be that way. The latest thing is that in the contract with the union anything over three years old goes out. If he flies a perfect three years, no matter what happened before, you can't use it."

The telephone rings. A secretary comes in with a letter to be signed. Someone sticks his head in the office with a reminder about a meeting.

"Eastern in my time paid me over a million dollars to fly their airplanes. And I would have done it for nothing if I could've found a way to live. Love of flying. A lot of guys coming up have that. It's what makes a safe pilot. But there are guys without that motivation. Flying for an airline doesn't mean much to them and they become bored.

"Lot of guys have businesses. We had a guy got down into the trees at one airport and then he got out and flew on to the airport. He owned a junkyard. A full-time business. That guy, that captain, is really not an airline pilot. I think the guy that is a pilot should be a pilot one hundred per cent of the time."

At ALPA headquarters in Washington, the airline captain, who spends much of his free time on union business, ponders a question. Do airline pilots have too much free time? Are they glorified bus drivers?

"Sure flying can be boring. You've heard that old saying. 'Hours of boredom followed by minutes of stark terror.' Lots of guys set up businesses. Others get involved in ALPA. But most of them try to regulate their lives so they're prepared. The day of a flight they'll knock off and rest. I'm sure there are guys that work too hard at their businesses."

One of the NTSB investigators ponders the question.

"Air carrier pilots do not devote the majority of their time and attention to their piloting job. Eighty hours a month. Check in an hour before the flight and stay an hour afterward. Course, they have layovers. Some do spend more than eighty hours a month on duty.

"I've been trying to catch one guy in connection with an investigation I'm working on who lives in Montreal and commutes by his company pass to New York to take his five trips a month.

"But they really are kind of bus drivers, some of them. Operate in a three-dimensional environment. Takeoff, climb, cruise, descend, land. Some pilots don't prepare themselves emotionally for a flight any more than a bus driver prepares himself. Does a bus driver really pump himself up in the morning to go out and cope with the traffic? Neither do most airline pilots. And that's part of the problem. It's the dull kind of flying these guys do that leads to this. What we got to do is find a way to psych the cockpit crew up as they begin their approach. That's where the accidents occur."

Down the hall at the NTSB, a colleague likens the problem of inattention in the cockpit to driving a car.

"You can drive down the street and stop at the stop sign and go on and five blocks later say, 'My god. Did I run that stop sign?' We drive at a less than conscious level. Some pilots fly at this level.

"So we have to wake them up when the approach starts, particularly a piece of cake approach. If it's a hundred-and-fifty-foot ceiling and a quarter mile visibility, they'll be psyched up already. It's when the ceiling is five hundred feet and visibility two miles that we have to worry. So we put in warning systems. Warnings upon warnings. Buzzers, beeps, bells, gadgets, gadgets, gadgets. An accident happens, we put in a warning system, the Band-Aid fix.

"As soon as you make it easier on the man with gadgets and devices he's no longer involved. You take him out of the loop. Instead of a participant, he sits on the sidelines watching. He's a monitor."

Down the hall, another NTSB colleague pursues that idea.

"You know, ever since airplanes have been built there has been an almost mom and apple pie goal that we've got to unburden the pilot, reduce the cockpit work load. And that has led to automation. I think it's possible for that pendulum to swing too far.

"There is a definite possibility too many safety systems lull the pilot. Or become a nuisance and are ignored. We've got to give attention to some basics, like cockpit fatigue. Warning systems don't do any good with tired pilots."

At ALPA headquarters, the question of fatigue touches a nerve with the airline captain.

"In 1940 the military looked at aviation problems. They found two problems—the pilot's ability to get adequate rest and the prudent scheduling of pilots. That was in 1940 and we still haven't learned.

"We still don't schedule pilots correctly. Computers schedule pilots. Nobody looks at the schedules from the human factors standpoint and says, 'Is that a flyable schedule?' Pilots bitch and complain and some companies will change a schedule. But other companies say to hell with it. The schedule's within the Federal Aviation Regulations and the union contract. Everything's legal. So you're going to fly it. We hire you to fly airplanes and we'll tell you when and where to go.

"I don't think there's any doubt you can fly all night, lay over the next day and then fly all night again. But you shouldn't be asked to be based in Seattle and be up all day during normal family life and then you're listening to the ten o'clock evening news, getting ready for bed, and the phone rings and they want you to deadhead to L.A. and depart L.A. at four A.M. for Denver, Kansas City, St. Louis, Washington and New York.

"Take the Pan Am and TWA guys who fly the North Atlantic. They leave New York at six P.M. and fly all night to Amsterdam or Paris or Brussels. Nothing wrong with that. But then they have to fly on all the next day for four consecutive additional landings all through Europe. They don't need that."

In Miami, the old Eastern captain has some parting advice.

"There are four things you have to know all the time if you want to survive. You have to know where you are. You have to know how high you are. You have to know how fast you're going. And it wouldn't hurt to know how much fuel you have on board."

He escorts his visitor to the door and down the hall to the elevators in Eastern's new, expansive training building.

"I always say you can make it foolproof, but you can't make it damn fool proof."

He chuckles, waves and starts back down the hall.

Captain James Reeves watched the numbers steadily flicking by in the small window in one corner of the navigation instrument that showed Eastern 212's track toward the Fort Mill VOR, the radio navigation station south of Charlotte. He was watching the DME—distance measuring equipment. It showed how many nautical miles distant they were from the station. Thirty-four. Thirty-three. Thirty-two. Thirty-one. Thirty. Their speed had picked up slightly in the rapid descent. He looked at the airspeed indicator: 340 knots.

Reeves looked down at the lower altimeter. 13,500 feet above sea level. 13,400. 13,300. 13,200. 13,100. 13,000. They were coming down quite fast now. His eye passed over the vertical speed indicator. Almost 3,000 feet per minute descent rate.

He reached down to the radio console and flipped the selector switch to "interphone." He picked up the microphone. They'd been too busy to jaw with the passengers.

"Ladies and gentlemen. We're now approaching Charlotte. So would you please recheck your seat belt so it is securely fastened and observe the no smoking sign when it appears," Reeves intoned.

Then the captain laced the fingers of each hand together and extended his arms in front of him, flexing his finger joints, his arm and shoulder and back muscles. He could hear his elbows pop. He yawned, making a guttural sound.

His eyes roamed the instrument panel, pausing at the altimeter.

"Eleven thousand for ten," he softly intoned. It wasn't a callout as much as it was an aside, like the tone a passenger in a car might use, when interrupting a conversation with the driver to point out a road sign they've both spotted.

CHAPTER TWENTY-ONE

7:25 A.M.

THE COFFEE WAS undrinkable. Jack Toohey accepted a cup from the stewardess and gingerly took a sip, wrinkling his nose with displeasure. He forced a second sip and then thrust the cup aside in disgust. He resumed leafing through the Eastern Airlines passenger magazine, pausing at an article about scuba diving in the Caribbean. He tried not to think about the solemn family awaiting him at the airport, about the wake and funeral mass, about his father's lingering illness and inevitable death.

Jim Toohey was only fifty-three when he died the morning before in Bridgeport, Connecticut, while Jack was at sea on the *Brumby*. The destroyer docked in Charleston later that day and Dorothy broke the sad news when she met him at the dock.

National Airlines, the airline of choice when flying from Charleston to the Northeast, was on strike, closed by a pilot walkout. After lengthy consultation with a reservations agent at Eastern Airlines, Toohey settled for leaving Charleston at 7 A.M. Wednesday for Charlotte, changing there for a flight to Philadelphia and then a tiny commuter airline to Bridgeport. He would be cutting it close, but if everything went smoothly, he would arrive Wednesday afternoon just in time for the wake.

Bridgeport, Connecticut, 711 Noble Avenue, an old two-story

Victorian era duplex. The Jim Tooheys lived downstairs with Mrs.
Toohey's parents, the Alfred Stokeses. Old Mrs. Waterbury, who
owned the house, lived upstairs. Alfred Stokes was a Dublin-born
Irishman, trained as an accountant in English schools. He won an
Irish lottery, "Not the sweepstakes," he always pointed out, and
used the winnings to book passage to America, where he went to
Hartford, met the young woman who became his wife and settled
in Bridgeport in the Waterbury house. The Stokeses made room in
their home for Jim Toohey when the young man married their
daughter. In all, the Stokeses and the Tooheys lived at 711 Noble
in the thick of Bridgeport's Irish neighborhood for thirty-five
years, until the 1960s, when Mrs. Waterbury, aged ninety-four,
died.

Jim Toohey was a second-generation Irishman whose first son,
Jack, was born two weeks after the Japanese attack on Pearl Harbor. Jack was only nine months old when his father left his job
servicing gas company meters and joined the Army. During the
war years Alfred Stokes became his grandson's surrogate father,
though the boy was reminded each day that the man in the uniform in the picture was his father who would return home someday.

Jim Toohey came home one night in 1945 after his son was in
bed. The soldier had often dreamed of his homecoming and the
moment of reunion with his son, now nearly four years old.

"Jack?" The boy wasn't asleep yet and he sat up in bed, rub-
bing his eyes in the light.

"Jack? It's me. I'm home, Jack."

The little boy was solemn. He studied the man. It was the face
in the picture.

"Are you going away again or are you going to be staying?" the
boy asked in a matter-of-fact tone.

"I'm home, son. I'm home for good. I won't be going away."

"Well, that's good. I have to go to bed now. I'll see you in the
morning." With that he lay down.

Jim Toohey stared blankly at his small son and then turned to
his wife, perplexed, disappointed. He hadn't imagined anything
like this.

"You just wait," his wife warned. "He'll be up at five o'clock in

the morning and he's going to come in and pounce on you in bed
and dissect you."

Jack did just that the next morning. He always thought he could
remember that homecoming scene with his father, though he was
never sure if he only remembered an early retelling, because it became a family legend, one of his mother's favorite stories. Jack's
brother Roger was born a year later. In many ways as the boys
grew up, particularly in their younger years, Roger was Jim Toohey's son and Jack was Alfred Stokes's son, although Grampa
never tried to be anything more than a grandfather. It wasn't a
divided house. When the older Stokes couple meted out discipline,
the Tooheys backed them, and the grandparents backed the Tooheys' discipline.

In Bridgeport, each ethnic group within the Catholic working
class had its own church and grammar school. The Polish Catholic
children went to St. Michael's, where they learned Polish and attended Polish masses. There was an Italian church and a Slovak
church. St. Charles was the Irish school and Jack Toohey went to
it, graduating to nearby Fairfield Prep, a Jesuit school where the
stern priests dispensed their discipline generously, an integral part
of the curriculum.

Jack was what now would be called a gifted child, although
such enlightened thinking had not then penetrated Bridgeport. His
superior memory permitted him passing marks with little effort
and left him chronically bored in school. He loved baseball,
adored the Brooklyn Dodgers—Gil Hodges, PeeWee Reese, Roy
Campanella, Sandy Koufax, Jackie Robinson. He collected bub-
blegum baseball cards and memorized batting averages, living from
day to day for the sports page in the Bridgeport *Post,* which he
delivered after school.

One Friday morning in late September 1955, in white shirt and
trousers and blazer with a book bag over his shoulder and lunch
inside, Jack Toohey caught the city bus into downtown Bridgeport, where he always changed for the bus to Fairfield Prep. In
his pocket he had almost twenty dollars collected from the paper
route.

He stepped off the bus and suddenly, on a whim, instead of
turning right and walking to the nearby Fairfield bus stop, he

turned left and headed for the old Bridgeport train station. He
shoved the book bag in a locker and inserted a dime, turned the
key and pocketed it. Then he stood in line with the commuters at
the New Haven Railroad ticket window, carefully counting out
$3.30 for a round-trip ticket to New York City. A few minutes
later he was sitting in a window seat beside a businessman reading
the New York *Times,* watching the bridges and factories and fields
and backs of row houses flash past, unmindful that he would be
reported missing, that his parents would become frantic with
worry, that Bridgeport police would flash his description throughout the Northeast, that the subway cops and the New York police
would add his name and description to their list of Holden
Caulfields who run away for their fling in the city. Too late he
remembered the lunch in his book bag in the locker.

Though Jack Toohey didn't know what impulse sent him to the
train station instead of the bus stop, once he stood in the cavernous Grand Central Station waiting room he knew what he would
do in New York City. As the throngs ebbed and flowed past him,
he read a discarded newspaper, poring over the sports pages. All
three New York baseball teams were at home. In Brooklyn that
night, his Dodgers, who already had clinched the National League
pennant, met the New York Giants at Ebbets Field. In the Bronx,
the Yankees played the Boston Red Sox. The Bombers, as New
Yorkers called the Yankees, were only one game behind Cleveland
in the American League pennant race. If they could win the pennant, New Yorkers would be treated to one of the classic World
Series battles between the Dodgers and the Yankees.

As he studied the newspaper, Jack knew which game he would
attend—the Dodgers' game, of course. Having sewed up the pennant the week before, the Dodgers promptly fell into a slump and
the night before had lost their fifth game in a row, in St. Louis to
the Cardinals 3–2. After their defeat they had flown home on a
chartered DC-4 with a slogan painted on its side—"Brooklyn
Dodgers, 1955 National League Champions." Although they arrived at LaGuardia Airport a few minutes before midnight, several
hundred fans had waited to whistle and wave and clap as the
ballplayers came down the airplane's steps.

He stopped in a hallway of the giant railroad station to purchase a hot dog, which he smothered with mustard and then ate as he walked down another hall to steps which descended into the subway. He purchased a token for a dime, dropped it into a turnstile and boarded the first subway train that came along.

Thus he spent the afternoon. The uptown Lexington Avenue local all the way to Jerome Avenue then back down to River Avenue and change to the IND train downtown to Chambers Street, switch to the IRT under the East River and into Brooklyn to Flatbush Avenue and then the IND back into Manhattan to Columbus Circle and then the IRT to Times Square and then the Flushing Local into Queens far out to Flushing Meadow Park then back to Queensboro Plaza and change to the BMT and into Manhattan on downtown and into Brooklyn again.

The roar of the wheels, the shriek of the brakes assaulted him through the open car windows, the ceiling fans washing tepid air over him as he sat on the benches, watching the doors open and close, open and close, gazing at the constantly changing kaleidoscope of clothes and faces and bodies. The New York subways were all that a young boy could want, hot dog and hamburger stands, bakeries, pizza, stores, pretzels, orange juice, candy bars, a steadily changing panorama, constant shifting entertainment, time unmeasured in the dim light of grimy cars and steel girders and dirt-blackened concrete, a civilization beneath the streets, all for a single price of admission, ten cents. He sensed the afternoon waning as the cars filled with homeward-bound workers, asked an elderly lady for the time and then began studying the route map in the car and finally asked a conductor and changed trains until he passed out of a turnstile and climbed the steps into the soft light of dusk within the shadow of Ebbets Field.

Jack carefully counted out seventy-five cents, the price of admission to the center field seats. He took up a strategic position, fortified with his fifth hot dog of the day and some popcorn.

When the Dodgers took the field in the top of the first inning, Duke Snider marked off his position in center field no more than thirty yards from Jack Toohey, who closely watched his every move, studying his face when he turned toward the bleachers between batters, noting how the Duke hunkered down into a ready position each time Billy Loes on the mound wound up for his pitch delivery. Then in the bottom of the first inning, his first time at bat, Snider belted a single into right field, driving in Junior Gilliam for the Dodgers' first run.

In the next inning, when the Dodgers came to bat, Gil Hodges hit a home run. Ah, to catch a Dodger home run and get the ball autographed. In the fourth inning with two outs and two men on base, the Giants' Ray Katt hit a long drive into center field that brought Dodger fans anxiously to their feet. It looked like a home run. It came straight at Jack Toohey. But Duke Snider was racing back, back, back toward the center field wall, now against the wall and up, up with a mighty leap, his glove outstretched, effortlessly grabbing the ball, ending the inning, preventing two Giant runs. Jack Toohey screamed his approval. "Way to go, Duke. Way to go, Duke baby."

The Dodgers won 4–3, snapping their losing streak.

Pushing another dime through the token window, Jack shoved through the subway turnstiles again and began the long trip back toward Manhattan, nodding off to sleep in his seat, waking with a start each time his head fell forward. His plan was to ride the subways all night, but he found dozing in the rocking cars difficult and there seemed to be more policemen now. One had eyed him steadily for a few minutes before moving into another car. So he made his way to the hard wooden benches in the Grand Central Station waiting room, patting his return ticket to Bridgeport from time to time, the ticket his ready explanation for being there alone at his age. About 1 A.M. a trainman, a conductor wearing a round, short-billed cap, stopped.

"You all right, boy? What're you doing here at this hour?"

"I . . . I . . . ah . . . I'm waiting to go home to Bridgeport. I missed the last train home," he replied, fishing in his pocket and bringing forth the ticket. The conductor nodded and went on.

Towards 6 A.M. he ate doughnuts and milk at a food stand and bought another subway token, resuming his underground odyssey. He studied the sports page in another discarded newspaper, eagerly reading the account of the Dodgers' victory, savoring the description of Snider's spectacular catch. He read about the Yankees' 5–4 defeat of Boston, which boosted them into first place in the American League by a bare two points. Both the Yankees and the Dodgers played again that afternoon and Jack resolved to watch his Dodgers meet the Giants again. But his father rooted for the Yankees and while the Dodgers had their pennant nailed down, the Yankees didn't. By 2 P.M., feeling a bit disloyal, he sat in the center field bleachers at Yankee Stadium. Mickey Mantle had pulled a leg muscle and didn't take his customary position in center field. He was replaced by Bob Cerv. Phil Rizzuto and Cerv managed a stunning double steal in the first inning and then in the fourth inning a stray pitch knocked Rizzuto to the ground, splitting his plastic batting helmet. The crowd stood up, strangely hushed as Rizzuto was carried from the field on a stretcher. The Yankees won 4–1.

Standing on the platform in the subway amid the crush of Yankee fans waiting for their trains, Jack suddenly felt weary, tired of riding subways, bored by wandering. Two hours later he nervously climbed the porch steps at 711 Noble, his book bag over his shoulder. He could see his mother through the screen.

"May I come in?" he asked meekly, rapping on the doorjamb.

She let out a shriek and rushed to the door, enveloping her son in her arms. Of course he could come in. Later his grandfather took him aside and gave him a gentle but stern lecture. He had no idea how much grief and worry he had caused. Why they'd even called the police. Had out bulletins for him. Bulletins in a dozen states for Jack Toohey. Thought he might have been kidnapped or fallen in with bad people. Just disappearing like that. You must never ever do that again.

When Jim Toohey came home, he stood with hands on his hips before his son, who anxiously stared at the floor, where his toe inscribed small circles. He could feel his father's anger.

"Well, I should tell you what's really on my mind," he said, his anger creeping into his voice. "I should maybe do what every father feels like doing in a case like this. Look at me, Jack. Look at me. But on the other hand I've been told that I shouldn't give in to my first impulse. I'm supposed to sit down with you and find out what the reason was, if there was any reason.

"You've already talked to your grandfather and your grandfather told me to take it nice and easy. He said everything's all right.

So I'm going to abide by your grandfather's wishes because he's close to you and he understands you."

Two weeks later Jack and his father—just the two of them—went into New York City and watched the Yankees and the Dodgers play in the World Series. They had seats in one of the best boxes. Duke Snider hit a home run.

Three years later, still frustrated by the same boredom with schooling that had nurtured the impulse to flee to New York, Jack Toohey dropped out of high school and persuaded his father to sign his Navy enlistment papers because he was only seventeen. Later, when Jack was a successful Navy medical corpsman with a wife and two daughters, Jim Toohey grew closer to his elder son, proud of his accomplishments.

Jack Toohey stared absently out the airplane window, unmindful of the throbbing whine of the jet engine just outside. He had last seen his father a few weeks before, when the *Brumby* put in at Newport, Rhode Island, and he took a weekend to go home to Connecticut.

He turned a baleful eye on the undrinkable coffee. The stewardess was passing with a tray of plastic glasses filled with soft drinks. He caught her attention.

"Could I have a Coke?"

CHAPTER TWENTY-TWO

7:27 A.M.

BURDETTE HEEMSOTH DRUMMED his fingers on the counter in front of the radar screen and hummed a nameless tune. He sat at the far right radar scope in the Charlotte radar room—sometimes called the Tracon—on the second floor of the Douglas Municipal Airport terminal building.

The Tracon is darker than the control rooms at Jax and Atlanta centers. It is also much smaller, just three radar screens and a spare set in a single bay along one wall of the long, narrow room, carpeted in brown. A small desk at a right angle to the wall opposite the radar screens is lit by an adjustable fluorescent desk lamp. The radar screens are powered by a different computer, called ARTS III, and small details of the controls are different, but otherwise, the air traffic controllers' positions resemble those in the two larger air route traffic control centers.

The Charlotte watch supervisor, Bill Sturkey, sat at the desk working on administrative forms, the light striking only his hands, arms and face, the darkened room giving them a disembodied appearance. He was smoking a cigar. Sturkey and his damned cigar. Even the strong air conditioning, beefed up to carry away heat from the radar consoles, couldn't suppress that cigar.

"Someday, Sturkey, we'uns is gonna take that see-gah and

shove it up yo' ass," a controller said, his voice an exaggerated characterization of a black man. Someone laughed. It was only half a joke.

There were four men in the Tracon besides Heemsoth and Sturkey. Two data men watching over the computer printer and the flight strips were also taking the manual hand-offs of traffic from Atlanta this morning because the Atlanta computer was down. Denny Hunter, the radar controller, was last to handle the airplanes before turning them over to the tower. The west arrival-departure controller handled the western hemisphere of airspace around Charlotte, assisted by his data man; and Heemsoth was handling arrival-departure east. He also was assisted by a data man.

When Hogan and Hare in the tower cab upstairs changed the active runway to Runway 36, Heemsoth's territory was redefined. Now it became all the airspace east of a line extending north and south from the centerline of Runway 36. A few minutes before, when the active runway was Runway 5, Heemsoth's responsibility had been the eastern hemisphere of airspace set off by a line extending southwest to northeast from the centerline of that runway. Heemsoth and the controller at arrival-departure west took aircraft when Atlanta, Jacksonville and Washington centers handed them over to Charlotte, and guided them around, lining them up for approaches to the active runway, readying them for transfer to Denny Hunter, today's final controller.

With Runway 36 active, Heemsoth would take aircraft arriving from the south and bring them into Charlotte's airspace by way of Richburg, a radio navigation beam intersection about thirty miles due south of the airport. Richburg Intersection would put them at Hunter's doorstep. As the final controller, Hunter was responsible for a ten-mile-wide strip of airspace extending from the end of Runway 36 to twenty miles south. The Charlotte controllers' blocks of airspace generally extended from the ground up to 6,000 to 8,000 feet altitude.

Heemsoth hummed on in casual anticipation of contact from the only airplane presently in his sector, an Eastern DC-9 handed off manually by Atlanta a few seconds before while the airplane was still at 13,000 feet. There had been no traffic below the DC-9, so Charlotte accepted the airplane even though it wasn't in their airspace yet. That was routine. Now the Atlanta controller would be calling the DC-9 pilots, telling them to contact Charlotte approach, frequency 124.0.

Heemsoth was also watching a Delta flight inbound to Charlotte from Atlanta. Atlanta Center had just handed it over to arrival west. Heemsoth pondered what to do with the Eastern DC-9. He already could see a conflict. The Delta DC-9 was coming in from the west. Arrival west was vectoring him so Hunter would have him about ten miles south of the runway. Then Hunter would turn him and give him an eight-mile straight final approach leg to Runway 36. A piece of cake approach through patchy ground fog.

Heemsoth, like other conscientious controllers, liked to save pilots as much time as he could, particularly commercial pilots, with all the screaming airlines did about the cost of fuel these days. But Delta was getting there first. If he gave Eastern a straight-in approach, the Eastern pilots would be up the tail of Delta, less than the required three miles' separation, less than the five miles Heemsoth preferred. What to do?

He considered this minor technical problem in a nearly subconscious manner. He didn't consciously ponder the situation and weigh the alternatives. Burdette Heemsoth had been faced with similar operational problems thousands of times in his six years with the FAA and three years before that as an Air Force controller. The solution was simple. He'd turn the Eastern DC-9 out to the right, from his present north northwest heading of 340 degrees to a north northeast heading of 40 degrees. He'd let the airplane track that way for three or four minutes, taking it southeast of the airport. Then he'd turn the pilots to the left, to curve them back nearer Denny Hunter's final approach corridor south of the airport. The Eastern airplane would inscribe a great letter *S* over the ground, perhaps ten or fifteen miles long from top to bottom. It would cost Eastern Airlines several hundred additional dollars in fuel and make the DC-9 two or three minutes later arriving. But Delta was arriving first. This way, Eastern would fall into sequence behind the Delta flight at just the correct distance. There would be no chance of a "deal." The aircraft wouldn't be permitted to come too close.

Burdette Heemsoth had routinely decided to do with the Eastern DC-9 what controllers throughout the world do thousands of times a day—use radar to vector airplanes away from established radio navigation courses, moving them in twisting, curving tracks over the ground to meld into the long string of aircraft moving toward a busy runway. Without radar vectoring, a busy airport would handle many fewer aircraft during periods of bad weather because much larger distances would have to be maintained between aircraft. Controllers couldn't constantly monitor the precise position and speed of each airplane.

Most pilots appreciate the convenience of radar, the ease of radar vectors to the final approach course, which is what Heemsoth planned to provide to the Eastern DC-9. The Eastern pilots had been carefully following a radio navigation beam bringing them into the Charlotte area. They could follow such beams right to the runway if need be with no radar help. But once Heemsoth radioed them with instructions to turn to a certain heading, taking them away from the radio beam that told them precisely where they were, the pilots counted on Heemsoth to guide them to their final approach to the runway. In effect, the pilots turned themselves and their airplane over to the controller and his electronic eye.

There is a subtle psychological danger present each time a controller begins giving radar vectors, a danger that varies from pilot to pilot but has the most ominous potential with airline pilots who may receive radar vectors to a final approach course during virtually every landing. Radar vectors invite lessened pilot vigilance, a disorientation about precise position, too much reliance on the controller to see that everything will come out all right in the end. They entice a small, unconscious transfer of cockpit command responsibility to the controller. Most pilots are aware of this potential danger, most guard against it, carefully monitoring their navigation radios and distance measuring equipment to track their position as the vectors twist and turn the airplane. A pilot never knows when the radar may suddenly fail, when the controller may announce, "Radar service terminated," leaving the cockpit crew to shift for itself.

Burdette Heemsoth bent closer to the radar screen, looking at the block of green letters printed beside the Eastern DC-9 target. It was Eastern 212. He glanced at the groundspeed, calculated and printed in the data block by the computer—315 knots. He studied the altitude readout from the airplane's transponder next to the groundspeed—12,500 feet.

Heemsoth turned to the flight data strip the data man had placed in the rack beside the scope. He wrote "125" on the strip and drew a line through the number. It meant he had assumed control of Eastern 212 at 12,500 feet altitude.

Heemsoth drummed his fingers, tapped his foot, hummed his tune. If he were an airline pilot, he thought, he probably wouldn't like being vectored all over Mecklenburg County, North Carolina, either.

CHAPTER TWENTY-THREE

7:28 A.M.

REAR ADMIRAL C. WARD CUMMINGS, Commander Naval Mine Warfare Force, painter of watercolors, accomplished pianist, holder of the Navy Commendation Medal, Bronze Star, Gold Star and Legion of Merit, and the life of every party, stared at the stewardess' breast nearly touching his nose. She leaned across his aisle seat to retrieve a coffee cup from Captain Felix Vecchione, a Cummings aide, who sat by the window. The breast, ample but not large, carefully sculpted and constrained by the elastic and cloth beneath the uniform, swept him away from the secret mine warfare technical papers in his lap and whisked him back to Long Beach. A smile tugged at the corners of his mouth at the memory.

He had been what then? A commander? Bucking for captain. It was the fall of 1965. He'd taken command of the *Coontz*, a guided missile frigate, a classy ship, a cherished command. She was in the naval shipyard in Long Beach for some work before deployment to Southeast Asia. He lived in the BOQ.

He and his officers developed a substantial reputation for prankish thefts. Hanberry and Kuhn stole some bushes outside the O Club. Someone else swiped a statue of the madonna. If something turned up missing, searchers came first to the *Coontz*.

One night he and his cohorts went to the O Club at Fort Mac-

Arthur to drink and sing and play the piano. He looked up from the keyboard and there, above the door, was a brace of old dueling pistols. They stashed the pistols in their coat pockets and swaggered off to the Diamond, a topless restaurant-night club.

"May I help you, gentlemen?"

The waitress was young, long brown hair spilling over her shoulders to the top of her large, surprisingly erect, completely bare breasts. She wore opera hose under a tiny skirt. Her lips were painted bright orange.

Ward Cummings turned at the sound of her voice, at an awareness of her approach. She stood at the table by his side. He started. Six inches from his left eye was the brightest, largest red nipple he had ever seen. His face broke into a sly grin. He felt the smiles, heard his officers snickering under their breaths as they watched to see what the captain might do.

Slowly, with elaborate, exaggerated stealth and a wink at someone across the table, he reached with his right hand into his inside jacket pocket, seized the dueling pistol hidden there and drew it out. Crooking his left arm in front of his face, he laid the pistol barrel on his forearm and pressed its muzzle against the woman's nipple.

"I'm going to blow your brains out," he proclaimed in a deliberate tone. He made a hissing sound like a child firing a toy gun. Coolly he raised the muzzle to his mouth and blew away an imaginary puff of smoke.

The table erupted into laughter.

The waitress smiled thinly.

"Can I get you gentlemen something to drink?"

They shipped out for Vietnam, designated as the flagship of a search and rescue task unit with the task unit commodore, Captain Fox, on board. Fox and Cummings quickly took a mutual dislike to one another. Their relationship was cool, distant, particularly after the helicopter trouble. Damned helicopter.

They built a special platform on 01 level, where the helicopter could be lashed down for transport across the Pacific. Then it would be moved to its launching pad on the fantail for rescuing downed pilots. The *Coontz* was the first ship so equipped, an example for the rest of the Navy, proof that the search and rescue force could handle such an important matériel transport job itself.

The helicopter tail protruded over the aft missile launcher, which had to be exercised each day at sea. He warned them, gave explicit orders: When exercising the launcher, beware the helicopter. Two days out of San Diego somebody brought the launcher around too far and sliced off the helicopter's tail.

Fox was outraged. The message traffic between the *Coontz* and San Diego was heavy. Commanders up the line became incensed. Fox requested and secured permission to conduct an investigation. The reputation of the SAR forces seemed to hang in the balance. They put in at Pearl Harbor while the investigation progressed. Fox rode Cummings unmercifully.

He knew of the whispers. They said he was to be relieved of his command, sent back to San Diego. He walked unexpectedly into the wardroom and caught several junior officers in an intense, hushed discussion. Someone hurriedly changed the subject, and like little boys caught with a hand in the cookie jar they sheepishly returned to their coffee.

His evaluation report came out. He knew from friends in Washington that he was up for promotion to captain. But Captain Fox had given him only a single "outstanding" mark—in ship handling. There was no "unsatisfactory" mark. But he would never make captain with such a lackluster report, not with broken service, not after resigning his commission early in his career then returning later to the regular Navy, not even with his connections in the Pentagon. "I'll never make captain. I just won't make it," he gloomily predicted, his head in his hands, to first one and then another of his senior officers when they sought him out as he brooded in his cabin.

The *Coontz* took its position at North SAR Station. The *Coontz* and a sister ship, the *Rogers,* steamed in tight circles, or back and forth, or lay dead in the water, maintaining a constant position off the North Vietnamese coast, fifty miles southeast of Haiphong. Airplanes from nearby carriers used the *Coontz*'s navigation radio signals to begin their bomb runs over the North and to return hours later. When a pilot bailed out, the two ships rushed to attempt a rescue before the North Vietnamese junks arrived to capture the flier.

On the last day of one stint on North SAR Station, the *Gurke* and the *King* arrived to relieve the *Coontz* and the *Rogers*. The new task unit commodore, the skippers of the two ships and their operations officers assembled in the *Coontz* wardroom for a briefing. An urgent message arrived. An airman was down far to the north, about thirty miles east of the North Vietnam-China border. The general alarm sounded, men scrambled down passageways and up ladders to duty stations. The four ships set sail at once, moving up the coast past a series of small islands, steaming farther north than any American vessels had gone during the war.

They found nothing as they searched under the scorching July sun. The four ships turned back southward and the wardroom briefing resumed. Suddenly it was interrupted by the strident blaring of the general quarters alarm. The *Coontz*'s Combat Information Center excitedly reported that the task force was under pursuit by three North Vietnamese PT boats, which had emerged from behind one of the small islands.

The commodore called in aircraft from the U.S.S. *Hancock* and a battle ensued. The aircraft attack with guns and bombs sunk two PT boats. Fox dispatched the *Gurke* and *Rogers* to pluck the drowning crew members from the water, as some gamely began to swim toward shore many miles away. The third boat sat low in the water, disabled, slowly sinking. Fox ordered the *Coontz* to move up, capture the crew and take the PT boat in tow.

Cummings watched through binoculars as the *Coontz* slowly moved toward the PT boat.

"Damn. He's got his gun trained right at us," Cummings said.

The knot of officers gathered at the rail stared tensely at the PT boat. One by one they lowered their binoculars. Now they were close enough to see without them. The PT boat's gun—it looked like a three-inch—was aimed directly at the bridge. A single burst from the gun could kill them all. "Don't fire unless fired upon," Fox had ordered. The *Coontz*'s guns were trained on the small craft. If the Vietnamese fired, they might damage the bridge, but the *Coontz* would blast the PT boat from the water.

The *Coontz* moved closer. They could make out the Vietnamese gunners clearly now, resolutely standing at their stations, training their gun at the bridge. Cummings felt like shrinking down behind the thin metal protection the bridge afforded. They drew closer.

"God damn. Why don't they lower their gun? They haven't got a chance." He gripped the rail tensely.

"Stop engines."

The sailor at the annunciator moved the handles, ringing the order down to the engine room.

"Prepare to launch the boat and boarding crew."

The talker repeated the order over the sound-powered phone.

The *Coontz* was slowing almost to a stop. The gun still pointed at the bridge. Cummings could hear the nervous muttering of the other captains and the new commodore. They stood helplessly by during the only naval engagement they were likely to see during their tour of duty.

"Find out if we have anyone who speaks French or Vietnamese. We'll order them to surrender."

Suddenly the PT boat's gun barrel moved. They gripped the rail, rigid with tension. Slowly the barrel moved away from the bridge, away from the *Coontz,* until it pointed amidships of the PT boat and into the air. The Vietnamese had surrendered.

They took seventeen prisoners, in all. The prisoners later complained to the Red Cross of brutal treatment aboard the *Coontz,* of beatings and abuse during interrogation. That led to a quiet investigation. They heard it even reached the White House, involving one of President Johnson's staff. But nothing came of it.

"Can I take your coffee cup, sir?"

"Why yes. Thank you," Admiral Cummings said, smiling at the woman and handing her the cup into which he had thrust the used napkin and plastic spoon. The toddler in line with them at the airport, laughing and giggling then, stared at him over its mother's shoulder one row up and just across the aisle. They were large, somber eyes. He smiled.

C. Ward Cummings had endured, despite the service break, despite the helicopter incident, despite Fox's fitness report. He'd made captain, commanded his own destroyer division during another tour in Southeast Asia, gone to the Pentagon on the staff of the Chief of Naval Operations. He sat through meetings and hearings sketching caricatures of the participants on his note pad,

sketches that won important friends, particularly among congressmen and senators' staff members. They remembered Ward Cummings next time he called to ask a favor, to solicit some information.

He made rear admiral in 1973 and eight months later the Chief
of Naval Operations, Admiral Elmo Zumwalt, handpicked him to
head the mine warfare force. It was a backwater assignment, a disappointment to a naval officer whose love was destroyers. He
wanted to command a destroyer group. But he had known Zumwalt since adolescence, when they were growing up together in a
central California farming community. Zumwalt was adamant.
Ward Cummings was what mine warfare needed. Do a good job
and then he'd get what he wanted.

He arrived in Charleston in midsummer. But only in the last
week had Lil moved and gotten settled into their base housing
among Charleston's admirals.

The airplane descended. He listened as the stewardess offered to
put ice in the hot chocolate she had given a young boy across the
aisle, to cool it enough to be drinkable before landing. He glanced
at his watch and reached down for the leather satchel. His fingers
brushed the gold-embossed lettering and he smiled.

His staff in Washington had bought the satchel as a going-away
present. They ordered the best gold embossing. He was fussy
about his name. C. Ward Cummings. How mortified they'd been
when the satchel came back Ward C. Cummings. But he liked it.
Just the right touch of eccentricity.

He shoved the papers in, closed the latch and leaned back in his
seat.

CHAPTER TWENTY-FOUR

7:29:20 A.M.

CAPTAIN JAMES REEVES collected signatures of the famous and near famous who boarded his flights. An autograph book lay in constant readiness in the flight bag beside his feet. Whenever a stewardess burst into the cockpit with news of some celebrity aboard the aircraft, he sent the book back with her. He even had her invite the famous person to the cockpit if the work load permitted. What celebrity could resist that?

He bought the autograph book after he joined Eastern in 1956. He asked each celebrity to address the autograph to one of his four children. "To Toni with best regards, Carl Sandburg." "To Terry, Dan Blocker." "To Jamie, from Shirley Chisholm." "To Jimmy, Eleanor Roosevelt." He bought the autograph book shortly after Jimmy, the youngest and only son, was born. As Jimmy grew and became his father's favorite child, the salutations changed until finally they all began, "To Jimmy." "To Jimmy." "To Jimmy."

Bill Russell, the pro basketball player, was a passenger in the first-class section. At an intermediate stop, Reeves pulled the book from his bag and walked down the aisle, proffering the book and a pen.

"I don't give my autograph to anybody," the basketball player snarled. "Nobody is good enough to have my autograph." He turned away and stared out the window.

Reeves felt his ears reddening, his face flushing. "O.K., if that's the way you feel." He stalked back to the cockpit, fuming. He burned with embarrassment and rejection and angrily told the story to his family when he returned home.

Each time Russell appeared on television commercials promoting long-distance telephone calls, Reeves fumed anew. "He's one of the rudest people. I don't see how he could be so famous and so many people like him, because he's just really nasty," Reeves said.

Eleanor Roosevelt graciously signed her name and at the end of the flight stopped at the cockpit door. "Captain," she called. "That's the nicest, the smoothest flight I've ever had." He never tired of telling the story.

Being "The Captain" was the most important status symbol in Jim Reeves' life. His mail came to "Captain" Jim Reeves. He wore a pair of pilot's wings on his red hunting cap. His two sons-in-law called him "Captain" as a term of endearment, and often his friends did, too.

Most of the Eastern Airlines DC-9 pilots based in Atlanta have a nodding acquaintance with one another and an impression, frequently based on reputation, of each man's skills in the cockpit. Best known are the pilots found at each end of the cockpit ability scale—the best captains and the worst captains, the best first officers and the worst.

In the dark in the bus at the Eastern parking lot that morning Jim Reeves and Jim Daniels quickly assessed one another's reputations. Each pilot was pleased to be sharing the next two days with the other.

Reeves had a solid reputation as a careful, deliberate captain. He was famed for his vast memory, his obviously high IQ, his expertise as a taxidermist and hunter. First officers who flew with Reeves regularly knew him as an opinionated man, quiet in the cockpit, not really a talker, more a whistler. He used his command authority but didn't throw it about. He believed in Eastern Airlines, would even go out in Atlanta while off duty and call on sportsmen's groups, urging them to use Eastern Airlines.

Jim Daniels had a solid reputation, too. His captains found him

agreeable, pleasant, a first officer who didn't constantly challenge
authority, who didn't make a captain uneasy through aggressive
assertiveness or sloppy flying. Daniels waited for his seniority to
grow until one day he would fly the left seat and command a left-
seat salary. "A copilot is a copilot. And that's all he is," Daniels
said. "There's only one way to operate and enjoy this business.
And that's to operate that way all the time everytime—as a copilot.
That way it's no strain on the brain. I won't get an ulcer. I've had
captains say when I give the altitude call-outs, 'Shut up. I don't
want to hear that crap.' So I say, 'Yes, sir. Out of a thousand. Out
of five hundred.' That's my job. So I do it. Sort of a robot doing
what it's supposed to be doing. That's not to say if a problem developed I wouldn't be ready for it any faster than the captain. But
there would be two men flying the airplane."

So Reeves knew when he flew the DC-9 he would have a complete copilot as his right hand; that when he relinquished the controls his copilot would become a competent, conscientious pilot.
And Daniels knew he would enjoy a relaxed cockpit free of tension.

Thus, in the operations office, the two men dispensed with the
briefing upon which some captains insist, particularly when the
crew is unfamiliar. Reeves might have gone over a variety of cockpit management points with his copilot—how he wanted to handle
altitude call-outs, approach speeds, descent rates, approach chart
use, flaps settings, weather, alternate airports and public address
announcements. But he didn't. He trusted his copilot. In the operations office he filled out the forms and Daniels inspected the airplane. Then they took off. The human factors aspect of flying, the
pilot as one of a complex system of components, didn't consciously
concern them. How they might interact with each other and how
that interaction might affect their instrument readings, response to
warning systems, perception of air traffic control instructions, recognition of visual and aural cues didn't cross their minds. They
had to fly from Atlanta to Charleston to Chicago to Orlando to
Dallas-Fort Worth and back to Atlanta in two days. They set out
to do that.

"Pressure altitude five forty," Reeves called out, reading the notes he'd made during the conversation with the Charlotte in-range man.

Daniels reached out to his altimeter and twirled the knob, setting the two small white hands on the inner scale to 540. The large white hands that measure altitude moved also, stopping at 9,800 feet. The aircraft was 9,800 feet above the touchdown zone of Runway 36 at Charlotte.

"Set here," Daniels responded. From the corner of his eye he saw the captain setting his upper altimeter, too.

Daniels' eyes made another circuit around the instruments. Airspeed 335 knots. Compass heading 342 degrees. The captain had asked that they pause in their descent at 10,000 feet before dropping into the 250-knot speed limit zone. Daniels eased back on the control wheel, raising the airplane's nose slightly, so the vertical speed indicator, which had read nearly 3,000 feet per minute descent rate a few seconds before now rapidly crept toward zero. The altimeter sweep hand, unwinding at a dizzying speed now slowed to a crawl. Daniels stretched his neck upward to see more clearly the captain's lower altimeter, the only one that now read altitude above sea level. Right on the money—10,500 feet. His eyes flicked to the airspeed indicator. Raising the nose to stop the descent, without adding more power from the engines, caused a reduction in airspeed. The needle was falling off toward 250 knots.

As the airspeed fell, the incessant cockpit noise, the whine the two pilots had endured since their speed picked up outside Charleston, began to diminish. They now spoke more naturally to one another. The radio traffic on the loudspeakers above their heads was clearer.

"Eastern 212, what's your altitude?" It was Atlanta Center.

"We're slowing at ten," Reeves answered.

The grating sound of the pitch trim buzzer sounded as Daniels adjusted the pressures on his control column.

"Eastern 212, roger," Atlanta replied. "Contact Charlotte approach on one two four zero."

"O.K.," Reeves said. He reached down and dialed in the new frequency.

"Charlotte approach, Eastern 212 descending to eight."

"Two twelve, Charlotte," Burdette E. Heemsoth replied. "Fly

heading zero four zero. Vectors to VOR final approach course, Runway three six. Descend and maintain six thousand."

"O.K. Down to six and . . . ah . . . zero four zero heading."

Reeves reached out to the glare shield and turned the altitude alert control knob until 6,000 appeared in the window. Daniels squeezed the red trim button on his control wheel and the buzzer sounded again. Then he slowly turned the control wheel to the right, gently rolling the DC-9 into a shallow right bank, beginning a gentle right turn. He watched the compass begin to rotate. Next he pushed the control column forward slightly, lowering the DC-9's nose, resuming the descent. He pulled the throttle levers back, reducing engine power so the airspeed wouldn't climb above 250 knots.

Reeves had been peering at a small card clipped to his control wheel, searching a chart for the correct airspeed during the last mile or so of the approach to the runway. This speed varies on each flight depending upon the amount of wing flaps used and the total weight of the airplane, weight that can be markedly different at the end of a long flight because of fuel consumption. The DC-9's takeoff weight had been 94,500 pounds; it would burn 4,500 pounds of fuel en route to Charlotte. Reeves's finger found the appropriate speed—122 knots.

"About a hundred and twenty-two," he told Daniels.

"Set," Daniels responded, reaching to the airspeed indicator and turning a knob that set a small reminder tab on the instrument face at 122 knots.

"Twenty-nine thirty-four?" Daniels asked, looking into the Kollsman window of his altimeter, wondering if after setting the pressure altitude hands at 540 earlier, he now had the correct reading in the window—the cross-check to ascertain that his altimeter functioned properly.

"Roger," Reeves said. Twenty-nine thirty-four was correct.

Daniels leaned over to get a closer look at the small window of the captain's lower altimeter. It had to be set to the Charlotte altimeter setting to read altitude above sea level correctly.

"Thirty twenty-four or thirty sixteen?" he asked Reeves.

Reeves glanced at the clipboard.

"Thirty sixteen."

The altimeter was set correctly. Daniels checked its reading again: 10,500 feet. He looked at his altimeter: 9,800 feet. Mentally he calculated the difference: 750 feet. Daniels turned to the Charlotte VOR Runway 36 approach chart clipped on the table beside his right knee. In the upper right corner it listed the Charlotte airport elevation: 749 feet above sea level. So the altimeters were all set. Set, checked and cross-checked.

Reeves reached back with both hands and grasped the two straps of his shoulder harness. Until now he had flown with just his seat belt fastened. Daniels had both his belt and shoulder harness connected. The captain drew the two straps across his chest and locked them into the connecting device in his lap. Pilots often leave the shoulder harness undone, although they shouldn't, because it is uncomfortable.

Reeves turned now to the checklist, also clipped to the control wheel, that listed the descent and in-range preparedness duties for landing.

Seat belt sign. He'd turned it on earlier. Airfoil, engine and windshield heat to prevent ice buildup. No need for that on this summer day.

Fuel system boost pumps. "Four and two," Reeves said aloud, making certain two fuel pumps for each wing tank were on and the two center tank pumps were off.

"Air conditioning and pressurization?" he asked the copilot.

"It's set," Daniels said.

Reeves turned to the hydraulic pumps, the source of hydraulic pressure to move aircraft controls and mechanical systems.

"Four on, system normal," he murmured, making certain the pumps were on, the pressure values in the green arc, the hydraulic oil quantity above the red line.

"Altimeters," the captain said, noting the settings.

"In range?" Reeves said quizzically.

"Check," Daniels said.

It had taken the two pilots a mere seventy-five seconds to complete the in-range and descent cockpit preparation. Both pilots performed the duties in the same unconscious manner that Burdette Heemsoth in the Charlotte Tracon decided to turn Eastern 212 to the right and vector it around to intercept the final ap-

proach course. Reeves and Daniels had gone through this descent
preparation thousands of times. Each knew the checklist by heart.
Nonetheless, Reeves ran through the list to make certain nothing
had been missed. It was a mark of the care with which he flew.
Some airline pilots don't routinely run through their lists, even
though airline policy and government regulation make it mandatory.

Just as a suburbanite may drive his station wagon to the neighborhood supermarket and not really be conscious of the stop signs
and traffic lights and oncoming cars as his mind dwells on work or
a ball game or any of a thousand things, Reeves and Daniels accomplished the in-range and descent check unconsciously. It was
second nature to them. Their conversation occupied them at a
more conscious level.

"It got so bad in Ben Hill they were havin' to get police in the
schools, in the halls," Daniels said.

"Yeah."

"Even so, they couldn't cover everything."

"Well, what they're doin' is they're forcing all the whites to go
to private schools and all the public schools're gonna end up
black. That's exactly what's gonna happen," Reeves said.

"I really . . ."

Reeves interrupted. "Then what they'll do is come out with a
law an' say, 'O.K. now. We're gonna integrate the private schools.
Therefore you white folks gonna have to pay for all these blacks
goin' to your private schools.'"

The captain looked out the side window. From Reeves' vantage
point at 10,000 feet altitude, the climbing sun had turned the
previously dark forests into greens and blues, broken by the
greenish-brown fields where crops were turning in anticipation of
fall. An occasional patch of white fog lay in low spots near a pond
or lake.

"Can't leave well enough alone, can they, the government?" the
captain said, turning back to the cockpit. They were passing
through 9,000 feet. Reeves pulled up his folding map table with a
clanging bang and hauled out the binder of airport approach
charts from his bag. He withdrew the chart for the VOR Runway
36 approach at Charlotte and clipped it on the table.

"Government's gotten so big that one out of sixteen people works for the government," Daniels said. He turned to his approach chart again and found the compass course to set into the navigation radio. It would pick up the radio beam to lead them to the airport when the controller finished his vectoring: 353 degrees. He rotated a knob on the instrument on his panel so it read 353 degrees.

"Two twelve, turn left heading three six zero," the Charlotte controller ordered.

"Three six zero. Two twelve," Reeves said.

Daniels turned the control wheel and the airplane rolled into a left bank. He thumbed the button and the pitch trim buzzer sounded. The speaker blared with instructions to other airplanes on the controller's frequency. Captain Reeves resumed the aimless whistling.

"Flaps five degrees, sir," Daniels said.

Reeves reached across the pedestal and hauled the flap handle into its first notch. The pressure on Daniels' control column immediately began to change. He thumbed the pitch trim button. The buzzer blatted once, twice. Daniels reached down to his radio console and flipped a switch. He wanted to hear the identifying code from the Charlotte VOR. He slipped his earphones in place. Dash, dot, dash, dot. Dot, dash, dot, dot. Dash. They spelled out C-L-T. He had tuned the correct station. He slid the earphones back on his head. Captain Reeves continued to whistle. The pitch trim buzzer sounded again.

"Seven thousand for six," the captain said, and kept on whistling.

"I was thinkin'," Daniels said. "I was thinkin' about it this morning. Just what we were talking about the presidential pardon, you know. If those crazy bastards don't quit screwing around I can see Ford gettin' his ass kicked out of there."

"Oh, yeah. 'At's what I think," Reeves said.

"He's not our elected representative," Daniels said.

"Right. I heard this morning on the news while I was . . ."

Reeves was interrupted by the whistle of the altitude alert, signaling passage through 6,250 feet.

Daniels turned the control wheel, bringing the wings back to level, the turn to 360 degrees complete.

"I heard they might start proceedings for impeachment because of . . . ah . . . givin' that pardon to Nixon and the Watergate people." The captain paused while he set his navigation radio to the 353-degree setting. Daniels had begun to stop their descent, to level out at 6,000 feet.

"Ol' Ford's beginning to take some of his hard knocks," Reeves added.

"Eastern 212, turn left, heading two four zero," the Charlotte controller ordered.

"Two four zero, Eastern 212. We're at six," Reeves replied.

"Eastern 212, roger. Descend and maintain four thousand."

"Awright. Down to four." Reeves twirled 4,000 feet into the altitude alert window.

Daniels cocked the control wheel to the left again, rolling into another left turn, around to 240 degrees, west southwest, seemingly away from the airport. Presumably the controller would turn them right in a few minutes and they would pick up the 353-degree radio beam to the airport. He pushed the control wheel forward, dipping the nose down, continuing the descent.

"Fifteen degrees, please," he called.

Reeves pulled the flap handle down another notch.

"Eastern 212, contact Charlotte approach on one one niner point zero," the Charlotte controller instructed.

"One nineteen nothin'. Good day," Reeves snapped.

So the pilots of Eastern 212 continued their descent, occupied by conversation touching mutual, strongly held views. They were unmindful of aviation's neglect of the human element of the system, unaware that human factors were playing a key role as they descended toward thin ground fog obscuring the airport.

Captain Reeves was tired, fatigued, in fact. He had flown on eight of the past nine days, taking time off only the Sunday before. He had amassed more than twenty-eight hours of flight time in that period with airport check-in times that varied from 6 A.M. to 6 P.M. Consequently he had alternated sleeping at night and sleeping in the daytime, both at home and in motels.

Dr. Stanley R. Mohler, a research physician with the FAA,

traveled with airline crews on international flights, to Hong Kong, New Delhi, Africa and the like, studying the effect of flight schedules on physiological performance. From his studies Dr. Mohler developed an index with which to assess the "physiological demand" placed on a pilot by his flight schedule.

An index value of 1.75 is a high but acceptable physiological pilot load. Values between 1.75 and 2.30 Mohler considers too high. He believes values above 2.30 to be dangerous.

Reeves felt tired, even remarked about it during the takeoff roll in Charleston. He didn't know about Dr. Mohler's index. But had he applied it, he might have been shocked. On Sunday, Reeves's day off, his index dropped to 1.10. But Monday he rose at 3:30 A.M. to begin the same two-day flight sequence he had started today. His index soared to 2.43. The next day, on the leg from Orlando to Dallas-Fort Worth and back to Atlanta his index was 1.72—high but just acceptable. Now, on his ninth day of flying with only one day off, his index came to 3.27, clearly dangerous.

Reeves had purposely arranged his schedule. He wanted to log as much flying as possible early in the month so he would have the last of it free. His parents were planning a visit and he also intended to make his annual hunting expedition. One advantage of being a high seniority captain is the opportunity to tailor one's working schedule.

If Captain Reeves and all airline pilots daily used Dr. Mohler's index or something similar to assess cockpit fitness, and followed the index's finding, many cockpit crews might be better prepared.

Human factors touched the two pilots elsewhere that morning.

They trusted one another, knew one another by reputation. So, even though they had flown together only once before—and that a full year earlier—the captain conducted no pre-flight briefing with his first officer.

In the past both men had misread altimeters, maps and charts, but they had read them correctly far more often. They may have disliked many of their instruments' display characteristics and might sometimes find the charts hard to interpret, but they had learned to live with them.

They were bothered by the noise of the air rushing past the windows, but the irritating whine was part of the job. The dual altimeters meant more cockpit work load, but it seemed a sensible system.

Like most Eastern pilots each felt annoyed whenever the altitude alert beeped its warning. The sound was irritating and they vaguely resented the beep, which might go off a dozen times during one flight. They tended to ignore its presence, but there it was, poorly designed or not, required by the government in every airliner cockpit.

They may have felt that their work load in the DC-9 was too fast-paced, that they needed a third pilot, like the flight engineer used in many other jet airliners. But the two-man cockpit debate had dragged on for years and wasn't likely to be resolved. They would just do the best they could, even if it was hard at times staying on top of a forty-five-ton airplane rushing along at six miles a minute.

Each had learned earlier in his career the necessity for constantly monitoring position when the air traffic controllers begin their vectors. Each felt a tiny bit of anxiety each time he was given vectors and, true, in the bustle of the cockpit work load they might not be precisely aware of their position or able quickly to ascertain it. But they did the best they could.

Daniels had listened to the ATIS, as much as he thought he needed. A pilot on first contact with an airport radar room or tower cab is supposed to inform the controller that he has listened to the ATIS, that he has all the necessary information about weather, runways and special problems. Captain Reeves didn't do that.

When a pilot failed to mention monitoring of the ATIS, Burdette Heemsoth was supposed to read up the current weather, runways and other information. He didn't do that either. A small slip, but the pilots doubtlessly were monitoring the ATIS. They would ask if they had any questions.

Captain Reeves dialed the new Charlotte approach frequency into the radio and picked up the microphone.

The controller on the new frequency was talking to another aircraft.

"Piedmont 917. Turn further right. Heading . . . ah . . . make it three six zero. You're through the final approach course now."

"Yeah. O.K. We've got it," the Piedmont pilot replied.

Reeves pressed the microphone button.

"Charlotte approach, Eastern 212. Descending to four. We're turning to two forty."

CHAPTER TWENTY-FIVE

7:29:30 A.M.

AL HARE STOOD AT the south windows by the stairway, his back to the other controllers in the tower cab, his eye following an imaginary straight line projected outward from the center of Runway 36. A miniature radar screen four feet to his left on the control console revealed a target about four miles out, Canair 101, a twin-engine Aero Commander 500U used to shuttle passengers between Charlotte and Hickory, North Carolina.

Every morning at seven, Canair 101 took off with passengers bound for Charlotte and connecting airline flights. Like others inbound to Charlotte, the Canair pilot preferred Runway 5 and the ILS, particularly since popping straight in would save fuel and money. The RVR fluctuated up and down after Al Hare and Pete Hogan switched to Runway 36. About ten miles northwest of the airport, when the RVR had risen to 6,000 feet-plus, Canair 101 asked to make an ILS approach to Runway 5. Denny Hunter, the final controller in the Tracon, vectored him to the ILS beginning point five miles off the end of the runway. Then the RVR suddenly dropped to 3,800 feet. When Hunter passed along this news, Canair 101 broke off the approach. Hunter gave him vectors to the 353-degree radio beam of the Charlotte VOR inbound to Runway

36. Then he turned the airplane over to Hare and Hogan in the tower cab.

Al Hare's gaze focused on a speck at the horizon, above the fog. He squeezed the microphone switch.

"Canair 101's in sight," he said into his headset.

"One oh one," the Canair pilot replied. "Looks like we got about three or four miles' visibility from where we are right now."

"Yeah. It's a little better on Runway three six," Hare agreed. He glanced at the small radar screen, known as the Brite Display, which reproduced the final controller's screen in the Tracon. He could see Canair 101's target outside the three-mile point.

Hare turned and glanced at Hogan, who stood watching, his headset plugged into Hare's local controller frequency. Having someone plugged in with him, even if it was for controller position check-out, and a nice guy like Hogan, made Hare nervous.

Al Hare began his air traffic control career in 1960 in the Air Force, right out of high school. He tried to get a job with the FAA four years later, when his Air Force tour ended, but the agency was in a controller-hiring slump. He went to work for the North Carolina Highway Patrol as a radio dispatcher in Asheville, his hometown. But he kept after the FAA, always seeking a controller's job. The chief of the Asheville tower was a friend—and in 1970 he was hired at Augusta, Georgia, a sleepy little tower. He spent four years there becoming a veteran, a full performance level controller. Five weeks ago he had transferred to Charlotte, a bustling facility with a large staff, not at all like Augusta.

Hare was disappointed to find that Charlotte Tower, for all its size and prestige, had no formal training program to indoctrinate an FPL like himself. He faced the prospect of learning every position in the tower under the watchful eye of veteran Charlotte controllers and then being certified as an FPL for the entire facility. In Augusta they checked out a new man position by position and certified him on each position as the facility check-out progressed. Hare also discovered a subtle pressure to be quick about his check-out.

"It's a hurry-up thing," he complained to his wife. "Get through and get on the position. We need the bodies. I'm not going to play their game. I'm going to make sure I'm ready before I take the responsibility."

He began early in August in the tower cab. The Tracon would come later. First he checked out on the data position—reading flight plans to pilots, handling the flight strips. Then he checked out on ground control, watching over all the aircraft taxiing on the airport to and from the runways. Finally, he began a check-out at local control, the runways themselves, the takeoffs and landings. Today was his third day as the local controller with Pete Hogan as his instructor.

"The pressure comes from above. From the chief. 'Why aren't you checked out? Why aren't you checked out?' So then your supervisor calls you in. 'I'm not ready,' I say. That's my personal opinion. If I'm not ready, I'm not ready and they can't say nothing about it. If the controller feels ready, they can turn him loose. If he doesn't, they can't.

"Training a guy is one of the worst jobs in the facility. Nobody wants to do training. They hate to train, because it is so confining. You're bothered with the responsibility of having to listen to somebody while you try to keep the picture. You're doing two jobs. I'm telling you, in the afternoon or evening shift and you're really busy and you have to monitor somebody for the whole eight hours, I'm telling you, it's a killer. You are completely, mentally exhausted."

Hare and Hogan watched silently as the Canair Aero Commander drew steadily closer. Three miles. Two miles. One mile. They could make out the distinctive Aero Commander fuselage hung beneath the wings, like a giant, unwieldy insect. Changing to Runway 36 was a good decision.

"The personality of the person checking you out is everything. Pete's all right. I like to kid around with him. He's one of the old controllers in Charlotte, although he's probably four years younger than I am. You know what I mean by 'old'? Probably knows more about it than any of the controllers at the airport.

"If you get somebody you can't work with on the check-out, then you have problems. Some of the controllers believe themselves to be superstars, which a lot of them are. And they'll tell you they are. They do good work, so why not? But if you can't conform to their superstar standards right off the bat, then it can become a personality conflict.

"Sometimes they try to break the shift up and let several guys monitor you. So maybe you'll work the position with this guy for an hour and he'll want you to do it his way. You work another position with another guy and he'll want you to do it his way, too. So how many ways are you going to do it? A man's got to develop his own technique.

"Hogan is more the instructor type. He's right there all the time and he stays there and makes sure you do it right. You can expect some kidding if you make a little booboo.

"I started out on flight data position and then ground control. And then you move over to local control and you say, 'Well, the terror is actually here now.' Local can be a bear at times.

"Sometimes local is really busy but you can't even talk to the man on final radar down in the Tracon. You'll punch into his line and all you hear are airplanes. You can't even take a second to talk to him about some airplane, he's so busy. And if he's working that many airplanes you think, 'Damn. They'll all be breathing down my neck in a few minutes.' So sometimes they bring in a cab co-ordinator and a radar co-ordinator who plug in and talk to one another and take some of the load off.

"Some guys call it 'gettin' in a box' when they work local. They say, 'Don't make any difference if you get in a box. Just don't let them nail the lid on.' Always have an out."

Al Hare had enjoyed being a radio dispatcher for the Highway Patrol, even though the pay was low. He co-ordinated some exciting highway chases when troopers pursued someone at reckless speeds. He hadn't been in bed very long after working a midnight shift one summer morning in 1967 when Trooper Bill Stiles excitedly telephoned. A Piedmont 727 airliner and a small airplane had collided and crashed a few miles south of the Asheville Municipal Airport, not very far from Hare's home. Stiles picked him up scarcely ten minutes later and they sped to the scene, red light flashing, siren blaring. The memories of that morning lingered and occasionally he told his controller colleagues about it. Few controllers see the aftermath of an airline disaster at such close quarters.

"What can I say? It dug a hole in the ground. We came down the interstate in the patrol car. It was right off the interstate. You could throw a baseball from the interstate to the crash.

"We parked and walked down there, walked real careful 'cause we didn't know if it was going to blow up or what. You could see the wreckage strewn about, the mass of the airplane where it hit the ground and was burning. Some of the fire people came and began to extinguish the fire. There were limbs off people everywhere. Bodies. Jeez, it was terrible. Now, I didn't see any looting, but others did. Some of the troopers said you just about had to physically restrain some people from taking wallets off those bodies and parts of bodies. The interstate was jammed up for miles with sightseers.

"They set up a temporary morgue at the National Guard Armory. We went up there. Boy, that was something. I didn't care for seeing that. The private airplane, it was a Cessna 310, that 310 just ripped the belly out of the Piedmont. Left a trail of baggage and people a mile and a half long. We went back and followed it.

"One body came out of the airplane and fell through the roof of a house, clear through to the basement. They said one stewardess jumped prior to the impact. Or maybe she was thrown clear. These are stories you hear. They say she was found on the bank of the interstate drove into the ground like a stake.

"Naw. I didn't get sick. I used to work in a funeral home in Asheville."

Canair 101 was almost to the runway threshold now. No trouble with the fog. The pilot hadn't even flown through any of it. Hare turned to the console and punched a button opening the line to Denny Hunter, the final controller in the Tracon.

"Hey," he called.

"Yeah?"

"Aircraft reporting visibility about three miles."

"About how many?"

"About three to four miles on Runway 36. They're seeing it about two or three out. Something like that."

"Pretty good."

Alden Hare. With a name like that, naturally they called him "Rabbit" in school. Rabbit Hare. Roy and Earl Williams were friends of Al Hare's father. They ran a family business, Williams Funeral Home. They needed part-time help, so Al went down one afternoon. He was in high school at the time.

Roy Williams talked to him in the office. "You may not want this kind of work," he warned. "Earl's in the back right now embalming. It's a bad one. Died of gangrene. If you can take that, you're pretty tough."

Earl had a giant exhaust fan roaring in the window and several little fans humming. It was gangrene, all right. Both legs amputated. It looked like burnt meat. The stench was terrible. Earl wore a gauze mask. Al watched the embalming. Again and again he wanted to retch. He fought it back. They gave him the job.

"Whaddaya say, Digger, old buddy?" "Hey, Digger, we'll be the last to let you down." "Try our layaway plan, Digs." "You stab 'em, we slab 'em, Digger." He liked to carry on with his friends. He dated girls. Working in a mortuary seemed to have some special appeal for them.

The funeral home was in a large old house. "We had an apartment upstairs right over the preparation room. We took turns sleeping there because we had a twenty-four-hour ambulance service. We'd back the hearse into the basement and open up those big doors. There was an elevator and arched hallways like an old dungeon.

"Lot of times you'd go to the hospital at two or three o'clock in the morning to get a body. You'd back the hearse in. Be dark as hell. I'd always be the one to go to the other end of the building in the dark and turn on the lights. God, it was scary. We'd wheel the body through there, by all these caskets and vaults. Wheel it up to the elevator and up to the preparation room and put it on the prep table. It was one of those old creaky hand-start elevators. Jerk the cable and it started."

Later, he lay in bed upstairs, eyes wide, staring at the shadows playing on the ceiling from rustling tree limbs and streetlights and car lights. Body tense, he strained for every sound.

The elevator creaked. Clank. Clank. Clank. Roy had come to embalm the body. Rattle. Rattle. Creak. Clank. Clank. Frankenstein's monster, loose in the Williams Funeral Home.

CHAPTER TWENTY-SIX

7:30 A.M.

RICHARD ARNOLD COULD see the airport. First he saw the buildings of downtown Charlotte, the Jefferson First Union Tower and a newer, black monolith, and then he glimpsed the airport, cars in the parking lot, portions of the runways.

He sat in seat 5E, on the right by the window in the first row of the coach section. It was Arnold's favorite airliner seat, a window in the no smoking section in front of the wing. It always provided an unobstructed view of the ground.

Arnold had flown into Charlotte many times. He had driven around the city, knew the road from downtown to the airport five miles southwest. He gazed out his window searching for a landmark.

First the pilots horsed the airplane around in a right turn, then straight, then left, straight again and another right. Before the last turn Arnold looked up from his *U. S. News and World Report* and saw the towering office buildings. Arnold searched southwestward to the ribbons of concrete and the parked cars at the airport.

He saw patches of fog dotting the airport perimeter. Directly below, the ground appeared through intermittent fog banks, the tops of the fog billows lighted by the low sun. They descended. He could make out the distinct boundaries of fields and forests, farmhouses, building clusters where a gas station and a general store broke the monotony of a rural highway.

Arnold was tired, weary from a restless depression. He spent the night before on his living room couch, reading, dozing, thinking about his boys.

He and Virginia married when he finished college in 1966, just before he went into the U. S. Air Force as a second lieutenant. "If you could spell lieutenant and had a college degree, then you were one," he was fond of saying. He had a degree in history, so they made him a computer programmer. He went to work for IBM after the Air Force, solving customers' software problems. They had two boys.

The marriage faltered. Virginia grew more liberated. Richard spent days, weeks away installing and debugging computer programs. He spent several weeks on a job at Hilton Head, South Carolina, the seaside resort. Virginia found the role of wife and mother to two small boys confining. She protested her husband's long absences.

"How many filet mignons can you eat in a row on an expense account before you lose your taste for filet mignon?" he answered. "All I want is a greasy old hamburger. All I want more than anything else is to be home. What I'd really like to do is tuck the kids in bed and talk to them."

Virginia sought her identity, a meaning to her life.

"Man, you've got it made here," he said. "You can sit and watch the birds. You can read. Go to the library. You can go to college. You can be anything you want. Just stay here and take care of the kids."

She returned to college, resumed studies interrupted by marriage. She searched for her place in life.

"I don't see why you have to get your identity in opposition to your role as a wife and mother," he argued.

Richard went to Atlanta to install a new computer system. One day a telephone call came while he was out. The Florida area code on the message the switchboard operator took meant only one thing. Virginia had gone to her parents, had left him. He ran from the data processing center, jumped into a taxi and rushed to the Atlanta airport. "Get me on the first flight out," he breathlessly ordered the ticket agents and used the last bit of change he had to take a taxi from the airport to Virginia's mother's house.

Virginia's stepfather threatened him. Her mother vilified him. Virginia finally consented to come out and speak with him. It's over, she said. Say good-by to the boys. The older boy tried to choke back his tears. I'll always love you and be your good friend. Don't worry, the boy told his father. The little one sobbed openly. It was good-by forever to him. Richard flew back to Charleston.

The house was a mess, mud everywhere. Virginia had taken much of the furniture. She rented a U-Haul and loaded and left. They had never been friendly with the neighbors, who grew alarmed at the unexpected goings-on and called the police. The police forced their way into the house but found no reason for alarm. Richard came back on a Friday and cleaned up. Bob from next door, whom he had never known well, came over. They sat in the living room and built a fire to ward off the January chill. They opened cans of beer. "There were such strange things happening," Bob explained. "We thought maybe Virginia had gone off her rocker and killed the children and herself. That's why somebody called the police."

He moved the remaining furniture into new corners, bought a rug for the bedroom and painted some walls. "Clay," he told the IBM salesman he worked with, "you know quitting time is five-fifteen. Right? Well I think starting at four-thirty each day we oughta start getting ready to quit. No overtime. No weekends. No nothing. We'll do everything cleanly. No sense getting the customers all upset thinking they've got a computer they gotta work on all night and all weekend."

Only once since then had he put in overtime, when the Medical University's accounting system broke down. He spent a weekend there. Fell asleep on the floor beside the computer cabinets. Never found the problem. Apparently made enough noise to scare the gremlins away.

The Medical University of South Carolina in Charleston was a favorite customer. They had challenging problems, truly humanitarian applications for computers. The university studied the possibility of a pilot project that would monitor data on patients. It might be initiated in the university's burn center, so he went there for a tour.

At the warning signs by the burn ward's entrance on the fourth floor of the red brick university hospital building he donned a surgical gown. No admittance without surgical gowns because of the burn patient's particular vulnerability to infection. A doctor met him and began the tour. Richard Arnold was immediately horrified and fascinated.

In the intensive care area a nurse sat on a raised platform behind a counter surveying the beds where the burn patients came first until the shock and fluid loss and respiratory ventilation problems had been surmounted.

The doctor pointed out a boy who had fallen from a tree onto the top of an electrical transformer only a few hours before. Both arms and legs were hideously burned. The electricity had burned off one ear. He certainly would lose an arm. The boy was conscious, even rational, groping for understanding of what had happened. They stopped by his bed to chat. What to say? You're still a person? Life will go on?

They entered a room of air beds—tanks of glass beads through which a fan underneath blew a strong stream of air, in effect fluidizing the beads. From intensive care the severely burned came to the air beds—sometimes for months, unless they died first. Lying on the fluidized beads was like floating in water. The bed prevented bedsores. He lay in one to get the feeling. It was like a water bed, but with more stability.

Then they went into the room with the tank—a stainless steel tank six by eight feet filled with warm water. A seriously burned man lay on a metal and canvas frame that had been lowered into the water. The doctors and nurses were working over him and the man moaned piteously, periodically uttering a muted scream. Arnold felt a dizziness creep over him, felt the perspiration under his gown. With scalpels they were cutting away the man's burned flesh on his back and chest, stripping away the dead material that would impede healing, that could become the breeding ground for an infection. They were literally skinning the man alive. Blood streaked the water. The hard pain, the agony the man felt frightened Arnold. It was etched on the man's face as he struggled to endure the pain, to choke back the moans and screams.

"It's called debridement," the doctor with them explained. "You cut off a little bit of dead material each day. Whatever area is ready. Whatever the patient can tolerate each day from the standpoint of pain. We usually give them some morphine or Demerol about forty-five minutes before. But you can't give a general anesthetic. We often have to do this every day for a month or two."

Arnold stared at the man in the tank with revulsion and fascination. How did he tolerate the pain? The doctors and nurses seemed casual in their attitude, even unfeeling. Was it just a job? Perhaps they couldn't indulge themselves with feelings about their maimed patients.

"The fear of the daily session in the tank is terrible," the doctor said. "No matter how much you anesthetize them you can't stop them from having some pain. Often these patients live in a kind of dread for two or three months from the debridement one day to the debridement the next day."

Later, in the burn ward staff's lounge they talked more.

"Infection of the wound is the single most common cause of death in the burn patient. Twenty, twenty-five years ago they died from shock and fluid loss. Now we know how to handle that. But the infection problem isn't so simple. 'Soupy.' That's the term for an infected burn wound.

"It's a digestive process, from enzymes secreted by the bacteria and from the white cells of the body that are fighting the infection. It liquefies, forms pus. Sometimes you say, 'That burn looks kind of soupy' and what you mean is it looks infected. A soupy burn wound is always a bad sign."

They talked about the patient's will to live—the key to leaving the ward alive.

"Well, if the patient isn't highly motivated to regain normal activity and get back to the way he was before, your battle is half lost in the beginning. Again and again we see a patient that is highly motivated get well and back to normal and the next patient with the same sort of burn will do all the same things. Except he doesn't care. And so he dies. It's terribly frustrating."

That night at home Richard Arnold fell into a deep depression. The tour unnerved him as nothing before. They never were able to design anything that would efficiently utilize a computer to help care for the burn patients.

Richard Arnold closed the magazine and laid it in his lap. He looked out again at the patches of fog. He no longer could see the airport.

CHAPTER TWENTY-SEVEN

7:32 A.M.

EASTERN 212 CONTINUED its descent.

First Officer James Daniels held the control wheel in his right hand and rested his left hand lightly on the throttle levers. He monitored their descent on the captain's lower altimeter, the only altimeter that now reported altitude in feet above sea level. The air traffic controllers' altitude instructions were in feet above sea level. Daniels craned his neck each time he looked at the instrument because his left arm concealed it.

The altimeter's white sweep hand moved counterclockwise, ticking off hundreds of feet of altitude loss—1,000 feet per revolution. They were descending at 1,000 feet per minute—a proper descent rate for this stage of the approach. Thus the sweep hand traversed the instrument face once a minute—moving at the same speed as the second hand on a watch. Daniels was aware of its movement, but he didn't concentrate on it. 5,500 feet. 5,300. 5,100. 4,900.

"Eastern 212," the radar controller called, "continue heading two four zero. Descend and maintain three thousand."

"Awright. On down to three," Captain James Reeves replied. He dialed 3,000 feet into the altitude alert system.

The radar controller's conversations with other aircraft blared from the speakers.

"Piedmont 917, contact tower one eighteen one. You're slightly left of course. Visibility on final three miles."

"O.K.," a Piedmont pilot replied.

Visibility three miles. Daniels arched his eyebrows. Much better than the official visibility, which was what, one and a half miles? Don't rely solely on weather reports. The weather is whatever you find when you get there.

The pilots continued their conversation.

"One thing that kills me so damn much," Daniels said, "is all this shit that's goin' on now. We need to be takin' definite steps to save the economy of this damn country. I think the A-rabs are takin' over every damn thing. They bought, shit they got so much damn real estate and land. They bought an island for seventeen million dollars off the Carolinas."

"Yeah," Reeves began.

"They got the stock market," Daniels added. "And the damn Swiss are going to sink the god damn money with their gold." He cackled wryly at the thought.

"Yes, sir. Sure are," the captain agreed.

The speakers rattled with the air traffic control instructions.

"Delta 608 is three and a half miles south of Ross Intersection. Turn left heading zero one zero. Cleared to the VOR three six approach. Contact tower one eighteen one."

"O.K. Ah . . . zero one zero. Cleared for the approach. One eighteen one," the Delta pilot acknowledged.

"Eastern 212. Reduce to one six zero knots," the controller continued.

"O.K.," Reeves said.

Daniels' eyes flicked to the airspeed indicator: 185 knots. The controller didn't say so, but he obviously sought a slight speed reduction to increase the distance between Eastern 212 and Delta 608 immediately ahead.

Daniels pulled back on the throttle levers slightly, just enough to slow their airspeed but continue the 1,000-feet-per-minute descent. Experience had taught him just how much to ease back. The change in power changed pressures on the aircraft control surfaces at the tail. Once again he squeezed the stabilizer trim button,

sounding the loud buzzer. The altimeter hand continued to re-
volve. 4,100. 4,000. 3,900.

"Yes, sir. Boy, they got the money don't they? Those Arabs got
so damn much money," Reeves said.

" 'At's right," Daniels interrupted. "It's coming in at such a fantastic rate."

"Yeah. I know."

"Hell, if we don't do something by 1980, hell, they'll own the
world."

The captain chuckled.

"Owned it all at one time," Daniels added.

"That's right."

"I'd be willing to go back to one car and . . . ah . . . lot of
other restrictions if we could get somethin' goin' here."

"Yeah."

"Four thousand for three."

The pitch trim buzzer blatted again.

"I'm car poor. I got, well, I just got two now. I just gave one to
my boy. But I'm buying a new one," Reeves said.

"Yeah."

"I ordered . . ."

"I thought about gettin' one, too, but . . ."

The radio loudspeaker interrupted.

"Eastern 212, turn right, heading three five zero. Cleared VOR
three six approach. You're six miles south of Ross Intersection."

"O.K. Three fifty. Cleared for the approach," Reeves replied.

The pitch trim buzzer sounded again. 3,500. 3,400. 3,300.

"I think I'll go ahead and keep that Toyota of mine for a
while," Daniels said. He squeezed the red button on his control
wheel and the trim buzzer sounded.

"It's a piece of shit. But it's cheap to operate."

The altitude alert beep sounded and the "ALT" light on each
pilot's instrument panel went out, signaling 3,250 feet, warning
that they approached the assigned 3,000 feet descent altitude.

Reeves pulled up on the seat latch lever and scooted his seat
forward so his feet were closer to the rudder pedals.

The VOR 36 approach to Douglas Municipal Airport is called a
non-precision approach. The pilots don't have a radio beam to

give them vertical guidance, so they cannot fly down the beam to the runway as they can with an ILS system. The VOR approach is based on radio navigation signals from the Charlotte VOR radio station at the airport. The station, located at the far end of Runway 36, broadcasts signals that permit an aircraft to fly to or from the station on any of the 360 points of the compass. A pilot who wants to fly away from the airport on the 97-degree point of the compass, for example, need only tune in the station, set his cockpit sensing instrument and keep a needle centered. It is the same needle that Jim Daniels kept centered with the autopilot as Eastern 212 flew direct from Charleston to the Fort Mill VOR station south of Charlotte.

The VOR 36 approach at Charlotte, depicted on the small chart each pilot clipped to his chart table, specifies that the cockpit VOR receiver be set so the aircraft flies toward the VOR station with a compass reading of 353 degrees. With the cockpit instrument set, the pilot who tracks the 353-degree beam by keeping his needle centered properly will find himself over Runway 36 at Charlotte.

But the VOR 36 approach provides no radio guidance about when or how fast to lose altitude, so the pilots control that with their altimeters. The VOR 36 approach has a minimum descent altitude, called the MDA. Once established on the proper course to the airport, pilots descend through the clouds or rain or fog— whatever is hiding Runway 36—until they reach the MDA, which is 1,120 feet above sea level. Then they level out and never go below that altitude until the runway is clearly visible. Once clear of the obscuring weather, they descend and make a safe landing. If the pilots level out and reach the VOR station but never see the runway, the weather is too bad to land. They climb back up and attempt the approach again or go on to an alternate airport where the weather is better.

An ILS approach is called a precision approach because pilots can land in poorer weather conditions than when flying a nonprecision VOR approach. If the Runway 5 approach lights at Charlotte had been operational, Reeves and Daniels could have made an ILS approach. With as little as one-half mile visibility they could descend to 200 feet above the ground before deciding whether to land or to go around.

But the non-precision VOR 36 approach required three-fourths mile visibility. They could descend only to 394 feet above the ground—1,120 feet altitude above sea level.

Airplanes flying the VOR 36 approach at Charlotte cannot descend below 1,800 feet above sea level until they reach Ross Intersection, a point directly south of Runway 36 and 5.5 miles from the Charlotte VOR. Pilots established on the inbound 353-degree VOR radial know they are at Ross Intersection when their distance measuring equipment—DME—reads 5.5 miles.

As Eastern 212 approached Charlotte, the controllers' radar vectors turned the flight out to the right and then curved it around to the left, heading it west southwest, and then turned it back to north again. The airplane's flight path inscribed a great S across the ground. When Denny Hunter, the final radar controller, gave Eastern 212 the final right turn to a heading of 350 degrees and told the pilots they were cleared to make the approach, he had brought them to within two miles of intercepting the 353-degree radio beam. The pilots knew they had merely to latch onto the beam, keep the needle centered as they tracked it toward the airport, descend to 1,800 feet and go no lower until they reached Ross Intersection. Then they could begin a descent to a minimum altitude of 394 feet above the ground. If the runway wasn't in sight then, they would level, fly until they reached the VOR, and then climb upward and decide what to do next.

But a "missed approach" seemed a remote possibility. Patchy ground fog at Charlotte was common. The controller had told Piedmont 917 visibility off the runway was three miles. The pilots had yet to fly through a single billow of fog. It seemed unlikely they would do so. All signs pointed to a routine approach, what pilots call a "piece of cake" approach. Why, they could look out the window and see the ground through the broken fog.

About 55 per cent of all aircraft accidents occur during the approach and landing phase of a flight. In some years the figure has soared to 65 per cent. In 1971, for example, there were 2,250 such accidents. The National Transportation Safety Board examined the growth of accidents and projected 4,500 approach and landing accidents by 1981.

Studies show that the chances of an approach and landing accident are four times greater if visibility is restricted. In a study of U.S. airline accidents between 1966 and 1970 in which 560 people died in 91 crashes, investigators found 40 per cent were identified with the approach and landing phase of a flight.

Investigators also have compared approach and landing accident rates between precision and non-precision approaches. In one study of 900 approach and landing accidents worldwide, only 15 per cent occurred on runways served by an ILS or precision approach radar. The highest susceptibility for an approach and landing accident is in reduced visibility conditions during a non-precision approach. In almost every case pilots in non-precision approach accidents descend below the MDA before it is safe to do so.

Pilots' groups, airlines, safety organizations and others have long called for installation of ILS systems on all runways on which aircraft make landings in instrument conditions. But thousands of ILS systems would be required nationwide and cost hundreds of millions of dollars. That a major airport as busy as Charlotte has only one ILS runway is indicative of how unlikely it is that smaller airports will ever be equipped with one. A non-precision instrument landing approach based on a VOR station on the airport grounds or nearby is much more likely. The Air Line Pilots Association estimates there are 200 airports in the United States at which scheduled airliners land that have no ILS system.

When pilots fly below the minimum descent altitude and crash, government bureaucrats call it "controlled flight into terrain." It is one of the most perplexing aviation safety problems, and numerous remedies have been sought to alert pilots to dangerously low descent. Most remedies involve installing more equipment in the cockpit.

In October of 1972 an Eastern Airlines flight inbound from San Juan, Puerto Rico to New York over the ocean began its descent on autopilot. A check captain was aboard, observing the flight. A stewardess stuck her head in the cockpit door to ask that the pilots radio ahead and request a wheelchair meet the flight. During that distraction, the pilots forgot to disengage the autopilot and level out. "What are you trying to do, dive into the ocean?" the check pilot shouted when he discovered the error. At that moment the airplane was below 500 feet, more than thirty miles from the airport. It would literally have descended into the ocean in less than a minute. Two months later an Eastern Lockheed L-1011 jumbo jet crashed in the Everglades because the pilots didn't notice their autopilot had accidentally disengaged and the airplane had begun a gentle descent.

As a result, Eastern engineers designed a terrain warning system that sounds an alarm each time the airplane descends to 1,000 feet above the ground. The system is built around the radio altimeter, an instrument that bounces radar beams off the ground and continuously reads the airplane's altitude above whatever terrain is below. They designed the warning system so that if the aircraft descends on an ILS the warning does not sound. But any other time the airplane passes through 1,000 feet above the ground, the crew is alerted.

Officials from several departments within Eastern Airlines pondered what warning sound pilots should hear when the aircraft reached 1,000 feet. It was suggested that the autopilot disconnect warning—a whistling whoop—be used. One possibility was equipping each system with a "voice chip," a piece of electronic circuitry that would make a voice announce "one thousand feet." But each chip cost $1,000—too expensive. Finally, although there was opposition, the airline decided to use the already installed altitude alert system's beeper because pilots associate that sound with altitude control. As a result, each time an Eastern aircraft descended through 1,000 feet, the altitude alert beep sounded, not once, but continuously until a pilot reached out and hit one of the "ALT" buttons, silencing the alarm. It was the same beep a crew may have heard a dozen times already during the flight. Instead of welcoming it, Eastern pilots quickly grew to detest the alarm. It went off during every non-precision approach, distracting them. Sometimes it went off prematurely when the aircraft passed over a hilltop or ridge within 1,000 feet of the airplane, even though the airport might still be many miles away. Pilots learned to hit the "ALT" button so quickly that the terrain warning alarm was silenced before it uttered a complete beep. Eastern Airlines failed adequately to assess the human factors aspects of the new system, so its intent was defeated.

Only in recent months had the system been installed in most of the Eastern DC-9 fleet. Reeves and Daniels hadn't been flying with the terrain warning system very long, but they too had grown to dislike it.

When Eastern 212 began its turn to a heading of 350 degrees, turning back to the right to intercept the Charlotte VOR radial for the beginning of the VOR 36 approach, Jim Reeves looked out his side window to a strange sight—a tall tower with a round doughnut-shaped structure atop it sticking out of the fog. It wasn't a radio antenna. It looked somewhat like a pencil with a thick round eraser on top, or a lollipop protruding from the fog. The sun shone on it. White warning strobe lights flashed from its top. It was the observation tower of Carowinds, an amusement park south of Charlotte that boasted a monorail, a roller coaster and other "theme" amusements patterned after those at Disneyland and other more famous amusement parks. The doughnut-shaped ring rode up and down the tower, carrying sightseers 340 feet into the air to survey the countryside.

"There's Carowinds. I think that's what that is," Reeves said.

Daniels had begun to monitor his altimeter, set to height above the airport, and pay less attention to the captain's lower altimeter, set to altitude above sea level. The white sweep hand of Daniel's altimeter also unwound counterclockwise, one revolution per minute. 2,700. 2,600. 2,500. It registered altitudes 750 feet lower than the sea level altimeter.

Carowinds? Daniels took his eyes from the instruments and raised up in his seat for a better look outside. The airplane's bank for the turn and its protruding nose made it difficult to see. Through the left front window he could make out the tower— three, perhaps four miles away. It was an intriguing sight, sticking up from the fog like that.

"Yeah," he replied, returning his eyes to the cockpit.

"Eastern 212, you can . . . ah . . . resume normal speed. Tower one eighteen one."

Daniels checked the airspeed indicator: 165 knots. They were about ten miles from the airport. They still could speed up and arrive sooner. He settled his hands on the throttles again and eased them forward slightly, watching the EPR gauges carefully. Then he gave the pitch trim button a push and the buzzer sounded. He watched the vertical speed indicator, holding the 1,000-feet-per-minute descent. His eye failed to stop at the altimeter, which was passing through 2,300 feet.

Reeves had the microphone again.

"One eighteen one and 212 good day," he acknowledged, then switched to the new frequency.

"Hello . . . ah . . . Charlotte tower. It's Eastern 212 about five miles south of Ross."

"Eastern 212 continue number two."

The altitude alert sounded. Reeves hadn't reset the alert system after the airplane passed through 3,000 feet, so it had beeped at 2,750 feet above sea level. But they had been cleared to the approach, which meant they now were authorized to descend to 1,800 feet and remain at that altitude until passing Ross Intersection. They no longer needed the alert system. Neither pilot paid any attention to the beep.

Daniels' field elevation altimeter continued to unwind. 2,200. 2,100. 2,000. But the copilot didn't glance at it when the beep sounded. The radio navigation needle had begun to move, indicating momentary interception of the 353-degree radial that would carry them to the runway. He cursed mentally. Damn. He hadn't turned quite soon enough or fast enough and he'd flown through the radio beam. He finished the roll-out from the right turn and eased the airplane into the merest hint of a left turn, correcting to bring it back on the exact track.

"Delta 608, you're cleared to land," the tower controller said on the radio.

"Delta 608 cleared to land three six," the pilot replied.

Reeves bent over his chart table, studying the approach chart.

"Ross is five point five and eighteen hundred," he announced, reading the crossing altitude of 1,800 feet and the DME distance from the VOR, 5.5 miles.

Daniels thumbed his pitch control button again.

"A thousand," Reeves murmured, noting one thousand feet altitude above the Ross Intersection crossing altitude. But the stabilizer trim buzzer sounded at the same moment. It drowned out his altitude call.

Daniels now had the correct heading nailed down, the navigation needle centered. They were on track to Runway 36.

On the instrument approach charts used by Eastern Airlines, critical altitudes are given in two values—height above sea level and height above the ground. At Ross Intersection on the chart Reeves read, the crossing altitude of 1,800 feet above sea level is shown in boldface type. Beneath it in parentheses and in smaller, dimmer type, is the altitude above the airport runway—1,074 feet. Reeves called out 1,800 feet without specifying whether it was field elevation or sea level altitude. Daniels, who was now flying the airplane using only his altimeter set to field elevation, assumed the crossing altitude Reeves called was a field elevation altitude. So the copilot made a mental note to stop the descent, to level out when his altimeter read 1,800 feet. They would be 1,800 feet above the runway.

The captain continued to peer outside. Now he tugged at his right ear, a perplexed look on his face.

"Carowinds is . . . ah . . ."

Daniels raised up slightly again to take a second look. He vaguely shared the captain's perplexity. The radar vectoring confused him, too. Where were they?

"Ah . . . would that tower, would that tower be it or not?" Daniels asked. He thumbed the pitch trim button again.

"No. I ah . . ." the captain said, the pitch trim buzzer drowning his voice. "No, I don't think it is. We're too far, too far in. Carowinds is in back of us . . . I think." Reeves rubbed his chin thoughtfully. If Carowinds was behind them, then where were they? No. He was wrong. It was Carowinds.

"By God that looks like Carowinds. I know that," he said.

Daniels looked outside again. The tower could be seen more clearly now. They were nearly abreast of it.

"That Carowinds is supposed to be real nice," Daniels said.

"Yeah, that's what that is," Reeves said. He was certain now.

"Gear down, please, before landing," Daniels called.

"That's what it is all right," Reeves said, taking a lingering look out the side window as he reached across the control pedestal to grasp the landing gear lever. The rumble of the wheels extending could be heard and then the whistle of air past the nosewheel and the nosewheel well doors. Reeves reached above his head and hit the switch lighting the no smoking sign. The no smoking chime sounded.

Through all this Eastern 212 continued its descent. The sweep hands on the three altimeters steadily revolved about their dials as Reeves took the radio calls, as Daniels adjusted their speed and as the captain puzzled over the tower protruding from the fog.

Occupied elsewhere, Daniels hadn't consciously perceived his altimeter for some time—not since it had read 2,500 feet. He hadn't looked at it when the second altitude alert beep sounded. The hand continued to spiral. 2,200. 2,000. 1,800. 1,600. 1,400. 1,200. 1,100. 1,000.

At last the copilot's eyes stopped at the round face.

They caught the white sweep hand then flicked up to the airspeed indicator. They didn't pass over the drum that read thousands of feet. He didn't see the crosshatch on the drum indicating an altimeter reading below 1,000 feet.

Daniels' eyes saw only the sweep hand. It was midway between the nine and the zero. The last time he checked they were just below 3,000 feet. Now his mind registered Eastern 212's altitude above the Charlotte airport—1,950 feet. He had to level out at 1,800 feet. The copilot eased forward on the throttles, adding a bit of power. He pulled back on the control wheel, raising the nose. He glanced at the vertical speed indicator, it was falling off toward 100 feet per minute.

He checked his altimeter. Damn. He'd leveled off a little late. The sweep hand was midway between the six and seven. He'd wanted 1,800 feet and had gotten 1,650. Oh well. They'd be at Ross Intersection in a few seconds. Then they could go on down.

The thousand-foot terrain warning beep sounded. Reeves, who after hitting the no smoking switch on the overhead panel had looked out at the Carowinds tower again, reached out with his right index finger and in a single motion so swift and sure that it certainly was born of long practice, punched the "ALT" button and silenced the annoying sound before it even had completed the first one-second beep.

Jim Daniels didn't notice. He had no reason to notice. He knew their altitude—1,650 feet above the airport, though in fact they now were but 650 feet above it.

Captain Reeves noticed the warning, but not at a conscious level. Like a man who deliberately lights and smokes a cigarette and can't remember it afterwards, he unerringly reached out and silenced the only warning that could have alerted the two pilots that an altimeter had been misread by 1,000 feet.

All the visual and psychological cues he received from inside and outside the cockpit told him that all was well.

"Carowinds," he said thoughtfully, looking outside once again. "That's it." He nodded his head affirmatively.

CHAPTER TWENTY-EIGHT

7:32:10 A.M.

IN ROOM 138 OF THE Airport Holiday Inn in Charleston, a wallpaper mural of trees and leaves and distant hills and crumbling Grecian columns looked down upon the two double beds. An air conditioner mounted in the wall below the window whirred steadily, bathing the room in a cascade of cold air and dimensionless sound. The curtain was drawn and only faint cracks of light at its bottom lit the room. In each bed a man slept, ready to rise and begin another day of business, waiting for the wake-up call on the telephone between the beds, the call that hadn't come.

Guy Henderson was twenty-eight, short and slender with muscular legs, a dynamic, nervous, demanding man with sun-bleached blond hair. He spent his weekends in Charlotte boating and waterskiing on the Catawba River. He was president of Concrete Drilling and Sawing, Inc. "We drill holes" was the company motto. Three years before he and his father had parted ways—but only in their business dealings—and Guy, whose personality demanded that he be in charge, that his hand always grasp the helm, took $6,000 in equipment and struck out. It was a test and he succeeded. Soon he would bill a quarter of a million dollars a year.

Steve Moore was a contrast in personality, a rural boy from the mountains of western North Carolina, a slow-talking, strong, deliberate man with brown hair and a moustache, an engaging smile. He was Guy Henderson's brother-in-law and his right hand at Concrete Drilling and Sawing, Inc. The two men were close friends as well as brothers-in-law and business associates. They had come to Charleston on business and were due in Charlotte that morning for a business meeting with Guy's father. Guy's company was to have additional autonomy and they were to sign the necessary legal papers. Steve would be given a small percentage of the company's stock in recognition of the hard work he had put into the Hendersons' affairs. But Guy and Steve hadn't always been close friends.

Guy and Steve had been heavily into drag racing at one time, four and five years before when Steve first came to work for the Hendersons, when Guy hadn't been married long to Elaine and Steve had just begun dating Roberta, Elaine's sister. The trouble between the two men began with problems at work. There were some troublesome drilling jobs. And then Steve's brother, who also worked for the Hendersons, was drafted. When he quit, Guy became angry because Russell hadn't given enough notice. Reports of Guy's anger and what he had said to Russell about quitting reached Steve, garbled in secondhand retelling. Steve dated Roberta, but he saw one or two other girls occasionally. That angered Guy, who took it as an insult to his sister-in-law.

Each Saturday they unloaded the coolers from the drilling trucks, filled them with beer and ice and went to the drag strip. Guy had a '69 Chevelle with headers and heavy valve springs that he ran as a stock dragster. Another man who worked for him ran a '70 Chevelle in gas class. They drank beer all day Saturday and Sunday, racing their cars, working under the hood, jacking them up, tinkering underneath, racing their engines, peeling rubber on the asphalt, drinking beer.

Steve came to the drag strip disgruntled about how Guy had treated his brother. Guy was too pushy, too demanding of those around him. Steve drank beer. Guy drank beer. Slowly they worked their way through the coolers of beer and ice. Steve's anger mounted with each beer. The two men could feel the tension building between them—little remarks, an occasional meeting and then quick diversion of the eye.

Finally, Steve could contain himself no longer. Guy lay under his car, just his feet sticking out. Steve leaned down.

"You think you're pretty fucking smart don't you?" he said.

"What?"

"Think you're pretty fucking smart. Mr. Big Man. That's who you think you are."

Guy scrambled from beneath the car, brushing dirt from his sweat shirt. He glared at Steve.

"Just forget it, shithead," he shouted. "I've had enough of your shit today. Always just hangin' 'round, hangin' 'round. Well, fuck you. I'm goin' home. I don't have to stay here and listen to your poor boy shit."

He turned and slammed down the Chevelle's hood and walked to the car door.

"Just shove it up your ass, Steve."

Steve grabbed Guy's arm in a viselike grip. Guy, who was smaller, exploded. He brought his free hand around in a wide arc, catching Steve in the chest while he wrenched his other arm free. Steve grunted at the blow and stepped back. With a flying leap Guy launched himself at Steve's middle, catching him in the gut with one shoulder and carrying them both to the ground, Guy on top. He pummeled Steve about the face and chest with his fists until Steve rolled away and scrambled up. They circled each other warily, their fists up, each watching for an opening.

"Where do you get off talking to my brother like that, you prick? You think you run everybody."

"Up yours, fella. How do you think I like you going out with Roberta? A nothing like you. Why don't you just fuck off."

Steve's fist shot out, grazing Guy on the cheek. Guy bobbed in with a left jab and then caught Steve on the shoulder with a right hook. Steve replied with a jab that caught Guy just above the left ear. He reeled back and someone grabbed him. They had Steve, too. "All right, you guys. Cool it," a voice said. It was over. Guy climbed into his car and roared away, spraying gravel.

The following Monday, Guy's father fired Steve. "Guy's my son," Mr. Henderson explained, the pain he felt obvious in his face. "I can't have you here if there's bad feeling between you."

Steve gathered his gear and left, avoiding Guy. They ignored

each other in the weeks following, often going to elaborate ex-
tremes to avoid meeting, even though Steve now planned to marry
Roberta and become Guy's brother-in-law. But one evening three
months later Guy and Steve found themselves helping move some
of Roberta's furniture. They were polite but pointedly cool with
one another. Neither spoke. But as they grunted with the furniture,
forced to communicate about who would lift this corner and who
that corner, straining with the heavy pieces, their animosity faded
away in the sweat. They finished, left Elaine and Roberta and
went off to a bar where they became deliciously, disgustingly
drunk. Steve had gone to work for Duke Power Company by then.
He remained there for a year after that. But one night Guy asked
Steve to come to work for his new company. Steve immediately accepted. The company prospered. Now the two shared that peculiar
bond that develops between men who have exchanged blows in
anger.

The sleeping men didn't know it yet, but the overlooked wake-
up call meant their legal paperwork in Charlotte would have to be
postponed. The next flight out wasn't until 11 A.M.

CHAPTER TWENTY-NINE

7:32:15 A.M.

COLLETTE WATSON HURRIED up the aisle.

"May I have your cup, please?" "Cup, please." "May I have your cup?" "Through with your cup? Want me to take that napkin too?"

Row by row she worked through the front half of the coach section to the row where the man sat with his two sons.

"Is it cool enough? Could you drink it?" she asked the younger boy. He smiled, mumbled something with an embarrassed look at his brother and handed her the empty cup with a napkin crumpled up inside. Whatever he said, she sensed it meant "Thank you."

Collette had flown the same DC-9 sequence the two days before —on Monday and Tuesday. She learned Monday how rushed the two stewardesses inevitably became during the short hop from Charleston to Charlotte as they hurried to complete the beverage service. So this morning while on the ground in Charleston she did as much as possible in advance. It paid off. The service went quickly. There were little problems, of course, always were.

In coach the boy had asked for hot chocolate. Hot chocolate! If it had been an adult, she might have put on her best sugar and honey South Carolinian voice and said, "I'm sorry, sir. We just don't have any hot chocolate. Could I get you something else?"

But it was a twelve-year-old boy. He asked so politely, so plain-tively, that Collette promised hot chocolate first chance she got.

She saw him watching each time she moved up or down the aisle, waiting expectantly. Finally she went to the galley and mixed the hot drink. By then it was late and she and Eugenia Kerth began collecting empty cups and squaring away the galley. The chocolate was too hot. What if she put some ice in it? she asked. Great, he replied. She did and he downed the cup in a few gulps.

Collette smiled as she hurried back to the galley to help Eu-genia. She loved her work when she could help like that, give pleasure, bask in the glow of genuine appreciation. The drunks, the blowhards, the pukers, the lover boys, the demanding, the rude and the pushy . . . well, they were part of the job.

"Boy, just made it," Collette sighed in the galley, leaning up against the wall for a moment. "I'll make the announcement, you check their seat belts and we're all set."

Collette Watson was the senior flight attendant. She joined East-ern Airlines in 1968—in fact, six years to the day before this flight —and Eugenia Kerth joined a year later. They had never flown to-gether, had met only that morning in Atlanta. But they took a quick liking to one another. Each was married and had no chil-dren. They lived only a few miles apart south of Atlanta. Each came from a close family.

Eugenia Kerth—high school homecoming queen, co-captain of the cheerleaders, teen board member—once wanted to be a doctor. Her grades were good in high school in Atlanta, but she did poorly in college in Augusta. Chemistry, biology and physics weren't her forte. After a year she transferred to Georgia State in Atlanta and worked as a department store sales clerk. She decided to become an airline flight attendant, was rejected by Delta as too short at five-two. But Eastern hired her on the strength of her languages—fluent Spanish and conversant French. She was born in Argentina, came to the United States as a small child and was naturalized only after joining Eastern. She met her husband in a pizza parlor in Alexandria, Virginia, while based in Washington with Eastern.

Collette was taking driver's license pictures in Columbia, South Carolina, commuting each day from her hometown of Batesburg, when a cousin who had been rejected by the airlines persuaded her to apply. The idea of becoming a stewardess seemed glamorous and sophisticated to a small-town girl.

She drove to an interview in Columbia and then five days later received a letter inviting her to a second interview in Atlanta. A ticket to Atlanta—her first airline flight—was enclosed. She flew from Columbia to Charlotte and transferred to an Atlanta flight. On the approach into Charlotte, the sudden rumble of the landing gear letting down startled her and she jumped up from her seat with a little cry. Passengers craned their necks and a lady across the aisle laughed out loud. Lady, if you only knew where I was going, she thought ruefully, her cheeks burning.

In Atlanta her heart thumped violently and she felt giddy sitting in a chair on one side of an imposing desk looking at an elegant woman who thumbed through her file. They chatted about inconsequential things and then the woman abruptly asked, "Collette, how would you like to come to work for us?" She wanted to jump up and scream, cry, hug the woman. She was the beauty contest winner at the moment of victory. "I'd like to very much," she answered demurely.

Her father, mother, little sister, Aunt Rae, Aunt Dot and some cousins waited at the airport in Columbia. They shouted and laughed and cheered and cried and generally made a spectacle of themselves. Local girl makes good.

She earned $378 a month plus a living allowance during the five-week training course in Miami. They wore heels, hose, dresses and gloves. They sat properly, ate properly, acted properly. It was like going to church every day. They studied all facets of the flight attendant's job. They even practiced evacuating airplanes, and they went on actual flights, wearing a pin that said "trainee," and served real passengers. She was based six months in Miami after graduation and then came to Atlanta. She and Mike had grown up together in Batesburg and dated through high school. Not long after her transfer to Atlanta they married.

Flight attendants who stay with their jobs do so because they love to fly, because they find satisfaction in a peripatetic life that telescopes time and distance. Periodically they have bouts with fear, vow to quit.

"Everybody goes through a period now and then," Eugenia

said. "They think, 'Well, gee, nothing has ever happened to me. It's all been so routine and nice, surely it's going to happen on this trip.' And maybe for a month or so you think about it on every trip. And if the weather is bad, that makes it that much worse. But it goes away. It's never enough to make me want to stop flying."

Collette lost her nerve during her first Christmas season.

"There had been some threats against the airlines, you know, bombs. The threats had said twenty airliners would crash during the Christmas season. I was in Miami then. Eastern had security agents sleeping on the planes. We went out there one morning and here came the security men getting off the darkened airplane with their blankets. Spooky.

"I thought, Ugh. This is no fun. I don't want to fly. So we had just taken off going to the Bahamas from Miami and when they raised the landing gear we lost one of the doors of a wheel well. There was this horrible rattle and a shaking. It scared me so bad. I just knew it was fixing to blow up.

"On that same trip I went back to Miami and then on to Chicago with a layover and check-in about three A.M. On the way to Indianapolis we lost an engine. It was a Boeing 727. Then on the way out of Indianapolis we lost another engine. I don't know if it was the same engine. It was a horrible icy winter day. It all really scared me. I mean, you know, bomb threats and two engine failures on the same trip.

"And when I got home for the holidays, fortunately I was able to go home for the holidays that year, I said, 'I'm not going to fly any more. I'm going to quit.' I was really scared. But my mother and Mike got me to go back. They've always been good encouragement to me, always tell me to go back. So I was back two weeks later and thought nothing of it."

The National Transportation Safety Board classifies airline accidents as "survivable" and "non-survivable," based on the stresses placed on passengers during impact. In the survivable accidents, flight attendants determine how many people walk away. Collette Watson and Eugenia Kerth had been trained to take charge in an emergency. They had practiced evacuating an airplane. They knew how to open the emergency exits, what to do if the airplane ditched at sea. They had watched films, listened to discussions,

read books and been thoroughly indoctrinated about their emergency duties. In the first seconds after a "survivable" accident, with
the aircraft almost always on fire, the lights gone, the cabin filled
with thick, acrid smoke that hides the exit signs, with frightened
passengers crowding the aisles, what they said and did would decide how many passengers lived. It was a burden each flight attendant carried, part of the job, like the vomiting passenger.

The NTSB studied "survivable" airline accidents between 1964
and 1970 and found that 43 per cent of the flight attendants in accidents occurring during takeoff were either killed or severely injured. In accidents that occurred during a landing, 48 per cent of
the flight attendants were killed or severely injured.

For several years the Association of Flight Attendants, the
union that represents stewardesses at most U.S. airlines, has cam-
paigned to have their members given safer seats on airplanes. In
most airliners, flight attendants are relegated to fold-down seats
bolted to cockpit doors, cockpit bulkheads, rear cabin doors, galley walls and storage closets. The seats frequently have no armrests or back or neck supports to absorb energy during an accident
and protect the flight attendant. By federal law, passengers are
well protected; flight attendants are not.

In the DC-9, Collette sat on a fold-down seat—a sort of ledge,
bolted to the back of the cockpit wall beside the cabin door. She
had no armrest or shoulder harness. Eugenia had a similar fold-
down seat attached to the rear emergency escape door in the very
back of the airplane. The door opened into a tunnel through the
tail cone of the airplane to another escape hatch. Her seat, too,
had no armrests or shoulder harness. Collette's and Eugenia's seats
were less likely to withstand the rigors of a crash than those of the
passengers they served.

Surviving an airline crash up to the moment at which the aircraft comes to rest often has little relation to the number of lives
finally lost. Intense fires, fed by ruptured jet fuel lines, erupt immediately, even as an aircraft is skidding to a halt. Flames can engulf
a cabin in seconds, filling it with dense smoke that blinds passengers. The cabin materials burn quickly, giving off large quantities
of carbon monoxide and hydrogen cyanide. Exit signs aren't visible. Emergency lighting systems often aren't bright enough. Evacu-

ation slides may malfunction and emergency exits may not open—often because panicky passengers neglected to read the safety information card in their seat-back pocket and then paid scant attention to the bland safety announcements flight attendants give at the beginning of each flight. Airlines traditionally have been hesitant to have flight attendants issue tough attention-getting safety instructions. Many stewardesses prefer stronger safety messages.

As a result, the airline passenger who boards an airliner and doesn't consciously spend a moment or two contemplating his course of action in an emergency—reading the emergency instructions card, noting the exits and studying how to open them—asks for trouble if an accident occurs. To imagine what an airliner evacuation might be like, a passenger need only look about when the airplane arrives at the gate and all the passengers stand up and crowd the aisle, eagerly waiting for the door to open. Then imagine that the aircraft is on fire, that the cabin is filled with smoke and frightened people are screaming and wailing in panic. At that moment, the passenger has thirty seconds in which to save his life.

In private moments Collette Watson and Eugenia Kerth each had wondered how they would react in an emergency, whether they would really think of the passengers and not themselves, whether they would remember their duties, whether people might die because they failed. These ponderings were reserved for sleepless nights in layover motel rooms. Right now they concentrated on fastening every galley drawer and compartment and latch, making the pre-landing announcement, checking the cabin, getting into their fold-down jump seats in time.

Collette stood at a small control panel on the wall beside the cockpit door, holding the microphone. Eugenia stowed the last container, latched the last door. The no smoking chime sounded, a combination bell and buzzer heard over the public address system.

"Ladies and gentlemen," Collette began. "The captain has turned on the no smoking sign and lowered the landing gear for our final approach into Charlotte. At this time please make sure your seat backs and tray tables are in their full upright position and that your seat belts are securely fastened. Please observe the no smoking sign until you are well within the terminal building. Thank you."

There was a rustling, a bustle up and down the cabin. Eugenia started down the aisle, touching the back of each aisle seat as she went, mentally ticking off each row. Right, left, right, left. She looked at the waist of each passenger for the seat belts and the buckle, checked the tray tables and seat backs, watched for a brief case that might have crept from underneath a seat into someone's lap or under someone's feet.

She stopped by a man in a naval officer's uniform.

"Will your seat back come up any more?" she asked. The man pressed the armrest button and leaned forward, but nothing happened. She leaned over and grasped the seat back and gave it a tug. It moved into place.

"There," she said, moving on down the aisle, left, right, left, right.

"Will you fold your tray table up now, sir?" she asked a man.

"Seat back all the way up, please. Thank you."

Someone handed her a coffee cup from which a soggy napkin and a plastic spoon protruded.

"Thank you."

She reached the rear of the cabin, folded down her seat and buckled the belt. It was her job in an emergency to open the hatch, lead her passengers across a metal grating catwalk in the cavernous tail cone and out a second hatch to safety.

In the front of the cabin, Collette folded down her seat and fastened the belt. She sat with her feet and knees together and her hands folded on her lap. The rear flight attendant wasn't on public display during the landing, but the forward attendant always was. It wasn't uncommon to sit on the front jump seat and gaze down the aisle to see several male heads casually leaning out, contemplating the flight attendants who sat there, flying backwards, waiting for the wheels to touch the concrete and the engines to roar as the thrust reversed.

CHAPTER THIRTY

7:32:35 A.M.

LIKE PILOTS, AIR TRAFFIC controllers chat as they direct the aircraft moving through their sectors of airspace. "Here's how I look at it," Pete Hogan instructed beginning controllers who came under his wing at the Charlotte tower. "You can control traffic and carry on a conversation about something else. But when it gets to the point you need to drop that conversation, you'd better know when to cut it off. Because air traffic control is the type of career field you need to be concentrating on your work. And if you don't, then you're looking for trouble."

Pete Hogan. His grandmother wanted her new grandson to bear the name Larry. His father preferred William. His mother liked Pete. They compromised. He became William Larry Hogan, but everyone called him Pete.

Pete Hogan and Al Hare had taken a liking to one another when Hare reported for check-out on the local controller position in the tower cab under Hogan's tutelage. They chatted about their work, their experiences, their roots, two North Carolinians, one from the flatlands, the other from the western mountains. Hare monitored the inbound aircraft and Hogan watched and listened.

"I joined the service in 1965," Hogan was saying. "Quit high school halfway through the eleventh grade."

"Yeah," Hare said.

"Charlotte tower, Piedmont 917 with you. We're showing . . . ah . . . Ross."

"Piedmont 917's cleared to land, Runway three six," Hare replied, glancing at the Brite radar, noting the target and data block just outside the three-mile marker on the screen.

"O.K. Runway in sight out here."

Hogan, like Hare and a dozen or more controllers in Charlotte and thousands of controllers throughout the FAA, had gotten his air traffic control initiation at Keesler Air Force Base in Mississippi.

"The first day of school at Keesler, this instructor came in and was asking about education," Hogan continued. "And there was several boys in there with from one to three years of college. But no graduates. So he asked if anybody didn't finish high school and I was the only one who volunteered his hand."

They stood side by side peering southward. Each caught sight of the Piedmont DC-9 at the same moment, about two miles away. In unison their heads turned to the Brite, confirming that the aircraft they sighted was the radar target now at the two-mile mark, Piedmont 917. They checked only the aircraft number on the data block. They had no reason to note the ground speed or the altitude. The DC-9 drew steadily closer.

"Anyway, this instructor told me, right there in front of the whole class, he told me that high school dropouts didn't make it through because it was such a hard career field."

"Yep. Yeah," Hare said, chuckling and nodding his head in recognition. "Those bastards. That's the way they are."

"Tower, Delta 608 over Ross for three six."

Both heads turned again to the Brite. They could see the Delta target at the five-mile mark.

"Delta 608. O.K.," Hare replied. He would wait until the Piedmont aircraft was closer to touchdown before issuing a landing clearance to the Delta DC-9.

"You've got the lights turned up haven't you?" the Delta pilot asked.

"Yes, sir. You should be able to see it three to four miles." The runway lights brightness control was on step 5.

"Well, that instructor was probably trying to motivate your ass," Hare said.

"Well, I don't know if he said it to motivate me or not, but it sure did. I was determined to show him. I finished the class with the highest grade average, including the college boys, and right after that I finished my high school work in the Air Force and got a diploma."

The Piedmont DC-9 steadily bore down on the runway, closer and closer, lower and lower. They could see the flashing red lights on fuselage, top and bottom. The landing lights were on. The gear was down, extended like the outstretched legs of a hawk settling gently onto the top of a fence post.

"Now I'm going to Biscayne Southern College. Guess I'll try for an associate degree in business management. Got better than a three point grade average so far," Hogan added.

He watched the DC-9. "I'm not as dumb as my education record makes it sound like."

Hogan trained at Keesler. Then he went to Craig in Alabama, where they were training pilots, gearing up for Vietnam. He shipped out for Thailand for a year and then to Polk in Louisiana and then—out of the Air Force and into the FAA.

"God, it was nerve-racking at times over there. If you sent five aircraft out, three of them would come back on emergency landings, all shot up. I worked some crashes.

"First one was a Skyraider, you know, an A-1. I was final radar, working him on a surveillance approach. No indication of a problem at all. Then two miles out on final I lost him. Just disappeared. So I went through my lost radar procedures. Called him. Told him to climb. Called him on the guard channel. He didn't acknowledge me.

"There was a thunderstorm out there on final, but that didn't mean nothin' to them boys. Didn't stop 'em from trying to land. 'Cause in Vietnam, being shot at all the time, hell, a thunderstorm was nothing. So the thunderstorm got him. You sit there and wonder if you did something wrong. But I was perfectly clean on that one. They played the tapes back and my phraseology was perfect. I can remember the squadron commander, a colonel. After he heard the tapes he come over and patted me on the back."

The U. S. Air Force. The all-jet air force. Hogan always chuckled when he heard that propaganda line. Sometimes they had
flown anything with wings over there.

"I was working one night and this A-26, which was really just a
modified B-26 from the Second World War, came along. I worked
him in the pattern and then on final. A real good approach. Right
down to the runway. It was raining. I got him down almost to the
runway and then I said, 'Take over visually. Tower one eighteen
one, or whatever.' I didn't have to monitor him any more. I was
through with him, so I took off my headset and had my mid-shift
stretch.

"We were in a van at the far end of the runway, maybe three
hundred feet from the runway edge, out in the bushes. You could
see each airplane on your scope as it landed and came down the
runway, about five thousand feet. I looked down at my scope and
saw this A-26 left of centerline, coming right at us. Well, I figured
maybe he'd had gear trouble or something at the last second and
was goin' around for another approach.

"I opened the door of the van and looked out and I just froze.
There he was, two giant propellers and landing lights comin'
across the bushes straight at us. No way he was going to miss us. I
learned later he landed and threw both propellers into reverse but
only one went in so he veered off the runway.

"Course you never know how you're going to react in a situation like that. I just froze. Just sat there and watched him come at
us. About a hundred and fifty feet from the van his nose gear hit a
hole and it flung him around and broke the whole nose off the airplane. Right at the cockpit.

"Then I came out of my trance. I was so scared that I went to
the direct line to the tower and said, 'Did he crash?' About that
time they rung the crash bell and all I could think about was a
five-hundred-pound bomb on that airplane exploding. We'd be
goners. So I shouted to a black staff sergeant who was sitting in a
corner of the van. 'Get out. Get out. It's gonna explode. Get the
hell out of here.' He came alive, his eyes as big as saucers. But I
didn't tell him what had happened. I just took off running, out of
that van and away from the airplane.

"I got clean away and the supervisor came up and asked if the pilots were O.K. And I told him that there was no way those pilots could have lived. The nose broke off right at the cockpit. About then the black staff sergeant came up. He was scared. But he was laughin' too. 'Na,' he said. 'They's O.K. Hogan jes tol' me to run. He didn't say which way. He didn't say why. So I ran toward the airplane and then I seed what happened and then I seed the pilots runnin' through the bushes with me right behind. They's all right. All I could see ahead of me runnin' was assholes and elbows. They's all right.'

"That was a very trying year for me over there. Always an emergency. Always shuffling traffic for an emergency. When I come back from overseas, my wife now, I was dating her then, she knows as well as anybody that I couldn't hardly drink a cup of coffee. I'd always have to hold it with two hands. Just the pressure. Took me about a year to get over it."

"Hello . . . ah . . . Charlotte tower. It's Eastern 212 about five miles south of Ross."

Again both controllers' heads turned toward the Brite. Piedmont 917's wheels were just touching the concrete. Delta 608's target was about three miles out. They could see a target about five miles behind the Delta aircraft. The data block said Eastern 212.

Hogan and Hare had no reason to examine the data block beyond confirming that the target was Eastern 212. They could have studied the numbers and seen that the aircraft was passing through 3,000 feet in its descent. They could have monitored the altitude of each airplane as it drew closer to the airport.

But they didn't. Procedures didn't require it. And if they had sighted an airplane lower than would seem normal that day, say an airplane crossing Ross Intersection 400 feet too low, they would only assume that the pilots had the runway in sight and, as procedures allowed, had begun further descent at their discretion for landing. Certainly if either controller had closely examined a data block and observed a dangerously low altitude, he would have called the aircraft and politely mentioned it, even if the pilot might think the controller intruded into his cockpit by doing so. But the pilots were sighting the runway, three, four, five miles out and descending at their own pace with no problems. The fog wasn't giving them trouble.

"Eastern 212, continue number two," Hare said. He turned to his left and watched Piedmont 917 slowing down on the runway. The thrust reverse buckets had opened at the rear of the DC-9's two engines, deflecting the jet blast forward, providing extra braking action. The spoilers on the wing tops were up.

"Nine seventeen turn left ahead. Contact ground control on point nine."

"O.K. Nine seventeen."

Hare glanced at the Brite. The Delta flight neared the two-mile mark.

"Delta 608 cleared to land."

"Delta 608 cleared to land, three six," the pilot replied.

"That's correct."

CHAPTER THIRTY-ONE

7:33:40 A.M.

ROLLING HILLS COVERED with poplars, gum trees, scrub pines and oaks extend southward from Douglas Municipal Airport. The hills are cut by brush- and vine-covered ravines, some of which have a trickle of water at the bottom of the dense foliage. Most are dry. Few have names.

It is an area in which agriculture, industrial manufacturing and suburbia co-exist, if nervously. The region, which slopes gently away from the airport toward the Catawba River, once was all farms and sharecroppers' cabins. That was before Charlotte's growth induced landowners to turn their backs on generations of ownership and sell out for subdivisions and industrial parks. Now the rolling hills are dotted with small manufacturing plants, warehouses and subdivisions—brick veneer frame homes set on one-quarter-acre lots and larger plots with room for a horse and a corn patch. There still are sizable tracts with nothing but trees and underbrush waiting for progress to push nearer. The skyscrapers of downtown Charlotte can be seen from the tops of many hills.

Five miles south of the airport and a quarter mile west of Interstate 77—close enough to hear the trucks rumbling southward to Columbia, South Carolina—the top of a knoll has been carved away and flattened by bulldozers, ripping out the trees and brush, cutting and filling, exposing the red clay, leveling the knoll into a football-field-sized plain. A development scheme of some sort began there but never matured. The flattened hill now is covered with weeds and brambles and a few pines that doggedly survived the machines. In the center of the plain is a boulder as large as a truck and flat on top, ample enough in size for a large family to spread a cloth and enjoy a picnic.

Airplanes frequently fly overhead, a thousand feet or more high. On the U. S. Geological Survey's topographic maps the boulder is 5.5 miles south of the Charlotte VOR, aligned on the 353-degree radial. The boulder, by coincidence, marks the general location of Ross Intersection. This is the point at which an aircraft flying the VOR 36 approach into Charlotte can begin to descend from 1,800 feet altitude above sea level for the final leg.

Interstate 77 is east of Ross Intersection, extending northward into Charlotte, skirting the west edge of the downtown business district. A half mile west of Ross Intersection, visible through the trees from atop the boulder, is a large automobile tire manufacturing plant. Noise from the factory drifts on the breeze through the trees to the boulder. A half mile further west is North Carolina Highway 49, known as York Road, extending northward into Charlotte, eventually becoming Tryon Street, downtown Charlotte's main street.

Two miles north on York Road, the York Wood Apartments sit on the slope of a hill. The sprawling eighty-nine-unit complex consists of brick and asbestos shingle two-story apartments with a slab of concrete at each back door, on which tenants pile their lawn chairs, bicycles and garbage cans beside small storage sheds. Rents are low, tenants change frequently, floorboards creak and carpets wear quickly. York Wood Apartments are workingman's apartments.

Across the road is a tract of trees and brush and an abandoned, decaying house and outbuilding contemplating collapse. The trees and brush climb the hill to its peak, where an old farmhouse with a sagging roofline, leaning porch and peeling paint sits back a few yards from the road. The pavement continues northward, dipping down the gentle north slope of the hill, passing the Charlotte pet cemetery on the right and a tar paper-covered sharecropper's cabin and a cornfield on the left. The cornfield extends a quarter mile back from the pavement to the lip of a ravine, a nameless dry ravine whose tangled bushes, vines, trees and weeds mark the perimeter of the farmer's efforts with his plow each spring.

On this morning patches of thick fog shrouded portions of York Road. The occasional early commuter using the two-lane road could race ahead for a quarter mile, then suddenly slide into a billow of the fog, his taillights glowing red in the mist as he hastily braked his car in the dangerously low visibility. The fog was thickest in the ravines, in the dips and hollows and creek bottoms, thinner on the hilltops. In the open areas, a hint of morning sun promised to burn the mist away.

Beside the pavement at the driveway entrance to the York Wood Apartments a gaggle of children began assembling about seven-fifteen to wait for the school bus. In September, when weather is still summerlike, when only the later sun and the browning leaves of the corn hint of approaching fall, and school has just begun, the waiting children romp playfully, shouting, arguing, teasing, pushing, accusing as they jockey for position in the line for the bus.

Ten yards away is the back door of the apartment of the York Wood's resident manager, Kathy Lawing, whose husband Tink is a Mecklenburg County parks policeman. Tink and Kathy lay in bed in the second-floor bedroom with the window open. The babble of children's voices slowly awakened them. They too had a child, a one-year-old boy still asleep in his crib in the next room. The young couple lay in that delicious state of dozing wakefulness before it's really time to climb from bed.

Suddenly the children began to scream, a frightened, despairing wailing and crying that knifed through the Lawings' somnolence, wrenching them abruptly awake.

At the same moment they heard an ominous whining, a high-pitched whistle, low at first but rapidly growing in volume, like the sound a falling bomb makes in a war movie. It approached them, trailed by a roar that steadily grew more intense.

An insistent banging began at the back door below the window, followed by the frightened howl of a child. It was David, a tenant's son. They recognized the voice.

"Kathy. An airplane. Kathy. An airplane," he screamed.

Kathy threw back the covers and leaped from bed, the terror in the child's voice knotting her stomach. The roar was intense now, drowning out the children's frightened voices, blotting out her surroundings, rattling the windows, shaking the nightstand. Her heart pounded. She stood, frozen, immobile. She wanted to clamp her hands over her ears and scream and scream and scream. The reading lamp on the nightstand toppled with a crash. From the corner of her eye she could see out the window. Across the road, 300 feet away, she sensed the passing movement of a massive object. The roar was at its loudest. In the next room the baby's wailing burst into her consciousness.

"Tink. Tink," she screamed, running into the hall and taking the stairs two at a time. "Get up. Get up." David was still banging on the back door.

CHAPTER THIRTY-TWO

7:33:56 A.M.

EXPERIENCED PILOTS HANDLE their airplanes differently when not flying in clouds or rain or snow or fog, when they can see outside the cockpit, when they can see the ground and expect to sight the runway three or four miles out during a letdown toward patchy ground fog. Experienced pilots scan their instruments differently then.

When a pilot can see the ground, when he can look out of his cockpit and have a sense of the horizon, even if portions of the ground are obscured, he flies more by the traditional seat of his pants. He uses visual cues gathered outside the cockpit to keep his wings level, to gauge where he has placed the nose of the aircraft in relation to the horizon to give him the correct amount of climb or descent or to hold the aircraft level. He visually monitors his altitude and descent rate, using the instruments to confirm the visual cues.

When descending toward a runway that he can see, or expects to see momentarily, the pilot in visual conditions pays less attention to altitude. Using long experience, even in a heavy, fast airplane like a DC-9, the pilot descending toward a runway gauges his altitude by watching the runway. The only critical instrument in the cockpit, the dial to which he must constantly return to check his approach, is the airspeed indicator. A pilot flying a visual approach must manage his airspeed carefully. He mustn't let it get too low. He mustn't come in too fast or he'll overshoot the runway. If a pilot knows his airplane, has amassed hundreds of hours flying it, you could cover every flight instrument in the cockpit except the airspeed indicator and you would likely see a smooth, faultless approach and landing, even in a DC-9.

Captain James E. Reeves and First Officer James M. Daniels had flown their DC-9 under an instrument flight rules flight plan, which required that they be under positive control of the air traffic control facilities along the way, and that they fly the prescribed approach to the Charlotte runways. But they hadn't encountered a single cloud or raindrop or fog bank. Theirs had been a visual flight all the way and they had little evidence it would end other than in visual conditions. They had heard the radio traffic—runway visible three or four miles out. Through the windows they could see the ground through holes in the fog below. The patches of fog obscuring the ground in front and to the sides of their field of vision did have a tendency to raise their horizon and, as a result, make them feel visually higher than they were. It was an effect Reeves and Daniels had read about but weren't conscious of at the moment. It didn't occur to them that it might be altering their perception of the distance to the ground.

So as they descended toward Douglas Airport, neither pilot scanned his instruments in the same way he would have if they'd been in thick clouds, their windshield battered by driving rain, the RVR at 2,400 feet and the ceiling measured at 300 feet. Daniels flew, concentrating on his airspeed indicator and the vertical speed indicator, so as to monitor the mix of power and nose angle to give a 1,000-foot-per-minute descent, which he would reduce to 500 feet per minute during the final phase of the approach. His attention also focused on the navigation radio needle, keeping the DC-9 on the 353-degree inbound radial. He watched the altimeter, but not as carefully as he would have in the clouds, because he knew he would see the ground—the runway—long before any inattention to the instrument might threaten their safety.

For his part, Jim Reeves was tired. He had a strong faith in his copilot. All the visual and audible cues he received, from inside and outside the cockpit, consciously and unconsciously, told him all was well. He too watched the altimeter, the airspeed indicator, the vertical speed indicator and the navigation needle. His copilot was on top of things.

When pilots descend in an aircraft they know well, when the descent is just like thousands of others they have made, they have a feel for the descent. They know how fast the altitude will bleed away, how fast the sweep hand on the altimeters will unwind, even in the jet transports which climb and descend so fast. Only a significant distraction can upset that sense of altitude.

Reeves and Daniels had flown a perfect flight—caught every radio call, stayed precisely on course, met every altitude, called out every critical altitude just as the manual of procedures required. Then they rolled into the final turn, coming out of the radar vectors, intercepting the inbound VOR radial. And there, there was the Carowinds tower.

It was a strange sight, a startling apparition protruding from the fog. It arrested their attention. Reeves and Daniels long since had ceased to marvel at the beauty of the weather, of clouds and fog seen from the airman's vantage point. But the observation tower was unusual. They knew what it was. But it seemed to be in the wrong place in relation to their position after the radar vectors.

And in those sixty-seven seconds as Reeves studied the tower outside his windows and as Daniels watched it intermittently while he nailed down the inbound radial and leveled out to wait for Ross Intersection, the sweep hands on the altimeters made an extra turn that the pilots' now distorted sense of descent didn't detect. And when eyes flicked back to each pilot's upper altimeter, they stopped at the pointed tip of the sweep hand resting between the six and seven, didn't linger to see that the crosshatch on the drums had come into view, that the instruments read 650 feet, not 1,650 feet.

Thus an improbable coincidence came to pass. Each man independently misread his altimeter by 1,000 feet. It wasn't the first time such a coincidence has occurred. Their mutual error was as improbable as the three Boeing 727 pilots who climbed to 19,000 feet, thought they were cruising at 29,000 feet and then descended to 1,000 feet, thinking they were at 11,000 feet. Now for Eastern

212 it remained only to see how long the pilots would continue their approach before discovering the error.

Jim Daniels watched the DME window, the tenths of miles ticking off: 6.0, 5.9, 5.8, 5.7. They descended slightly, 200 feet per minute. Airspeed, 170 knots. The VOR needle centered.

Jim Reeves ran through the final before-landing checklist, glancing at the list clipped to the control wheel.

"Ignition," he said, reaching above his head and pushing the switches to the continuous position.

"No smoke." He already had turned the sign on.

"Radar's up and off," he said, checking two switches on the center control pedestal beside the small weather radar screen.

He glanced at the red landing gear handle on the edge of the center instrument panel. "Gear down." His eyes traveled up to the annunciator panel above the center windshield, the panel of small black squares which light up with verbal warnings. Every square was black, unlit.

"Annunciator panels clean."

He reached to the center control pedestal and grasped the spoilers lever, pulling it up into the armed position. When the wheels touched pavement, electrical circuits would sense the landing and raise the spoilers, flaplike devices on the top surface of each wing, reducing the wings' aerodynamic lift, helping the DC-9 stop more quickly.

Daniels thumbed his stabilizer trim switch again and the buzzer sounded. The copilot bent over the map table and studied the bottom of his VOR 36 approach chart. The minimum descent altitude was 394 feet. He musn't let the airplane go below 394 feet unless the runway was in sight.

"Three ninety-four," he called out.

"Got it," Reeves said.

The captain's eyes ranged over the instruments, pausing at the altimeter. The sweep hand was at the six: 1,600 feet. His eye moved on to the DME window in the corner of the navigation course indicator. He watched it. 5.6. Pause. 5.5.

"There's . . . ah . . . Ross. We can go on down now."

Daniels saw it too and had already begun to lower the nose. He pulled back gently once again on the throttles, reducing the engine power slightly.

"O.K. How about fifty degrees please?" he said.

Reeves reached across and pulled the flap handle down into the final notch, locking it there.

"Fifty," he acknowledged, and then picked up the microphone.

"And Eastern . . . ah . . . 212 by Ross."

"Eastern 212 cleared to land three six."

"Awright."

Both pilots were looking out the window, peering into the fog in the distance, studying the point where they expected to see the runway, three, four miles away. Reeves looked down and grasped the seat handle, moving his seat nearer the rudder pedals.

At that moment, for the first time during the flight, the DC-9 flew into a fog bank. The mist at once enveloped the cockpit completely, suddenly giving the light a ghostly white quality, a sterile eeriness. Simultaneously the pilots' eyes darted back to their instruments. Their eyes swept the instrument panels, peered at them with a new interest, a careful intentness. They could no longer see the horizon, or any visual cues that revealed their altitude. Daniels' gaze returned first to the flight director. Keep the wings level, hold the heading. Airspeed indicator 160 knots, decreasing. Vertical speed 300 feet per minute descent, approaching 400. The altimeter. Come down to 394 feet and level out.

"We're all ready," Reeves announced. "All we've got to do is find the airport," he quipped wryly. They were on course, on time, all set. The runway should come into sight any second.

Daniels saw the trees first, rushing at them through the fog, a blur of green, the brown of cornstalks and beyond that more trees. Thousands of hours of flying, years of training, hundreds of make-believe emergencies in cockpits and simulators commanded his hands. His left hand, resting on the throttle levers, shot forward, ramming the levers against the stops at the front of the pedestal, stinging his palms. At the same moment, his right hand came back with the control column, hard and fast, tight against his crotch. Full power. Nose up. Climb. Climb, you son of a bitch. The trees rushed at his face.

"Oh, oh. Damn," he screamed. But at the same moment, from a

detached perspective, as a distant observer of the catastrophe rushing at Eastern 212, a single thought flashed through his mind, over and over and over.

"The fucking FAA. The fucking FAA. The fucking FAA."

A single moaning shout of alarm and recognition and doom broke from Jim Reeves's throat, drowned out even as it began by a deafening, sickening grinding and tearing and crunching.

CHAPTER THIRTY-THREE

7:34 A.M. and Beyond

AT THE TARAGATE FARMS subdivision south of the Charlotte airport, in the upstairs master bedroom of a four-bedroom tract house, Kent Winslow, assistant airport manager, pulled his sports jacket from the hanger in the closet and shrugged his long arms into the sleeves. Downstairs his wife supervised three young girls who fussed with one another as they ate breakfast and prepared to catch the school bus.

He padded across the carpet to pocket some change lying on the dresser. Just as he reached out, the windows unexpectedly rattled and the muffled "karoomph, karoomph" of a distant explosion startled him. An explosion? He cocked his head in puzzlement as if to catch further sounds. He furrowed his bushy eyebrows.

"Kent? What was that? You didn't drop something, did you?" his wife called from the kitchen.

"No. Sounded like an explosion. Not too far away," he answered.

He went to the east-facing window and gazed at billows of fog in the distance catching the morning sun. At the horizon, a mile or less away, a thin streamer of black smoke rose out of the fog. Suddenly the wisp of smoke thickened, grew blacker, spread out over the top of the fog. An explosion and a fire?

He sat on the bed and dialed the telephone on the nightstand. First his office in the terminal building. The secretaries didn't come to work until 8 A.M., but someone else might be there. He let it ring five times and then pressed the receiver button and dialed the airport maintenance shop, where the crew came to work at seven. Tommy Mason picked up on the second ring.

"Tommy? Kent. Is everything all right? We've had an explosion somewhere out here. Now I can see some smoke."

"Everything's quiet here."

"Well, we definitely felt something. I heard it."

"Haven't heard anything. You say an explosion?"

"Yeah. Rattled my windows. And now I can see some smoke."

"Oh, my God. We've bought the farm," Jack Toohey shouted. A thousand hands seemed to claw at him, pummeling, slapping, shaking, punching his body while the DC-9 cabin in front of him began to disintegrate. A cloud of debris filled the air. Papers, coats, hats, brief cases, seat cushions, carpet, overhead racks, wires, windows and panels washed over him amid a cacophony of screams and wails and shrieks and rippings and tearings as trees grabbed at the airplane and gouged holes in it, as they skidded across the ground, bumping, bouncing, coming apart.

The hands beating at his body lessened and Toohey sensed the fuselage beginning to come to rest. He gasped in fright. Rolling down the aisle, with a great "whoosh," reaching from floor to ceiling, taller than he, was an orange fireball. He felt the heat on his face, knew the flames that washed over him were singeing his eyebrows and hair, scorching his skin and the arm he threw up.

Suddenly they were stopped, stilled. The banging and crunching and grinding ceased, replaced at once by the roar of the fire, and panicky screams. His seat seemed canted backward. The two officers next to him were gone. Ahead he could see only flames, scorching flames, the heat growing more intense. He was going to burn to death.

He looked down, fumbling with his seat belt. By his feet, to the right and back a bit, was a hole in the fuselage. The seat belt fell away and Jack Toohey bent down, reached the hole, grabbed a tree branch, ducked his head into the hole and tumbled through the opening, falling into dense underbrush, into thorns that tore at his skin and clothes. He scrambled frantically through the vines and brush and briars to an open space and began grabbing handfuls of leaves and beating them against his smoldering socks, snuffing out the flames. Then he fought his way further from the wreckage, away from the crackling flames and the screams, suddenly emerging from the brush into a cornfield.

With a thundering sound like a gas oven lighting in a kitchen stove but much, much louder, the cabin erupted in flames. They surrounded Richard Arnold. "Hold your breath. Hold your breath. Hold your breath. Don't breathe the fire in," a voice inside him cried out. He held his breath. The sailor in the next seat was screaming, flailing at Arnold with his hands. Arnold's lap was covered with debris. Part of the overhead rack had collapsed into his lap.

Flames were everywhere. Still he held his breath. It was like swimming, like swimming in yellow water. The seat belt buckle was scorching his hand. He fumbled it loose. There was a hole above him, in front of him, a hole in the fuselage. He reached into it, feeling for something to grasp. Nothing. The debris held him in his seat. "This is what it's like to die. I'm going to die."

He reached into the hole again and grasped something and pushed off from the seat arm with his left hand and jumped. Suddenly, he was free, teetering on the edge of the broken fuselage, one shoe gone, standing on the trunk of a fallen tree. He tumbled into a thicket of briars, the thorns stripping the molten double-knit nylon clothes from his back and legs. He scrambled through the brush. To his amazement he could hear birds singing in the trees, interspersed with the screams.

Pete Hogan stared at the smoke. A trash fire? A pain suddenly began to gnaw at his stomach, growing larger, rising up into his chest. His eyes darted to the Brite. Eastern 212's data block was there, moving steadily nearer the airport. He looked closer. The tiny green triangle, the target itself, was gone. The data block was in "coast." The radar had lost the airplane, but the computer kept the data block moving, projecting where the airplane should be.

"Shit, that's no trash fire," Hogan burst out, stepping forward to the console, past Hare.

"Eastern 212. Charlotte tower. You have the runway in sight," he barked into his headset. He listened intently for a reply. The smoke was turning black now, thick black smoke, flattening out against the inversion layer. Hogan punched a button on the console.

"Hey final."

"Uh huh," Denny Hunter drawled.

"Eastern 212, Charlotte," Hogan called, while Hunter listened.

"Eastern 212, tower one eighteen one," Hunter called on his frequency. He listened. "Not on me," he told Hogan.

"Hey final?"

"Yeah?"

"There's a large bunch of smoke out there . . ."

Hogan stared at the smoke, still boiling up. Stay calm. Stay calm. Stay calm.

"We mighta lost 212 out there on final. Send Sturkey up to the tower right away."

"O.K."

They chuckled wryly later, looking back. It was the fastest Bill Sturkey had ever come up the tower stairs.

The woman sat screaming on the ground, amid the debris before the DC-9's smoking tail section which had broken from the fuselage and skidded down into the bottom of the ravine, lying on its side. She was burned. Already the swelling distorted her features. Fire fed by the jet fuel danced around her. Her screams mingled with those coming from the gaping hole in the tail where it had been severed from the fuselage. There were still people alive in there. There were bodies and pieces of bodies strewn through the brush and trees and Jim Stanley stepped on some and around some as he stumbled toward the frantic woman, fighting to keep from vomiting.

"Oh, God damn. Somebody help me," she screamed. The woman had either been thrown from the tail section or crawled from it. Jim Stanley shouted at her as he fought through the brush, shoving aside pieces of airplane.

Stanley had been hurrying to work in his dune buggy, a vehicle he'd built from Volkswagen parts, with a roll bar and no windshield. He'd been shaken by an explosion in the trees ahead as he drove north on York Road. Then the column of smoke billowed up. He turned into the wood opposite the York Wood Apartments, gunned his machine up beside an abandoned house and into trees, then backed out to the road when he couldn't get through. A big beefy man in a white T-shirt and jeans, wearing heavy work shoes without socks, appeared. He was a park policeman who lived in the apartments. He climbed into the buggy and clung to the roll bar as Stanley roared up York Road to the top of the hill and then whipped down into the narrow ditch and up into a field. He plowed through chest-high weeds and grass 200 yards or more to the lip of a ravine and slowed to a stop in the soft earth.

The broken remains of the jet lay before them, scattered down the ravine slope, on fire, dense smoke mingling with the thick fog, fire dancing over the ground, the smell of burning flesh mingling with the smoke and putrid odor of jet fuel, hanging heavy in the air. The airplane had hit in a cornfield to the left, and then plunged into the ravine, down the tree- and brush-covered slope. The trees sheared away the wings and broke the fuselage into three pieces. The midsection lay just below the crest of the slope, burning fiercely. The front of the airplane tumbled further down into the ravine, lodging itself finally in a thick grove of trees at the bottom. The tail section had skidded another fifty yards along the airplane's direction of flight, coming to rest on its side, the jet engines nearby.

"God, oh, God, somebody help me. Somebody help me," the woman in front of the tail cried.

Jim Stanley reached out and grabbed her arm. She was charred, blackened by the fire. He pulled on the arm and suddenly drew back in horror. The woman's burned flesh had come off in his hand, a loathsome jelly. He felt his stomach heaving and turned aside and bent over, his mouth filling with vomit. He vomited and

vomited. Willing his heaving stomach to cease, he gamely turned
back to the woman, seized her arm again, and pulled her away
from the flames and the hot metal, into an open space. He
straightened and looked about through the smoke and fog. He
could hear sirens. Other passersby arrived now. Some, like him,
ran desperately through the brush trying to help the broken and
burned bodies strewn about. Others walked calmly about, offering
no aid, merely staring with morbid curiosity. Stanley's eyes came
to rest on an object in the bushes nearby. It was a leg, a leg completely clothed, with pants, sock and shoe, lying alone in the
brush.

Jim Daniels watched the small finger of flame beneath his legs
steadily reaching upward toward the cockpit, creeping through the
fractured floor, licking electrical wires and insulation and grease
and oil. He was paralyzed. Only his left arm and hand seemed able
to move. The pain grew worse.

He looked at his legs, familiar, but strangers. He couldn't feel
them. His legs seemed pinned under the instrument panel, each
one doubtlessly broken. His pants were torn open and one knee-
cap had been struck. He could see the shattered bone through the
torn flesh. It looked like someone had smashed an ice cube with a
hammer. There were more flames now. Smoke drifted through the
cockpit and out the open side window.

The side window. Moments before the stewardess had screamed
at him from the other side of the cockpit door. The impact had
knocked the door lock open, but the anti-hijack latch was bolted
from the inside. "Jim. Open the door. Open the door, Jim," she
had pleaded. Slowly he reached back with his left arm and undid
the latch. The stewardess and a passenger had climbed over the
captain's seat and jumped from the window into the brush outside.
The cockpit was canted, its nose resting against a barricade of
small trees.

The captain. Jim Daniels passed out as they plowed into the
trees, first one tree, then another whipping them to and fro. When
he awoke, Captain Reeves lay across the control pedestal, his head
by the flap handle, the rest of his body folded up in the mangled

seat and control wheel. "Jim?" the copilot called. He reached out to touch the captain and at that moment the older pilot seemed to sigh, a small bloody bubble forming in one nostril. The captain was dead.

The fire was much closer now, more flames. Daniels could feel the heat. The fire burned steadily upward toward the cockpit.

An immense sense of disappointment settled over him. I'm really going to hate to die, he thought. I'm not ready to die. It's finally happened. The fucking FAA will have my ass now. I'm going to hate to die.

He reached out with his left hand, stretching as far as he could across the radio console between the seats. He grasped the back of the captain's chair and pulled as hard as he could, squeezing his eyes shut in concentration and pain. Slowly, slowly, he pulled his frame sideways until he lay across the radios, his legs hanging limply, but free of the instrument panel. He rested, his chest heaving, gasping for short breaths. The smoke was thicker.

He turned sideways and craned his neck to look out the open cockpit window, his escape route, conscious of a rustling in the bushes, of voices calling. He fought the pain, concentrated on remaining conscious as the window shimmered in his blurring vision. Something was in the window. A man. Oh, God, don't make this man mad. Don't make this man mad. Here's your last chance. Don't make him mad.

"Sir," Daniels croaked. "Would you mind helping me out? I can't get out."

One after another the ambulances whipped down the driveway, the sirens moaning, red lights flashing, directed by the uniformed security officers, screeching to a halt in the covered driveway at the rear of Charlotte Memorial Hospital. Immediately each vehicle was surrounded by waiting doctors and nurses and television cameramen and newspaper photographers who moved as close as permitted to film the action as drivers leaped from their seats, swung the rear doors outward and swiftly but gently lifted out the wheeled stretchers and rushed them through the sliding doors.

Inside, the outpatient clinic waiting room had been cleared and

dozens of wheeled hospital stretchers and wheelchairs and large
carts of medical supplies and linens moved into place. Phase II of
the hospital disaster plan had been activated, preparing the hospital to receive from fifty to seventy-five crash victims. Staff doctors
and private doctors who happened to be making patient rounds
rushed to the clinic waiting room, ready to go to work as the flood
of injured arrived.

The ambulances came in a flurry. The patients were rushed inside for initial examination and then referral. Most were burned,
some quite badly. Hospital staff members gasped but plunged
grimly on when they recognized one of their own, Dr. William
Shelley, seriously burned.

Then abruptly, no more ambulances came. The doctors and
hospital officials and orderlies and nurses standing in the drive
could hear no more sirens wailing in the distance, growing closer.
They waited. Then word came from the Emergency Room via the
police and hospital staff physicians who had rushed to the scene of
the crash. No more survivors. The all-clear code message sounded
throughout the building. "Attention, all interns, residents and hospital staff physicians. The briefing in the ground floor doctors'
lounge has been canceled."

Orderlies began removing the stretchers and wheelchairs from
the clinic waiting room.

"How many did we get altogether?" someone asked at the elevators as the supply carts were wheeled aboard.

"Twelve. I heard somebody say they took a stewardess to Presbyterian. So I guess there must of been thirteen who weren't
killed."

"How many were on the plane?"

"I don't know. I heard Eastern told us to be ready for as many
as seventy-five people."

Mark Ethridge strode boldly to within ten feet of the charred
seat sitting in an opening amid the trees and brush. He had heard
firemen talking about it, the charred seat in which a charred
woman held a charred infant, both burned beyond recognition. He

forced himself to look, to study the details, to be a careful and accurate observer. He moved a step closer.

Mark Ethridge was a reporter for the Charlotte *Observer*. He and Bill Fuller, another newspaper staff member, had raced to the scene south of Charlotte, abandoning their car when they could go no further in the traffic and the police roadblocks. They walked a circuitous route through someone's watermelon patch to the farmhouse atop the hill by the cornfield. Police had set up a command post there and permitted no one beyond, not even reporters. He hung about the farmhouse yard, interviewing police, firemen, anyone who trudged up from the ravine.

Then an ambulance arrived, not to carry away corpses or the survivors, but to carry in refreshments for the workers at the crash. A woman's auxiliary had thoughtfully loaded the ambulance, now parked in the farmhouse driveway.

Ethridge stuck his head in the window. Please, could he get in the back and go in with them. I'm with the *Observer*. I have to get down there. If I don't get down there, I'll be fired when I get back to the office. My editor will fire me. Please, I've got to get in there. The old reporter's trick worked, and he hid under a stretcher as the ambulance passed through the police line and bounced down the rutted path through the field.

He walked through the trees and brush, now considerably beat down by the firemen and rescuers, staring in horror at the gore.

"Careful where you walk," someone warned. "Some places you take a step and the ground just spurts blood."

Mark Ethridge studied the seat and its charred remains. It definitely was a human figure, probably a woman, holding something, cradling it just as a mother would cradle a baby. Yes, it was another human form she held in her arms. He turned away, perspiring. He swallowed with difficulty, making a gulping sound.

Elaine Henderson sat on the edge of the king-size bed in her bedroom choking back loud sobs as she listened to the telephone ringing at the other end of the line. Guy and Steve were on the airplane. Certainly dead. They said they would be on it. They had a morning meeting. She collapsed on the bed sobbing when Guy's secretary called and the portent of her news first struck. Then, on an impulse, Elaine went to the telephone, dialed directory assistance, obtained the Airport Holiday Inn number in Charleston.

"Hello. Is this the Holiday Inn?" she asked, her voice catching. The sobbing began anew. "It is? The Holiday Inn by the airport? Yes? Well, can you tell me if Mr. Henderson and Mr. Moore have checked out yet? Yes, that's Henderson and Moore."

She waited, trembling, while someone checked. She knew what the answer would be.

"What?" she screamed. "They what?"

But the line was dead. The clerk answered her question and then hung up. Were they crazy? Her hand trembled violently now. She tried to dial the number again and had to start over. She waited. The phone rang. Answer the phone. Answer the phone. Answer the phone.

"Hello. Would you please ring the room of Mr. Henderson and Mr. Moore. Yes, Henderson and Moore."

She waited tensely while the telephone rang. Once. Twice.

"Oh, Guy. It's so good to hear your voice. Oh, thank God. You're alive. You missed it. You missed it."

She fell back on the bed, sobbing joyfully.

A few minutes later Guy's stricken parents pulled into the driveway. They had rushed to their son's home at first news of the crash. Elaine saw them through the window, climbing from the car. She burst through the front door, down the steps and ran into the driveway, shouting joyously.

"They're alive. They're alive. They missed the plane."

Guy's father rested his head against his forearm on the roof of the car and began sobbing.

Jim Wilkes quickly flipped through the Eastern 212 ticket coupons he'd stuffed in an envelope earlier. The telephone receiver lay off the hook by his elbow. At the other end someone in Miami Dispatch waited while he counted. They wanted an exact count. Wilkes picked up the phone.

"I have seventy-eight. That's seven first-class and seventy-one coach."

"Are you sure?"

"Yeah, sure I'm sure. That's what I just counted."

"O.K. Thank you."

"Hey, what's going on?"

"Well, we have a report that 212 has crashed outside Charlotte. We'll call you back in a couple of minutes."

Dispatch hung up. Wilkes sat in his chair, holding the telephone receiver, staring at the wall, dozens of faces suddenly marching before him.

Richard Arnold lay in a stretcher suspended in a rack inside a U. S. Army helicopter parked on the lawn outside Charlotte Memorial Hospital. He never had flown in a helicopter before. Through the haze of heavy sedation that masked the pain of the third-degree burns over half of his body, he was aware of a massive black Army corpsman wearing a crash helmet standing beside the stretcher. Arnold wanted badly to raise up and look around inside the helicopter. Each time he raised his head the great hulk of the corpsman was there, gently pushing him down, quietly admonishing him. "Now, you just lie still, fella. We'll have you in Charleston before you know it. Just lie still."

The pain had been intense at first, before the morphine. He'd remained rational. Where did he want to go for treatment? they asked. Home. I want to go home to Charleston, he replied. Home. I want to go home.

So he was going home, or nearly home, to the hospital at the Medical University, to the Charleston burn center, one of the finest in the Southeast. The irony of his serious condition and his destination hadn't yet struck him. The doctors and nurses in Charleston were expecting him.

Arnold tried again to raise up. The large black hand was there by his face, gently shoving him down.

"I've never been on a helicopter. I just want to look around," he mumbled. He felt as if he were swimming away, looking back at his body lying there in the stretcher hanging from the rack. He'd never flown on a helicopter.

"We'll have you in Charleston in no time, fella. Just take it easy."

Bruce Thingstad stood in line at the check-out counter, holding an armful of groceries, odds and ends picked up on the way home from work. He'd spent the day working on satellite communications gear aboard a destroyer escort. The lady ahead of him and the checker talked about the plane crash in Charlotte. Bruce had heard somebody mention it shortly before noon. He'd paused then, frowning. A midmorning flight from Charleston had crashed. He shrugged. Karen was already in Chicago waiting for the connecting flight to Minot. He stood with his back to the woman and the checker, surveying the store.

". . . and on the radio they said that because it happened so early in the morning that all the traffic of people going to work and the school buses and what not held up the firemen getting there," the checker said.

Bruce wheeled, a panic rising in him.

"What time did you say it crashed?" he asked fiercely. The two women stared at him, alarmed by his tone.

"What time did it crash?" He wanted to grab her arm, shake her. "What time did it crash? I thought it crashed at ten-thirty."

The checker got her voice back first.

"Well . . . ah . . . no, sir. I think it crashed earlier than that. It's one of the first airplanes each day."

Bruce dropped the items on the counter. "Excuse me," he mumbled, and stumbled from the store, dazed. He blindly gunned the Camaro from the parking lot, rushing toward home, snapping on the radio. Soon a summary of news headlines began. The lead item was the crash, the crash of Eastern 212 in Charlotte.

He slid to a halt in the driveway and ran inside and turned on the television.

The news began. The crash, the big story. There were survivors.

They read the names. The telephone rang. He picked it up. He knew from the crackling on the line that it was long distance.

"Bruce?" It was Edie Iverson. She was crying.

It was night. A sedan pulled into the driveway of the Holiday Inn, where several Eastern Airlines officials stood waiting, among them Frank Borman, a former astronaut who joined the airline and became its executive vice-president, later its president.

Collette Watson sat in the back seat of the sedan with her husband, Mike. A passerby, a daughter of an Eastern employee in Charlotte, had driven Collette from York Road to Presbyterian Hospital. Except for a few bruises, the loss of her glasses and a thorough jostling, she was uninjured. From the hospital she went home with the woman and spent the day there, resting, avoiding reporters. Mike had flown from Atlanta and joined her. Now, dressed in a nightgown, Collette hoped to slip into the hotel where the airline had set up its headquarters.

As the car pulled to a stop Borman leaned in the open window and smiled at the flight attendant. She recognized him at once.

"Hey, Collette. How are you? Listen, Collette, we need you for a DC-9 trip tomorrow. Can you be ready?"

She started, looking at him in alarm. He smiled. He was joking. Collette laughed thinly.

"Oh, that's O.K. Perhaps some other time," she said, trying to joke back. She hurried into the hotel. They didn't want any reporters spotting her.

Mike trailed his wife and Borman spoke to him.

"Listen, Mike. You and Collette can have a trip anywhere you want to go. Whenever you're ready. Just let me know."

In the ABC television studio, Harry Reasoner sat at the desk, holding the script lightly in his hands, waiting for the red light atop the camera. The floor manager intoned the cues.

"Five seconds. Four. Three. Two."

The light came on. Reasoner began.

"I'd like to take this space today to mark the death of John

Merriman, killed in yesterday's plane crash in North Carolina. John had been with CBS News practically forever. He started in 1942 as a page and for the last eight years he was the editor and in many ways the conscience of the CBS Evening News.

"His conscience was particularly touchy in areas where journalists do violence to the English language. He not only knew the rules and made writers keep them, he had that rarer thing, an ear for the clunking phrase and illiterate sentence. Even at his death I have to remember him with smiles because we always had a couple of language projects going that made us laugh.

"We kept track of journalistic clichés. He would call me and say, 'The wires say that a giant pall has settled over Washington. Did you fellows get pictures of it? Oh well, I suppose under the pall it was too dark for pictures.' Or he would call back and say, 'Do you suppose that's the same giant pall that covered Paris when De Gaulle died?' We'll miss those calls. And the trouble is, more sloppy writing may go unnoticed in this craft without John around.

"John was fifty—too young to die, especially when you like good food and good language and good sports as much as he did. He was a qualified judge of food and wine and he knew New York's restaurants better than most people. But he also liked the natural food of the South and he had been there probably enjoying some country ham and pork barbecue just before his last flight. He had only one fault in my view. A strange fondness for horse racing. But nobody's perfect.

"I tried to be very careful in writing this piece because I have the strong feeling that if a sloppy cliché crept in John would know about it wherever he is and he would object strongly. Just the same, his friends do feel there is a sort of giant pall over the day."

The camera light went out and Reasoner began gathering up his script.

The two men paced carefully through the ravaged cornfield, studying the deep grooves gouged from the earth. They were accident investigators from the National Transportation Safety Board. One, a member of the NTSB's "Go Team," had been in Charlotte within hours of the accident. His colleague had come down later and now toured the scene.

They began under a pine tree whose top the DC-9 had sheared off, the first object it struck. Then the airplane hit the ground, the first time in the cornfield, then bounced, hit again and began striking trees. The duo stopped to study a single groove in the soft dirt, gouged by the protective skid on the bottom of the airplane's tail.

"See, this is the tail skid mark. So you can see he'd rotated the nose at this point," the Go Team investigator said. "When they get through with the cockpit they'll probably find the throttle levers all the way forward. So he rotated and he went to the throttles. He was trying . . . trying to fly it out."

The other man grunted. They walked on, pausing to examine parallel grooves made by the landing gear. They stopped next at a tree stump. Something had cleanly severed the eight-inch trunk.

"See, he got the nose up and then the wheels touched and then he bounced and then . . ." He fell silent. The stump told the story. Nose up, full power, the jet engines just beginning to spool up because they take several seconds to respond. Then the wing struck the tree and the tree ripped the wing apart.

"Oh, I don't know. He tried. He certainly tried," the NTSB man said. "It's hard to say. Maybe if he'd seen it earlier, gotten the power on sooner, if he hadn't hit that tree . . . that tree really did them in, though. There was no flying out of here after hitting that tree."

The other man nodded and they walked on, stopping to study more stumps as they descended into the ravine.

Slowly, with a steady rumbling and a relentless squeaking and clanking of its cleated tracks, the bulldozer marched across the field toward the ravine. Once, it had been a cornfield. But the fire trucks, ambulances, police, accident investigators and hundreds and hundreds of the curious in nearly two weeks had trampled every last stalk into the ground.

Seated on the dozer's seat, using his feet to steer the massive machine, braking first one track and then another so that it slued right and slued left, waddling across the field, was Robbie McDowell. His father, John McDowell, was the farmer who owned the cornfield and ravine and lived a half mile northward up York Road.

The last body long ago had been removed. The last investigator had left after carting away the last instrument and the last control surface for study, after taking the last picture. Now only the carcass of a fallen airliner remained, a constant temptation to the steady stream of curiosity seekers. So Robbie McDowell had come to bury Eastern 212.

He began at the lip of the charred ravine, thrusting the dozer blade deep into the soft earth with each cut, the powerful diesel engine laboring as he shaved away the hilltop and pushed it downward, sending dirt and brush and saplings cascading over the burned hulks. It took nearly a half day. But when he finished, the hilltop was stripped bare, the red earth pushed into the bottom of the ravine, the DC-9 buried under ten feet of soil, only a charred tree trunk protruding here and a neatly severed tree stump there to bear witness.

The doctor, a pathologist who taught and also served as a medical examiner, sat at his desk talking on the telephone. The caller was a newspaper reporter. The doctor nodded as he listened, a look of tolerant forbearance crossing his face. He and other pathologists involved with the accident had received several such calls. It was a story to which the press persistently returned.

The caller sought to ascertain whether or not the medical examiners had found, in the wreckage of the airplane and the bodies and pieces of bodies, any evidence of an infant, a child, a year or perhaps eighteen months old.

"You see," the caller was saying, "Richard Arnold definitely recalls seeing an infant in the line at the ticket counter in Charleston and he clearly remembers it in the cabin with a woman sitting near the admiral. And the ticket agents agree that a baby could get aboard unnoticed. It would be difficult, but it could happen.

"Then you have witnesses at the scene. A Charlotte *Observer* reporter says he saw a woman strapped in a seat holding a baby.

He wasn't more than ten feet away. Now, he agrees that she could have been holding a pillow or a blanket or something. But it sure looked like a baby."

The doctor interjected a grunt from time to time as the caller laid out his hypothesis.

"There's another eyewitness, Jim Stanley, who saw it up close. He says there is no doubt in his mind that it was a small child."

The doctor began to speak. No. No small child's body was ever found. They were very careful, quite meticulous, both in gathering the remains at the scene and examining them and performing autopsies. Every passenger was accounted for. Traumatic injuries killed thirty-one passengers and the captain; thermal injuries and smoke inhalation, twenty-three passengers; thermal burns alone, eight passengers; combined thermal injury and traumatic injury or carbon monoxide poisoning, seven passengers; one passenger and the flight attendant died of smoke inhalation only.

No. No, they really would have found some indication if there had been an infant. It's conceivable there could have been one, but unlikely. No. No reason to think an infant had been aboard. Yes. Well, sorry I couldn't be of more help.

THE MAIN COURTROOM is the jewel of the old federal building in downtown Atlanta on Peachtree Street. Ornate gold drapes frame windows that reach from the floor to the high ceiling, which is ringed with intricate decorative plaster molding. The walls are paneled in delicately carved dark wood. The bench, the counsels' tables, the jury box, the witness stand and the spectators' benches are old, richly built, deeply burnished by frequent polishing. An old pendulum clock hangs on the wall, permanently stopped at nine-forty, replaced by a nearby electric clock, the electric clock and fluorescent light fixtures suspended from the ceiling the only visible concessions to modernity.

One day in late 1975, deep into the afternoon, a short man with sagging jowls and snow white hair sat behind the high bench. His name was Robert R. Boyd, Administrative Law Judge, National Transportation Safety Board. Judge Boyd carefully regarded a man who sat in the witness stand, below the bench and to the left. The witness had a smooth, handsome face, hooded eyelids that sometimes seemed to form slits from which his eyes watched the world. Though he was clearly twenty-five years younger than the man behind the bench, his hair, trimmed to the top of his collar, was almost as white. Sprinkled strands of brown gave a slight salt and pepper effect. It was James M. Daniels, the surviving pilot of Eastern 212. He wore the same gray suit he had worn thirteen months before, when they wheeled him into the large meeting room in the Holiday Inn in Charlotte, in a wheelchair with his leg out straight in a cast, the television klieg lights blinding him, the cameramen crowding in close with their whirring machines. The room was overflowing with newsmen, dozens of lawyers representing those killed and injured in the DC-9 crash two months before and the relatives of many of the passengers he had flown to their deaths in that cornfield and ravine. He had come to testify then before a National Transportation Safety Board fact-finding hearing. He was the star attraction, the pilot unfortunate enough to survive. He had never been so frightened. To him, the hatred in the room that day had been palpable. He had sat at the microphones, under the hot lights, on display, all afternoon.

But today, it was different. There were only five reporters, all seated in the jury box by the witness stand, the better to hear. On the spectator benches a dozen people sat in various states of inattention. Witnesses mostly, air traffic controllers, some Air Line Pilots Association representatives, Federal Aviation Administration officials and Richard Arnold, one of the surviving passengers. Arnold had taken off from work and come to Atlanta, he told reporters earlier that day, speaking loudly because he knew the pilot was in earshot then, sitting at the table with his lawyers, to find out how Daniels could have flown the airplane into the ground. "I mean, even I could see the airport. If I'd known, I'd have gone up and flown the airplane for them." If Daniels heard, he didn't flinch.

The FAA revoked Daniels' commercial pilot's license. He appealed. The matter had come before Judge Boyd as provided in aviation regulatory law. At the prosecution's table sat John C. Callahan and Ronald R. Hagadone, FAA attorneys. At the defense table Daniels sat in the middle, flanked on the left by John T. O'Brien and on the right by John G. Loomis, both ALPA attorneys. The two attorneys frequently leaned forward in front of Daniels, conferring in whispers.

Through two days of hearings, the pilot, who had been fired by Eastern Airlines and also faced legal battles over that action, sat immobile, staring straight ahead, hands clasped in his lap, never turning to look at the reporters or the spectators or the FAA counsels' table. He seemed to read the pages of a book only he could see somewhere on the wall behind Judge Boyd's head.

Air traffic controllers testified, then instrument experts, FAA inspectors. The hearing dragged on. Finally the FAA ended its presentation. John Loomis called only one witness to present the pilot's case—James M. Daniels.

Loomis guided him through the questions, pacing to and fro between the witness box and the ALPA table.

"Now, it was your testimony, sir, that you made call-outs during the flight into Charleston from Atlanta. Did Captain Reeves make any of these call-outs during . . . on the final approach into Charlotte?"

"No."

"He didn't make the thousand foot call-out?"

"No. If he did I didn't hear it."

"The five-hundred-foot call-out?"

"No."

"During the descent, the en route descent and the approach into Charlotte, were you monitoring the flight instruments?"

"Yes."

"At what point did you become aware of the fact that your aircraft had descended below one thousand feet above the terrain?"

"I think possibly a split second prior to impact."

"Before impact, where did you think you were in relation to the ground?"

"I thought I was above a thousand feet. I never knew I was below a thousand feet. I didn't know."

"You were monitoring your raw data flight instruments?"

"I was setting the airplane up for the approach. I was flying the airplane. I was holding a heading. I was monitoring my systems and any other controls that may have been functioning to check response of these controls and everything seemed perfectly normal to me at the time. I just had no suspicion that things had gone amuck."

"I'm ready to excuse this witness, your honor."

Hagadone took up the questioning, retracing the same ground, firing his questions from behind the FAA's table, conferring frequently with Callahan.

"Do you feel that you misread the altimeter for a full minute?"

"It's evident to me that I did, that I misread it. How exactly I picked it up, I have no idea, nothing was brought to my attention, that I had descended below an altitude. The captain said nothing about it whatsoever, no indication there was anything amiss. He also was reading his instruments. He has two altimeters. I only have one and he has one that reads in both modes and I only have the one altimeter. No indication was made of this. It may have happened at such a time that I misread it, I don't know for sure, but it's the only thing . . . are you listening to me?"

Hagadone had bent over, whispering with the other FAA attorney while Daniels spoke. He straightened abruptly and blushed.

"Yes, sir. I'm sorry. I'm still listening."

"It's the only thing that makes sense to me. I had to misread the altimeter or something happened like the gear going down or anything and I missed a cycle on it perhaps. I don't know. I'm no expert on altimetry."

He fell silent and after a couple more perfunctory questions, Hagadone ceased his questions.

Now Judge Boyd leaned forward, studying the witness, who suddenly, passionately, his voice quavering, almost breaking at times, had begun to speak.

"If I may say something, your honor." His voice was low, almost a whisper. The judge and attorneys and reporters leaned forward.

"I'm terribly sorry about the accident. I'd give anything in the world if it hadn't happened." He stopped and swallowed, then plunged ahead. He was near breaking.

"But I did my job. At no time was there any intent on my part to commit or violate any of the company operating procedures or the Federal Aviation Regulations or anything like this. I think it's pretty evident if you've been reading some of this information . . . I think I misread the altimeter. I think I made a mistake. I'm human and I made a mistake."

His voice trailed off, leaving an embarrassed silence in the courtroom. Judge Boyd cleared his throat and looked down. John Loomis nervously fingered a pencil. Daniels swallowed.

"I'm sorry," he whispered, his eyes brimming.

Loomis jumped to his feet.

"Your honor, I can't hear the witness," he said loudly. As he hoped, his voice broke the spell. Spectators coughed. The reporters furiously scribbled in their notebooks. Judge Boyd slumped down in his chair. An ambulance, its siren wailing, passed in the street. Hagadone began gathering papers on his table. Jim Daniels stared at the ceiling.

Judge Boyd's ruling, issued four months later, was sympathetic to First Officer Daniels' plight. But Boyd upheld the Federal Aviation Administration's revocation of Daniels' commercial pilot's license.

The copilot appealed to the five-member National Transportation Safety Board, whose members are appointed by the President. In September 1976—just six days after the second anniversary of the crash of Eastern 212—the NTSB reversed the earlier rulings and ordered that instead of a license revocation, Daniels be subjected only to the lesser penalty of a six-month license suspension. The board ordered that Daniels' license be reinstated in April 1977.

Life moved forward for Jim Daniels. Under pressure from the Airline Pilots Association, Eastern Airlines provided the copilot with a medical disability retirement. Kathy Daniels went to work to help support Jim and the twins. They sold their house in Roswell and moved into a cramped apartment. Jim enrolled in a junior college outside Atlanta, resuming college studies broken off two decades before, struggling each night with freshman physics and biology. Each news account of the latest lawsuit brought against Eastern Airlines by crash survivors or relatives of the dead reopened the wounds. He gave away his extensive aviation library.

Jim Daniels faces more hospitalization as surgeons continue work to repair his broken body. He awakes from nightmares filled with screams and smoke. He ponders a basic question that transcends his anguish: When he can fly again, will he want to?

EASTERN AIRLINES FLIGHT 212

September 11, 1974

SURVIVORS

First Officer James M. Daniels, Jr.

Senior Flight Attendant J. Collette Watson

Richard Arnold IV

Robert Miller Burnham

Royal Felix Hendrix

Scott Richard Johnson

Francis Charles Mihalek

James Lee Schulze

John T. Toohey

Charles Joseph Weaver